*Dedicated to the great state
of Northern California*

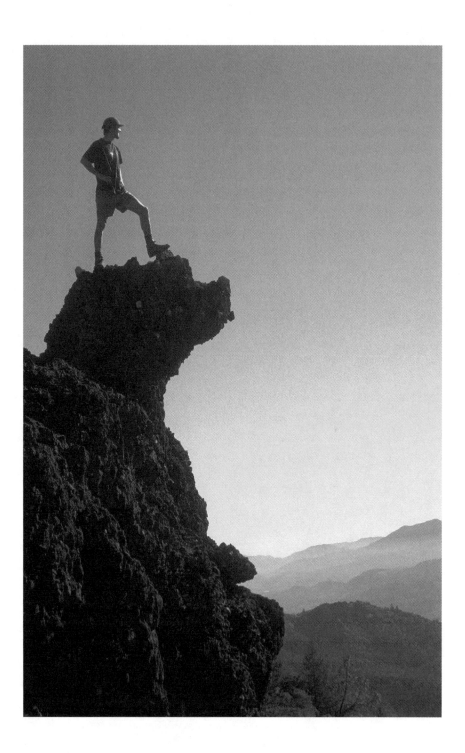

101
HIKES
in
Northern
California

Exploring Mountains, Valleys, and Seashore

Matt Heid

 WILDERNESS PRESS · BERKELEY, CA

1st EDITION December 2000
2nd Printing July 2001
3rd Printing January 2004

Copyright © 2000 by Matt Heid

Photos and maps by the author
Cover photos copyright © 2000 by Matt Heid
All topographic maps © 2000 National Geographic Maps with trails added by the author
Locator maps (pp. 11–12) by Jaan Hitt
Book design by Margaret Copeland—Terragraphics
Cover design by Larry B. Van Dyke

Library of Congress Card Catalog Number 00-053426
International Standard Book Number 0-89997-257-8

Manufactured in the United States of America

Published by   **Wilderness Press**
                1200 5th Street
                Berkeley, CA 94710
                (800) 443-7227
                FAX (510) 558-1696
                mail@wildernesspress.com
                www.wildernesspress.com

                Contact us for a free catalog

Cover photos: **Castle Dome**, Trip 51 (background)
               The Lost Coast, Trip 39 (top inset)
               Burney Falls, Trip 63 (bottom inset)
Frontispiece: **Table Rock, Robert Louis Stevenson State Park,** Trip 32

Library of Congress Cataloging-in-Publication Data

Heid, Matt, 1975–
    101 hikes in Northern California : exploring mountains, valleys, and seashore / Matt
Heid ; [photos and maps by the author].-- 1st ed.
        p. cm.
    Includes bibliographical references and index.
    ISBN 0-89997-257-8
    1. Hiking--California--Guidebooks. 2. Trails--California--Guidebooks. 3.
California--Guidebooks. I. Title: One hundred one hikes in Northern California. II.
Title: One hundred and one hikes in Northern California. III. Title.

GV199.42.C2 H45 2000
917.94--dc21
                                                                        00-053426

Acknowledgments

Thanks go first to the countless rangers who aided me in my research and patiently answered my long lists of questions. While too numerous to name individually, each contributed valuable information to this book in an ever-friendly and knowledgeable fashion—I owe them all a debt of gratitude.

Many wonderful people joined me on my hikes: Pogen MacNeilage, Gretchen Ela, Chuck Kapelke, John Heid, Analise Eliot, Ben Hart, Erich von Ibsch, Leslie Rubin, Big Tom Hruschka, Cindy Miner, Julio Gutierrez, Dan Hruschka, Sean Fitzpatrick, Jan Heid, Sid Bean, Marsha Lewis, Lindsay Lewis, U.G. Stone, Mike Jones, Kara Forman (and Sonoma), Genevieve Juliard, David Doostan, Kevin Daly, and Ethan Phillips. The Professional Outdoor Team!

Thank you to all who supported me during this seemingly endless project, especially my parents. Thanks to Janet Muzinich for her amazing hospitality. Thanks to the folks at REI Berkeley. Finally, a tremendous thanks goes to all the wonderful people at Wilderness Press, especially Mike Jones and Caroline Winnett, who provided me with this opportunity; and Paul Backhurst, whose care, patience, and hard work shine through in these pages.

Matt Heid
Pacifica, CA

Disclaimer

Hiking in the backcountry entails unavoidable risk that every hiker assumes and must be aware of and respect. The fact that a trail is described in this book is not a representation that it will be safe for you. Trails vary greatly in difficulty and in the degree of conditioning and agility one needs to enjoy them safely. On some hikes routes may have changed or conditions may have deteriorated since the descriptions were written. Also trail conditions can change even from day to day, owing to weather and other factors. A trail that is safe on a dry day or for a highly conditioned, agile, properly equipped hiker may be completely unsafe for someone else or unsafe under adverse weather conditions.

You can minimize your risks on the trail by being knowledgeable, prepared and alert. There is not space in this book for a general treatise on safety in the mountains, but there are a number of good books and public courses on the subject and you should take advantage of them to increase your knowledge. Just as important, you should always be aware of your own limitations and of conditions existing when and where you are hiking. If conditions are dangerous, or if you're not prepared to deal with them safely, choose a different hike! It's better to have wasted a drive than to be the subject of a mountain rescue.

These warnings are not intended to scare you off the trails. Millions of people have safe and enjoyable hikes every year. However, one element of the beauty, freedom and excitement of the wilderness is the presence of risks that do not confront us at home. When you hike you assume those risks. They can be met safely, but only if you exercise your own independent judgement and common sense.

Contents

Preface

Welcome to the total Northern California outdoor experience. Every aspect of the region's incredible natural diversity is found within these 101 Hikes—the jagged granite of the High Sierra, the crashing surf of the Pacific Coast, the volcanic landscape of the Modoc Plateau, the rich diversity of the Klamath Mountains, the magnificent redwoods of the North Coast, the spectacular views of the Bay Area. Lakes, peaks, rivers, creeks, waterfalls, valleys, beaches, forests, meadows, wildlife, wildflowers, lighthouses, volcanoes . . . they can all be found within these pages.

This book describes a greater area than most Northern California guidebooks. Stretching north from Sequoia National Park through the Modoc Plateau of northeast California, it includes virtually all of the Sierra Nevada. Sweeping north along the coast from Big Sur to the Oregon border, it contains the Coast Ranges, the San Francisco Bay Area, and the Klamath Mountains. In total, this book covers the entire northern two-thirds of the state.

The 101 Hikes were selected using three basic criteria and each adventure will include some combination of:

- **Isolation** Wilderness is freedom, an escape from the trappings of society. The fewer the people you encounter, the deeper your experience.
- **Scenic Beauty** Sweeping 360° vistas, exquisite works of Nature, the splendor of Northern California.
- **Unique Destinations** Redwood forests, giant sequoias, granite domes, marble mountains, thundering waterfalls—places unlike anywhere else on Earth.

While all of the hikes can be completed in a single day, many can also be done as overnight backpacking trips. Each hike description includes an easy-to-use header outlining the basics of the trip, detailed driving directions, an in-depth trail description, and the location of the nearest visitor center and campground. Backpacking information is provided for appropriate hikes. The hikes are broadly distributed across Northern California; no matter where you are, an adventure awaits nearby. Enjoy!

How To Use This Book

To prepare for the total Northern California outdoors experience, first carefully read the following chapter on "Safety, Gear, and the Wilderness Ethic." Selecting a hike can be an absorbing process. Those unfamiliar with the state or unsure about where to visit should consult the "Where Should I Go Hiking?" chapter. For those looking for a specific feature, the hikes are grouped by theme in the back of the book (see Appendix 1). Otherwise, just flip through the pages to your desired area and evaluate each hike based on the standard information provided.

The 101 Hikes progress in clockwise order around the state. Beginning along the Pacific shore with the Big Sur region, the listings proceed north through the Bay Area, Coast Ranges, and Pacific Coast to the Klamath Mountains, then inland east across the Modoc Plateau, and finally south through the Sierra Nevada to end in southern Sequoia National Park.

Each hike utilizes a standard, easily understood template. Going from top to bottom, the template is composed of:

The Header

- **Title** Something fun to intrigue the reader, most hike titles are the author's own creation and will not appear on maps, signs, or be known to those not holding this book.
- **Location** The location immediately below the title identifies the area or specific destination visited by this hike.
- **Governing Agency** The third line of the header identifies the governing agency for this hike. Contact information is listed at the end of each description.

- **Highlights** The most exciting features of the hike.
- **Distance** The total mileage of the hike. For point-to-point hikes, the one-way distance is listed.
- **Total Elevation Gain/Loss** The total amount of climbing and descending on the hike. It can be significantly greater than the difference between the hike's lowest and highest points.
- **Hiking Time** This indicates the total amount of time required for the hike, including time for brief rest stops and a meal break on longer trips. As this varies markedly depending on physical fitness and pace, a range of times is usually given. The lower number indicates the amount of time a fit hiker can complete the hike, pausing only briefly for short breaks. The higher number is for hikers moving at a more leisurely pace and for anybody who likes to take extended breaks over the course of a journey. Remember that these times are only rough estimates and hikes can potentially take longer for slower hikers and those with heavy backpacks.

It is important to be aware of your physical capabilities and limitations when selecting a hike. As a general rule of thumb, a reasonably fit hiker can expect to cover 2–3 miles per hour over level ground and on gradual descents, 1–2 miles per hour on gradual climbs, and only about 1 mile—or 750–1,000 feet of elevation—per hour on the steepest ascents.

- **Difficulty** This book utilizes a five-level rating system of one to five stars. While all factors contributing to the overall challenge of the hike are taken into account, some general criteria for each level are as follows:

★ *Easy.* Typically short and level, these hikes can be done by anybody and will have less than 500 feet of total elevation gain.

★★ *Moderate.* Hikes on good trails with roughly 500–1,000 feet of total elevation gain. Suitable for any reasonably fit hiker.

★★★ *Strenuous.* Longer hikes with approximately 1,000–2,000 feet of elevation gain on trails that are often rocky and steep. Good fitness required.

★★★★ *Challenging.* A very strenuous hike with roughly 2,000–3,000 feet of elevation gain in often remote regions on challenging trails. Experienced wilderness users only. Many are good overnight trips.

★★★★★ *Epic.* An adventure with an elevation gain in excess of 3,000 feet on rough and difficult trails. Cross-country navigation skills are often required. Only the fittest individuals can complete them in a single day. Excellent for overnight trips.

- **Best Times** The best times to do the hike. Note that many of the hikes can be done outside of the times listed, but weather or crowds will probably make them much less appealing.
- **Optional Maps** Usually the appropriate USGS 7.5-minute topographic maps but occasionally a Forest Service Wilderness map. Many of the hikes can be completed using only the maps in the book or those available near the trailhead, but greater safety and enjoyment come with more detailed and comprehensive maps— especially on the more difficult and remote hikes. All USGS maps can be ordered online at *www.usgs.gov*. Most Forest Service maps are available for purchase online at *www.r5.fs.fed.us*.
- **Symbols**

 An out-and-back hike that returns to the starting trailhead by retracing its route.

 A loop or semi-loop hike that retraces little or none of its route to return to the starting trailhead.

 A point-to-point hike that ends at a different trailhead. Two cars or shuttle required to return to the starting trailhead.

 All hikes that can be done as overnight backpacking trips will have this symbol. Specific backpacking information is listed at the end of each hike.

A hike that requires some travel through thick or overhanging brush. Long pants and a long-sleeve shirt are recommended to guard against ticks and scratches.

A hike well-suited for young children. A hike bearing this symbol will be short, easy, and often have educational interpretive signs.

Hike Description

The body of the hike is broken down into three main sections:

- **The Hike** Following introductory material and background information is a brief overview of the hike discussing seasonal differences, crowds, recommended equipment, special regulations, fishing possibilities, and the availability of water both at the trailhead and along the hike.
- **To Reach the Trailhead** Concise driving directions to the start of the hike. This book assumes that you have a basic highway map of California. Mention is made if access requires a 4WD or high-clearance vehicle. Entrance fees are also included in this section.
- **Description** The hike itself. Parenthetical notations such as (10320) indicate elevation in feet. Parenthetical notations such as (2.7/8750) are included in many longer hike descrip-

tions at important junctions or landmarks. The first number represents
the total distance from the trailhead
in miles. The second identifies the elevation of the location in feet.

Listings

Following each hike are up to four
listings:
- **Nearest Visitor Center** The closest
source of information to the trailhead
and the best place to call for general
information. Opening hours are
included but be aware that schedules
are subject to regular change and
these times should only be considered
approximate. Unless otherwise mentioned, assume the hours are year-
round.
- **Backpacking Information** If the hike
can be done as an overnight backpacking trip, this section discusses
required permits, fees, quotas, and
crowds. Campsite locations may be
briefly mentioned but they are not
described in detail or discussed in the
main body of text.
- **Nearest Campground** The closest
organized campground to the trail-

head. "Organized" means that there
are at least picnic tables, fire rings,
and toilets. Water will be available at
the campgrounds unless specifically
mentioned otherwise. Where information was available, the total number of sites and camping fees are
included as well. Be aware that prices
always increase and those listed here
should only be considered approximate. All state park campgrounds
operate on the same reservation system—call 1-800-444-PARK or go
online at *www.reserveamerica.com* to
reserve a site.
- **Additional Information** Any recommended Web sites.

The Maps in This Book

The maps in this book were created
using TOPO! software from National
Geographic Maps. Because they are only
intended to convey very basic route
information, most hikers will want to
purchase the Optional Map. For several
hikes, where the route is obvious or very
short, there are no maps. Note that the
maps are reproduced at different sizes,
and scale varies from map to map.

Above the Lost Coast

Safety, Gear, and the Wilderness Ethic

Safety

Always tell somebody where you are hiking and when you expect to return. Friends, family, rangers, and visitor centers are all valuable resources that can save you from a backcountry disaster when you fail to reappear on time.

Know your limits. Don't undertake a hike that exceeds your physical fitness or wilderness abilities.

Try not to hike alone. A hiking partner can provide the margin between life and death in the event of a serious backcountry mishap.

Drink lots of water. Prevent dehydration and its accompanying dangers by consuming as much water as possible. Always purify water taken from rivers, lakes, and streams in the backcountry.

The Animal Hazards

Bears The grizzly bear is extinct in California and only its smaller cousin the black bear still roams the mountains. Seldom dangerous, black bears will usually run away as soon as they spot you. In popular areas—Yosemite being the prime example—resident bears have learned that people mean food and exhibit no fear of humans. If a bear approaches, be loud and obnoxious, bang pots, throw small rocks, and try to frighten the animal away. Always avoid females with cubs as the maternal instinct can make her attack if she feels her young are threatened.

Whenever camping in bear country it is imperative that you safely secure food and any scented items (toothpaste, deodorant, etc.) away from the campsite. Plastic bear canisters are the most effective and can be purchased or rented at many outdoor equipment shops. Hanging your food from a nearby tree is a good option in less-traveled areas, but is all but ineffective in the popular national parks. To hang your food, divide it evenly between two stuff sacks and find a tree with a long thin branch extending at least 10 feet from the trunk and at least 20 feet from the ground. Throw a rope over the branch using a weighted object of some kind, tie one of the stuff sacks to the end, hoist it to the branch, attach the second stuff sack as far above the ground as possible on the other end of the rope, and use a stick to push the second sack upward until it is level with the first.

Rattlesnakes Common throughout Northern California below approximately 6,000 feet, these venomous snakes like to bask on hot rocks in the sun. They usually flee at the first sight of people and will only attack if threatened. Be wary when cruising off-trail and don't put your hands where you can't see them when scrambling on rocky slopes. If bitten, the goal is to reduce the rate at which the poison circulates through your body—try and remain calm, keep the bite site below the level of your heart, remove any constricting items (rings, watches, etc.) from the soon-to-be-swollen extremity, and *do not* apply ice or chemical cold to the bite as this can cause further damage to the surrounding tissue. Seek medical attention as quickly as possible.

Ticks These parasites love brushy areas at low elevations and are common throughout the state, especially during the rainy season. Always perform regular body checks when hiking through tick country. If you find a tick attached to you, *do not* try and pull it out with your fingers or pinch the body; this can inject tick juices under your skin and increase the risk of infection. Using an appropriate tool, gently pull the tick out by lifting upward from the base of the body where it is attached to the skin. Pull straight out until the tick releases and do not twist or jerk as this may break the mouth parts off under your skin. A small **V** cut in the side of a credit card works well for this operation.

Lyme Disease is present in Northern California but only one of the 48 tick species found in the state is capable of transmitting it—the western black-legged tick—and chances are low for exposure. Caused by a spirochete, this potentially life-threatening disease can be hard to diagnose in its early phases. Common early symptoms include fatigue, chills and fever, headache, muscle and joint pain, swollen lymph nodes, and a blotchy skin rash that clears centrally to produce a characteristic ring shape 3–30 days after exposure. If you fear that you have been exposed to Lyme Disease consult a doctor immediately.

Giardia *Giardia lamblia* is a microscopic organism occasionally found in backcountry water sources. Existing in a dormant cyst form while in the water, the critter develops in the gastrointestinal tract upon being consumed and can cause diarrhea, excessive flatulence, foul-smelling excrement, nausea, fatigue, and abdominal cramps. While the risk of contraction is very slight, the potential consequences are worth preventing. All water taken from the backcountry should be purified by boiling or chemical treatment.

Deer Mice There is no known cure for hantavirus, a rare but usually fatal pulmonary syndrome acquired by ingesting urine, droppings, or saliva from infected rodents; or by touching your nose, mouth, or eyes after handling infected rodents, their nests, or droppings. Deer mice are 4–7 inches long, gray to brown in color with white fur on the belly, and have large ears. They are common around the state. Never handle rodent nests, avoid buildings they inhabit, and never leave food sitting out.

Mountain Lions Common throughout the state mountain lions are rarely seen. If you do encounter a mountain lion acting in an aggressive manner, make yourself look as large as possible and do not run away.

Plants To Avoid
Poison Oak If you learn only one plant in California, it had better be this one. Poison oak grows throughout California below approximately 4,000 feet. A low-lying shrub or bush, its glossy oak-like leaves always grow in clusters of three and turn bright red in the fall before dropping off in the winter. Both the leaves and stems contain an oil that causes a strong allergic reaction in most people, creating a maddening and long-lived itchy rash that can spread across the body. Wash thoroughly after any exposure. It is mentioned in the hike description if it occurs along the trail.

Stinging Nettle Common along the coast, this spiny plant causes an unpleasant stinging sensation when any part of it comes in contact with your skin. It is mentioned in the hike description when it appears along the trail.

Physical Dangers
Lightning Thunderstorms are common during the summer months and often bring lightning—especially at higher elevations. If you see a thunderstorm approaching, avoid exposed ridges and peaks, take shelter in low places, and sit on some sort of insulating material if you feel in real danger—your backpack, sleeping pad, or anything else you might have handy.

Hypothermia This occurs when the body is unable to stay adequately warm and its core temperature begins to drop. It is a life-threatening condition whose initial symptoms include weakness, mental confusion, and uncontrollable shivering. Cold, wet weather poses the greatest hazard as wet clothes conduct heat away from the body roughly 20 times faster than dry layers. Fatigue reduces your body's ability to produce its own heat; wind poses an increased risk as it can quickly strip away warmth. Immediate treatment is critical and entails raising the body's core temperature. Get out of the wind, take off wet clothes, drink warm beverages, eat simple energy foods, and take shelter in a warm tent or sleeping bag. *Do not* drink alcohol as this dilates the blood vessels and causes increased heat loss.

Heat Stroke The opposite of hypothermia, this occurs when the body is unable to control its internal temperature and overheats. Usually brought on by excessive exposure to the sun and accompanying dehydration, symptoms include cramping, headache, and mental confusion. Treatment entails rapid, aggressive cooling of the body through whatever means are available—cooling the head and torso is most important—and drinking lots of fluids. Stay hydrated and have some type of sun protection for your head if you expect to travel a hot, exposed section of trail.

Sunburn The Northern California sun can fry you quickly—especially at higher elevations where the air filters less of the damaging rays. Always wear sunscreen of sufficiently high SPF.

The Pacific Ocean The dangerous waters of the Pacific are frigid, swirling with strong currents and undertows that can instantly suck the unwary out to sea. Rogue waves can always occur, sweeping the unsuspecting from seemingly safe rocks and beaches—especially during times of large swell. Unless you are confident in your abilities and knowledge of the ocean, don't tempt fate by going in the water.

Gear
Survival Essentials
You should always have:

Water Carry at least one water bottle, drink frequently, and have some means of purifying backcountry sources (chemical treatment or filter).

Fire Waterproof matches to help build an emergency fire.

First Aid Kit A basic kit should include at least the following: some type of painkiller/swelling reducer (ibuprofen is always good), an ACE bandage, a topical antibiotic (like Neosporin), and sterile wound dressings. Prepackaged kits are readily available at any outdoor-equipment store.

Warmth A warm sweater can be critical in the event of an unexpected night out. At the minimum, carry an emergency space blanket. Made of thin foil designed to reflect radiating body heat, they are cheap, compact, and lightweight.

Knife A good knife can be invaluable in the event of a disaster. Pocket knives and all-in-one tools have many other useful features as well.

Extra Food In case you are out longer than expected.

Map and Compass To find your way home.

For Your Feet
Your feet are the single, most important component of your total hike experience. If they are unhappy, you will be even more so. Appreciate them. Care for them.

Footwear The appropriate hiking footwear provides stability and support for your feet and ankles while protecting them from the abuses of the environment. For most hikes in this book, a solid pair of mid-weight hiking boots is recommended. When selecting footwear, keep in mind that the most important feature is a good fit—your toes should not hit the front while going downhill, your heel should be locked in place inside the boot to prevent friction and blisters, and there should be minimal extra space around your foot. Stability over uneven ground is enhanced by a stiffer sole and higher ankle collar. Allleather boots last longer, have a good deal of natural water resistance, and will mold to your feet over time. Some boots have Gore-Tex, making them totally waterproof. Be sure to break in new boots before taking them on an extended hike—simply wear them around as much as possible beforehand. While many of these hikes could be completed in sandals or tennis shoes, their use increases the risk of twisting an ankle, offers minimal protection from rocks, and is generally not recommended.

Socks After armpits, feet are the sweatiest part of the human body. Unfortunately, wet feet are much more prone to blisters. Good hiking socks will manage foot moisture, keep a dry layer next to your skin, and provide padding for your feet. Avoid cotton socks at all cost as these quickly become saturated, stay wet inside your shoes, and take forever to dry. Many socks are a confusing mix of natural and synthetic fibers. *Wool* provides warmth and padding and, while it does absorb roughly 30 percent of its weight in water, it is effective at keeping your feet dry. If regular wool makes your feet itch, try softer *merino wool,* which is obtained from the first few shearings of a sheep. *Nylon, polyester, acrylic,* and *polypropylene* (also called *olefin*) are all synthetic fibers that absorb very little water, dry quickly, and add durability. *Liner socks* are a thin pair of socks worn underneath the principal sock designed to more effectively wick moisture away—good for really sweaty feet.

Blister Kit As everybody knows, blisters suck. They are usually caused by friction caused by foot movement inside your shoes and are best prevented by buying properly fitting footwear, wearing appropriate socks, breaking your shoes in ahead of time, and using some simple preventative items. Always carry moleskin or the equivalent, and apply it as soon as you notice a hot spot developing.

Clothing

Get dressed and go. The following information is helpful for staying warm and dry on the trail.

The Fabrics *Cotton* is generally a lousy outdoors fabric. It absorbs water quickly and takes a long time to dry, leaving a cold wet layer next to your skin when you stop hiking. In hot, dry environments, however, cotton is useful as the water it retains helps keep you cool for longer periods of time. *Wool* is a good natural fiber for hiking. Despite the fact that it retains up to 30 percent of its weight in water, it still insulates when wet. *Polyester* and *nylon* are two commonly used synthetic fibers in outdoor clothing. They dry almost instantly, wick moisture effectively, and are generally much lighter weight than natural fibers. They will melt quickly, however, if placed in contact with a heat source (camp stove, fire, sparks, etc.).

Raingear/Windgear There are three types available: waterproof/breathable, waterproof/non-breathable, and water-resistant. *Waterproof/breathable* shells contain Gore-Tex or the equivalent and effectively keep liquid water out while still allowing water vapor (i.e. your sweat) to pass through. They keep you comfortable during heavy exertions in the rain but are generally bulky and expensive. *Waterproof/non-breathable* shells are typically rubber or coated nylon and keep water totally out but hold all your sweat in. Seams must be taped for them to be completely waterproof. Although wearing these while hiking strenuously is a hot and sticky experience, they are inexpensive and often very lightweight. *Water-resistant* shells are typically lightweight nylon windbreakers coated with a water repellent that wears away with use. They will keep you dry for a short period of time but will quickly soak through in a heavy rain. All three are good in the wind. Unless you are planning some rainy winter hikes, a simple coated waterproof/non-breathable nylon shell should be more than adequate and can remain hidden in your pack until the day you need it.

Keeping Your Head and Neck Warm The three most important parts of the body to keep warm are the torso, neck, and head. Your body will strive to keep these a constant temperature at all times. Without any insulation, the heat coursing through your neck to your brain radiates out into space and is lost. Warmth that might have been directed to your extremities is instead spent replacing the heat lost from your head. A warm hat and neck gaiter are small items, weigh almost nothing, and are more effective at keeping you warm than an extra sweater.

Keeping Your Hands Warm Hiking in cold and damp conditions will often chill your hands unpleasantly. A lightweight pair of polypropylene liner gloves will do wonders.

Important Hiking Equipment

Backpack The ideal daypack is big enough to easily carry everything you need and should have between roughly 1,000 and 2,000 cubic inches of volume. For shorter dayhikes a large fanny pack is often adequate. For overnight trips, a pack with at least 3,000 cubic inches is required and more than 4,000 cubic inches recommended. The pack should ride principally on your hips, not on your shoulders—look for a comfortable hip belt that effectively transfers loads to the lower body. Outside water-bottle pockets and an abundance of compartments are nice.

Flashlight Hiking after dark is no fun without a flashlight. Even if you plan on returning well before sundown, unexpected delays and extended periods of enjoyment can leave you on the trail past dusk. Headlamps keep your hands free and are recommended.

Trekking Poles Spare your knees. While somewhat cumbersome, trekking poles are highly recommended for steep descents and rough off-trail adventures. They provide stability, transfer some shock absorption to the upper body, and will save your knees for later in life.

Essential Overnight Equipment

Sleeping Bag Nights are surprisingly cold in Northern California, especially at high elevations. *Down* sleeping bags offer the highest warmth-to-weight ratio and are incredibly compressible. However, down loses all its insulating ability when wet and takes forever to dry. *Synthetic-fill* sleeping bags retain their insulating ability even when wet but the increased bulk and weight are drawbacks. Polarguard 3D is currently the best synthetic fill. A temperature rating of 20°F or lower is recommended—keep in mind that the bag will lose some of its loft and insulating ability over time.

Sleeping Pad Inflatable pads are the most compact and comfortable to sleep on. Foam pads are lightweight, cheap, and virtually indestructible.

Tent or Tarp? During the Northern California summer, a tent offers little more than privacy. Extended rains are very infrequent—especially in the Sierra Nevada and Modoc Plateau—and there is little to prevent you from sleeping under the stars. Thunderstorms do occur but are usually short-lived. A large tarp is always useful: emergency tent, sunshade, groundcover, rain shelter...but don't forget the rope! Due to fog and wind, a tent is always advisable along the coast. In winter and spring, a tent is essential across the state.

The Kitchen Sink All your cooking and eating supplies: stove, fuel, cooking gear, silverware, dish (a Frisbee or gold pan is good), mug, pots (at least one big one), pans, lighter/matches, spices, oil, and plenty of food!

Campwear Time to kick it. A nice pair of thick fleece pants, sandals/camp shoes, warm long underwear, and collapsible furniture all come highly recommended.

Other Good Stuff A collapsible water bag (5+ liters), sun hat, sunglasses, sunscreen, waterproof backpack cover, towel, toiletries, Zip-Loc bags, garbage bags, scissors, duct tape (tape some around your water bottle), and trowel.

Fun Equipment

Still have room in your pack?

Camera Make sure it is ready for outdoor abuse. Protective camera bags cost much less than new cameras. A polarizing filter is good for taking outdoor pictures with lots of sky and water. Shady forests are challenging to photograph when the sun is out—wait for foggy and overcast days.

Fishing Equipment Fly-fish or use very lightweight spinning tackle in the mountain lakes and streams. A valid fishing license is required for all anglers 16 or older and can be purchased at just about any store that sells outdoor equipment.

Altimeter A fun toy for tracking your progress and identifying your location. While they are generally accurate to within 100 feet, greater precision requires constant recalibration. Elevation is measured by change in barometric pressure and regular fluctuations in air pressure make it necessary to input a known elevation at least once a day to maintain accuracy.

Other Fun Stuff You can see more with binoculars and play more with a Hacky Sack, Frisbee, or cards.

The Wilderness Ethic

In order to preserve the wilderness for future generations, follow some simple guidelines to leave no trace of your passage:

Do Not Scar the Land Do not cut switchbacks. Stay on the trail as much as possible.

Camping Camp at established sites. Select a location that has adequate water runoff and do not dig ditches around your tent. Keep your camp clean and never leave food out.

Fires Campfires should always be made in a fire ring. Use preexisting rings if available; otherwise, scatter the stones and ashes before you leave. Keep fires small and use only material that is already dead and down. Avoid making campfires in heavy use areas and at high elevations where firewood is scarce. *Make sure the fire is completely out before leaving.*

Sanitation Choose a spot at least 200 feet away from trails, water sources, and campsites. Dig a cat hole six inches deep, make your deposit, and cover it with the soil you removed. Do not bury toilet paper.

Garbage Carry out all garbage and burn only paper.

Group Size Keep groups small to minimize impact. Maximum group size allowed varies by location but is usually 10 or less.

Animals Do not feed wild animals.

Noise Be respectful of other wilderness users. Listen to the sounds of nature.

Meeting Stock on the Trail Move off the trail on the downhill side and stand still until the animals pass by.

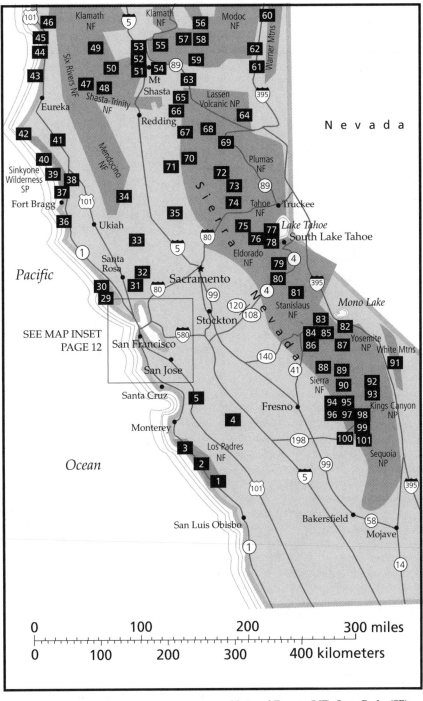

Pacific

Ocean

Nevada

Six Rivers NF

Klamath NF

Klamath NF

Modoc NF

Warner Mtns

Mt Shasta

Shasta-Trinity NF

Eureka

Redding

Lassen Volcanic NP

Mendocino NF

Sinkyone Wilderness SP

Fort Bragg

Ukiah

Sierra

Plumas NF

Tahoe NF

Truckee

Lake Tahoe

South Lake Tahoe

Santa Rosa

Sacramento

Eldorado NF

Stockton

Nevada

Stanislaus NF

Mono Lake

SEE MAP INSET PAGE 12

San Francisco

San Jose

Yosemite NP

White Mtns

Santa Cruz

Monterey

Sierra NF

Fresno

Kings Canyon NP

Los Padres NF

Sequoia NP

San Luis Obisbo

Bakersfield

Mojave

0   100   200   300 miles

0   100   200   300   400 kilometers

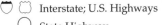 Interstate; U.S. Highways

State Highway

National Forests (NF); State Parks (SP);
National Parks (NP); Mountain Ranges

Lakes; Ocean

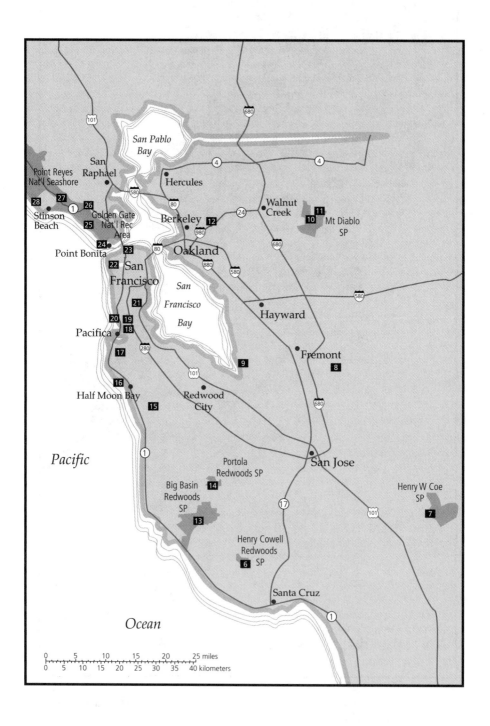

Where Should I Go Hiking?

Because the 101 Hikes range from the supremely easy to the incredibly difficult, you should be able to find a hike that fulfills your personal sense of adventure in the region you wish to visit. For an overview of the difficulty rating system, please see "How To Use This Book." For those looking for a specific trail feature, the hikes are organized by theme in Appendix 1. Those unfamiliar with Northern California's geography and weather patterns should read on.

California Dreaming

For the purposes of this book, Northern California can be divided into four regions that share similar characteristics. Each is described briefly below.

The Central Coast, Bay Area, and Coast Ranges (Hikes 1-38)

Stretching from the southern end of Ventana Wilderness in Big Sur north to the Lost Coast, this region encompasses the stretch of coastline accessible from Highway 1, all of the Bay Area, and the interior Coast Ranges as far north as Snow Mountain Wilderness. The overall topography is one of low mountain ranges divided by broad valleys—interrupted by the unique world of the San Francisco Bay Area. While the coastline is generally rocky and characterized by steep bluffs and headlands, beaches are also common.

Annual precipitation is high on the coast but diminishes rapidly as you go inland, creating habitat for lush redwood and mixed-evergreen forests near the Pacific, and extensive oak woodlands farther east. Going from south to north, precipitation generally increases while average temperatures decrease, leaving the southern regions hotter and drier for most of the year. Dense fog is common along the coast during the summer months, snow seldom falls anywhere in the region, and most of the hikes can be done year-round. Highlights of the region include rolling oak woodlands flushed green in spring, foaming surf on the dramatic Pacific Coast, lush redwood forests, and the endless variety of hikes and views available in the Bay Area.

The North Coast and Klamath Mountains (Hikes 39-53)

Stretching north from the Lost Coast to the Oregon Border and east to Mt. Shasta, this region includes the hard-to-access strip of coastline north of Highway 1, the magnificent old-growth redwood forests along Highway 101, and the convoluted ranges of the Klamath Mountains. The coastal topography is usually rocky and often dominated by sheer cliffs. Inland, the Klamath Mountains compose a variety of smaller ranges incised by deep river canyons. Elevations rarely exceed 8,000 feet. The Trinity Alps and Marble Mountains are two of the more notable subranges.

Annual precipitation is high throughout the entire region and creates thick forests that blanket all but the tallest ridges and peaks. Snow occurs down to 3,000 feet in the winter and dense fog envelops the coast during the summer. Highlights include remote locations, luxuriant forests, and some of California's choicest wilderness.

Shasta and the Modoc Plateau (Hikes 54-68)

Including all of northeast California from Mt. Shasta east to Nevada and Lassen Peak north to Oregon, this region is a starkly different place. The landscape is entirely volcanic, an extensive plateau averaging around 4,000 feet in elevation dominated by two active volcanoes—Mt. Shasta and Lassen Peak. Cinder cones, defunct volcanoes, lava flows, and the notable Warner Mountains add a distinctive topography to the land.

Annual precipitation is low and summer temperatures are high, creating deserts and dry forests. Snow falls across the plateau in the winter. Highlights include the volcanic wonderlands of Mt. Shasta and Lassen Peak, the Warner Mountains, and some of the emptiest corners in the state.

The Sierra Nevada (Hikes 69-101)

For the purposes of this book, the Sierra Nevada stretches from southern Sequoia National Park north to Keddie Ridge just south of Lake Almanor, and includes a few locations east of the range. Ranging in height from over 14,000 feet at its southern end to barely 7,000 feet at its northern terminus, the range is characterized by jagged peaks, major rivers, and countless alpine lakes. While naked granite composes much of the range, a more complicated geologic mix is prevalent in the northern regions.

Annual precipitation is high and arrives in the form of heavy winter snows that melt throughout the summer, creating a broad forest belt that extends upward to about 10,000 feet. The highest elevations support only bare expanses of rock, snow, and hardy low-lying plants. Highlights include spectacular alpine scenery, unique landforms, deep river canyons, and the magnificent giant sequoia.

Northern California Weather

The overall weather in California is closely linked to the sun's relative position with the Earth. As the sun's rays strike more directly north of the equator in spring, the air it warms in the tropics rises into the upper atmosphere and moves north over the Pacific Ocean. Cooled as it travels, the air sinks back

down to the surface to form an area of high pressure over the north Pacific known as the "Pacific High." As the summer progresses, the high becomes increasingly stable and prevents low-pressure storm fronts in the Gulf of Alaska from reaching Northern California. As a consequence, summers are almost entirely devoid of rain. Localized thunderstorms do occur—especially in the high mountains—but generally the entire state basks in never-ending blue skies and sunshine. Summers on the coast are remarkably different, however. The same Pacific High that keeps storms away also creates northwest winds that almost continually buffet the shoreline. Warm moisture-laden summer air condenses into fog over the cold Pacific waters, which is then pushed onshore by wind and the land/sea temperature differential. Summer on the coast can seem a lot like winter.

As the sun begins to strike north of the equator more obliquely in October, the entrenched Pacific High keeps storms away for most of the month while the decreasing temperatures greatly reduce the incidence of fog. It is California's choicest month of weather. Storms return by November, striking the North Coast first and then gradually reaching farther south as the Pacific High deteriorates. By January, storm after storm is hitting the state, inundating it with heavy rainfall and deep snow. Sunny breaks do occur between storms but they are generally short-lived. February is the wettest month and storms can continue well into April, although spring days usually begin to occur in March. As a more direct angle of sunlight hits the north once again, the cycle repeats itself.

A Month-by-Month Playbook

The following is a brief description of the hiking opportunities available each month. Bear in mind that many hikes can be done year-round or at times not explicitly mentioned below.

January Winter storms begin drenching the cold state and only low-elevation regions near the coast are free from snow. Last year's brown slopes begin to explode with green grass and powerful winter waves often break, making a coastal trip very worthwhile during sunny spells. The storms also cleanse the pollution from the air, making this the start of prime hiking season for views in the Bay Area—try Mt. Diablo (Hike 10), San Bruno Mountain (Hike 21), or Mt. Tamalpais (Hike 26). Redwood forests are always open for hiking on rainy days. Crowds are all but non-existent.

February The wettest month of the year hammers at the state and hiking is challenging. Stay coastal and in the Bay Area if the weather breaks. Pinnacles National Monument (Hike 4) is an awesome place to visit on sunny days. The adventurous can go looking for bald eagles around Cache Creek (Hike 33), in the Great Central Valley (Hike 35), or at

Tule Lake (Hike 56). Crowds remain absent.

March A highly variable month, March can continue to bring wintry storms or break into long stretches of warm sunshine. Regardless of how frequently they come, the first spring days arrive this month and herald the start of wildflower season. Open slopes along the coast burst with color, views remain generally clear throughout the Bay Area, and oak woodlands flourish green. Big Sur (Hikes 2–3) can be downright hot during sunny spells.

April Though much like March, April has increasing sunshine and warm weather. Fog can already begin to reappear on the coast, making this the last good month for fog-free coastal adventuring. Oak woodlands explode with wildflowers and Henry W. Coe State Park (Hike 7) is a choice destination. Bidwell Park and Ishi Wilderness (Hikes 70–71) make a great combination trip. This is also a great time to tackle the North Coast (Hikes 39–46). Pummeled

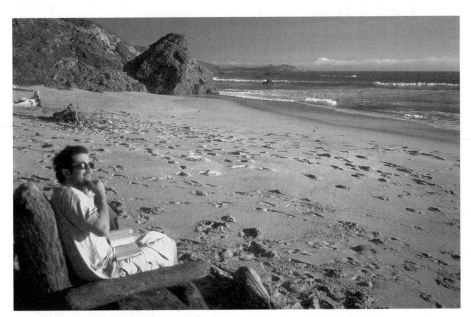

Hmmm, where should I go hiking next?

by rain and/or fog much of the year, the region experiences some of its nicest weather this month, when tourist crowds are absent.

May The winter snowpack begins to melt at higher elevations and hikes below 5,000 feet open for the season. Mountain rivers rage with snowmelt, the waterfalls of Yosemite Valley are spectacular (Hike 83), and deep river canyons offer summer heat and wildflowers. Warm sunny days at the coast are intermittent as the fog begins to increase, hills in the Coast Ranges begin to brown, and summer haze begins to collect, ending the prime Bay Area hiking season. Crowds remain surprisingly light until Memorial Day, when the summer hordes instantaneously appear.

June The winter snowpack continues to melt but hikes above 8,000 feet usually remain snow-covered and inaccessible all month. The cable route on Half Dome (Hike 84) is usually put up in the middle of the month, and Sequoia and Kings Canyon national parks (Hikes 94–99) offer great early summer adventures. Coastal fog continues to increase and heat in the Coast Ranges and Sierra foothills starts to become oppressive. The summer crowds are out in force at popular destinations.

July Unless it has been an unusually heavy winter, virtually all hikes are open by July and the three-month high-elevation season has begun. While the Sierra Nevada is the destination of choice with its wide variety of alpine hikes, also consider a trip north to Mt. Shasta and the Klamath Mountains (Hikes 47–55). Wildflower season begins to taper off as the month progresses. Fog and crowds are heavy along the coast. Avoid the July 4th weekend if at all possible.

August Though much like July, the very highest elevation hikes to Palisade Glacier (Hike 93) and Sawtooth Peak (Hike 101) are sometimes snow-free for the first time. Coastal fog is as thick as it gets, statewide temperatures max out,

and crowds remain heavy all month long.

September This is a great month to be anywhere in the mountains. Summer vacation ends for a lot of people on Labor Day and crowds suddenly vanish, yet the weather remains absolutely ideal across the state. It's a good time to visit Lake Tahoe (Hikes 77–78) or the Trinity Alps (Hike 47–48). Coastal fog begins to diminish and high elevations become increasingly cold at night.

October This is a great month to be anywhere in California. It is the month of Indian summer when the sun shines day in and day out, coastal fog finally disappears for the season, and fall colors fluoresce in the mountains. Hot summer weather lingers on the Modoc Plateau and the aspens of empty South Warner Wilderness (Hikes 61–62) rustle gold in the breeze. Higher elevation hikes usually remain open but nighttime temperatures often drop below freezing. Be aware that hunting season opens early in the month on National Forest lands, and bright colors are good for hikers. Near the end of the month temperatures begin to swing markedly and the first rogue winter storm often strikes the state.

November Much of California closes to hiking as snow begins falling in the mountains and a chill sets in at higher elevations. Intermittent winter storms occur and air quality and visibility start to improve in the Bay Area. Fall lingers in the low-elevation foothills of the Sierra Nevada for the first half of the month—Rubicon River (Hike 76) is a pleasant destination. Stay coastal or in the Bay Area otherwise.

December Daylight dwindles to a minimum as California slips into the depths of winter and hiking days are short. Weather is variable; long stretches of rain, cold snaps, and sunshine can all occur. Remain strictly coastal or enjoy views in the Bay Area.

The Different Governing Agencies

This book visits a wide variety of parks and forests managed by several different governing agencies. Rules and regulations often vary by location, but generally are the same within each group. The four most commonly visited areas in this book are **National Parks, State Parks, National Forests,** and **National Forest Wildernesses.** A miscellany of other governing agencies occurs as well, including the BLM and various city and county parks.

National Parks Run by the federal government (Department of the Interior), national parks are designated to preserve and protect unique natural features and wilderness. Generally very user-friendly, they tend to draw the largest crowds and often have amenities like small stores, hot showers, and well-maintained campgrounds. Free park maps are handed out and driving is easy. Regulations are generally strict—car camping is permitted only in designated sites, wilderness permits are always required for overnight trips into the backcountry, trail quotas are common, and dogs are never permitted on the trail. While entrance fees between $5 and $20 are charged for all national parks, purchase of a Golden Eagle Pass ($50 as of 1999) allows free entry into all national parks across the country for one year.

State Parks Run by the state of California, state parks are generally small and protect a wide variety of natural features. They are common along the coast and tend to be the most costly places to visit—day-use fees between $3 and $7 are always charged, campgrounds are expensive, and even park maps (when available) cost $1. As of July 1, 2000, however, many state park fees were reduced, and prices listed in this book may be overstated (at least for now). Roads are good and driving is easy. Regulations are generally strict—car camping is permitted only in designated campgrounds, backcountry camping (when possible) is allowed only at designated trail camps, and dogs are never allowed on the trail. All state park campgrounds operate on the same reservation system—call 1-800-444-PARK or go online at *www.reserveamerica.com* to reserve a site.

National Forests As "the land of many uses," national forests are America's playgrounds. Run by the federal government (Department of Agriculture), the U.S. Forest Service manages the land for a wide variety of purposes—logging, ranching, hunting, and hiking are all permitted—and regulations are generally few. Dogs are allowed, camping is permitted virtually anywhere on national forest land, no wilderness permits are required for backcountry camping, and no use fees are charged. A **campfire permit** is required for the use of stoves and campfires, obtainable free from any Forest Service ranger station and valid across the state for the entire year. Roads are generally poor, commonly unpaved, and often challenging and confusing to navigate. National Forest maps are usually remarkably accurate, indicate areas of private property, and are highly recommended for road navigation. While organized National Forest campgrounds are plentiful across the state and tend to be inexpensive or even free, they generally lack amenities (pit toilets are common).

National Forest Wildernesses Managed to protect the land's wilderness aspects, designated wilderness areas are much like national forests but with a few more restrictions. No roads exist, all motorized vehicles are prohibited, and logging is not permitted. Wilderness permits are required in all but the most remote areas and can be obtained free at any nearby ranger station. Due to heavy use, the wilderness areas in the Sierra Nevada are more heavily managed and trail quotas are often in effect for back-packers. Dogs are usually allowed and backcountry camping is permitted almost anywhere. Facilities and amenities are non-existent—come prepared.

Other Agencies City and county parks are common in the Bay Area and are almost all day-use only. Entrance fees ($3–6) are usually required. Dogs are generally not permitted but there are some exceptions. The BLM manages a few regions covered by the book. Much like national forests, they have few regulations and almost no amenities or facilities. Dogs are permitted.

Other Factors

Children While this book is not designed for families with young children, several short hikes are perfectly suitable for the youngest hikers; look for the symbol in the trip header or the complete list in Appendix 1.

Campgrounds Campgrounds vary markedly depending on location. State and national park campgrounds are generally the most luxurious, but are often expensive and crowded. Forest Service campgrounds are usually much more basic, smaller, cheaper, and good if you can cope with pit toilets.

Hike 1—Burnt

Location	Ventana Wilderness
Agency	Los Padres National Forest
Highlights	Unobstructed views atop the highest coastal summit in California.
Distance	3.0 miles round trip
Total Elevation Gain/Loss	1400´/1400´
Hiking Time	2–3 hours
Difficulty	★★★
Best Times	April through November
Optional Map	Forest Service *Ventana Wilderness* topographic map

Three miles from the ocean, Cone Peak rises a mile to the sky. In the summer of 1999, most of Ventana Wilderness burned. Cone Peak, the dominant mountain of the southern wilderness, burned with it. Now nothing hides the seamless joining of ocean and sky, the towering coastal vistas, or the sweeping panorama of the Santa Lucia Mountains.

The Hike climbs to the fire lookout atop Cone Peak (5155) on steep but short Cone Peak Trail. The recent fires and ensuing rains badly eroded the trail over the '99–00 winter and trail conditions were poor the following spring, increasing the overall difficulty of the hike. Call ahead to check current trail conditions and be prepared for loose, rocky slopes. Los Padres National Forest requires visitors to purchase a Forest Adventure Pass ($5/day), available inland at King City Ranger Station (see below) and on the coast at Big Sur Station (see Hike 2) but not anywhere close to the trailhead. The 6-mile dirt access road closes after the first heavy winter rains (typically in December) and usually reopens in March. Crowds and coastal fog are heaviest in the summer. No water is available at the trailhead.

To Reach the Trailhead, take Nacimiento Rd. east from Hwy. 1—the turnoff is by Kirk Creek Campground 4 miles south of Lucia. Be aware that Hwy. 1 is subject to frequent washouts and closures, especially in the winter. Follow sinuous Nacimiento Rd. as it climbs 2,800 feet in 7 miles to the divide, and turn north on rough and unpaved Cone Peak Rd. Low-clearance vehicles should have no problem making it to the trailhead, located 6 miles down this road on the left at a sharp **U.**

Approaching from the east, take Hwy. 101 to the Hwy. G14/Fort Hunter Liggett exit just north of King City. Follow G14 south for 17 miles and turn right (west) on Mission Rd., passing immediately through an always-open fort entrance gate. Bear left on Nacimiento Rd. 2.8 miles past the gate and left again 0.8 mile farther—be watchful as the intersection signs are not obvious. From here, it is 16 increasingly narrow miles to Cone Peak Rd., where you proceed as described above.

Description: From the trailhead, the trail initially strikes west to quickly attain the nearby ridgetop. The cliffs of Cone Peak and the fire lookout are clearly visible to the northwest, and Hare Canyon can be seen slicing southwest down to the ocean. Far down the canyon is a dense patch of green, a stand of coastal redwoods very near the extreme southern limit of their range. Briefly remaining on the ridge, the trail then drops inland and passes through a few shrubs before switchbacking up to the ridgetop.

As the trail begins its long coastside traverse to approach the peak from the west, the devastation of recent fires is evident in the bare hillsides. Fires sweep through the dry chaparral about once every 20 years as part of a natural process of plant regeneration. The 1999 Big Sur fire began during a dry lightning storm in September, a blaze that eventually consumed almost 90,000 acres—more than half the area of Ventana Wilderness—and went down in the books as the 10th largest wildfire in California's recorded history.

Only a few scraggly oaks survived the blaze and Coulter pine snags protrude from the slopes like burnt matchsticks. The exposed trail traverses below the summit cliffs before beginning a tightly switchbacking ascent along a steep and rocky spur ridgeline. A small patch of unburned forest grows below the trail as it climbs to a junction immediately below the summit—to the lookout!

The walkway surrounding the lookout is usually open to the public and views are tremendous. Looking southwest, the scale of land and sea is distorted by your elevation—notice the tiny bridge of Hwy. 1 at Limekiln State Park far below. Turning northeast, the tall rise of Junipero Serra Peak (5862) is one of the few distinguishing peaks in this land of sheer, naked topography. Southeast, the broad valley of Fort Hunter Liggett can be distinguished beyond the low

nearby ridges. Heading downhill, you return the way you came.

Nearest Visitor Center: King City Ranger Station, (831) 385-5434, located at 406 S. Mildred St. in King City—take the Canal off-ramp from Hwy. 101, go east on Canal, right on Division, and left on Mildred. Open Monday through Friday 8 A.M.–4:30 P.M.

Backpacking Information: Due to the recent fire devastation, backpacking in southern Ventana Wilderness is not recommended. No wilderness permit is needed but a valid campfire permit and Adventure Pass are required.

Nearest Campground: Kirk Creek Campground, located at the Hwy. 1/ Nacimiento Rd. junction (33 sites, $16). Inland try Nacimiento Campground, located on Nacimiento Rd. 3.5 miles east of Cone Peak Rd. (7 sites, $12).

Additional Information: *www.r5.pswf.gov/lospadres/index.htm*

BURNT

Hike 2—*El Sur Grande*

Location	Ewoldsen Trail
Agency	Julia Pfeiffer Burns State Park
Highlights	Quiet redwood forest. Aerial ocean views.
Distance	4.5 miles
Total Elevation Gain/Loss	1500´/1500´
Hiking Time	3–4 hours
Difficulty	★★★
Best Times	September through May
Optional Map	USGS 7.5-min *Partington Ridge*

Big Sur is exceptional country. Open redwood forest lines creeks gurgling clear as glass, mountains rise thousands of feet above the foaming surf, and bare golden hilltops offer sweeping vistas of it all.

The Hike, a steady ascent along Ewoldsen Trail, takes you through a creekside redwood forest on your way to a viewpoint atop an open bluff more than 1,600 feet above the sea. Crowds are constant on the Big Sur coast and—due to the limited amount of public land directly along the coast—all hiking trails receive heavy use. Not a hike for solitude, summer months are the worst for crowds. Water is available at the trailhead.

Julia Pfeiffer Burns State Park

To Reach the Trailhead, take Hwy. 1 to the Julia Pfeiffer Burns State Park entrance, located 10 miles south of Pfeiffer Big Sur State Park on the central Big Sur coast. There is a $6 day-use fee.

Description: From the trailhead in the upper parking lot (0.0/280), the path immediately enters the redwood forest and passes along a wooden fence before dropping down to a picnic area by McWay Creek. The open forest here is much different than the temperate rainforest more commonly associated with redwoods farther north. Here, at the southern limit of their range, the trees are only able to find adequate moisture for growth along the small creeks and rivers that slice the Big Sur coast. The drier conditions prevent the redwoods from obtaining the colossal size of their northern counterparts and also eliminate the dense understory and thick moss normally present. A few small patches of redwood sorrel, ferns, and seasonal wildflowers can be found among the litter of the forest floor, but generally the forest is remarkably open.

Crossing the clear creek by a rundown barn, the trail begins climbing through an area good for bird-watching. American dippers can often be observed ducking in and out of the water as they look for aquatic insects and other snacks on the creek bottom. Small brown creepers are easily identified overhead by their ability to ascend trees vertically, spiraling around the trunk as they go. The junction for Canyon Trail is soon encountered (0.2/400), a quick and worthwhile 0.1-mile side trip leading to a delightful bench by a cascading ribbon of water.

Back on the main trail, you climb steeply above the canyon on a few switchbacks as tan oak begins to appear trailside. After crossing the south fork of the creek, the trail traverses the slopes and passes through a dramatic vegeta-tion change, where redwoods suddenly disappear into thick chaparral. Large redwoods reappear as you rejoin the creek and reach a junction by a small bridge (1.6/880). This is the start of the loop. Go right, passing several substantial trees as the trail winds along the creek. You next turn west and ascend through coast live oak and California bay to the high point of the hike where spectacular views await (2.7/1700).

Highway 1 winds along the edge of the continent below and the aquamarine clarity of the ocean often allows you to distinguish a sandy bottom. Looking south, several drainages are identifiable beyond that of McKay Creek, overshadowed by peaks of the high ridge rising abruptly and paralleling the coast a short distance inland. From this viewpoint, the ridgetop is still more than 2,000 feet above you, and the tallest summit visible south is nearly 4,000 feet high and less than 3 miles from the ocean. Imposing topography indeed. This is also a good spot to look for red-tailed hawks and other raptors scanning the bare hillsides for lunch. From here, the trail drops behind the ridge, losing views as it makes a half-mile traverse before cutting back to quickly descend to McKay Creek and the junction at your loop's end. Head right to retrace your path to the trailhead.

Nearest Visitor Center: Big Sur Station, (831) 667-2315, located 10 miles north of this park's entrance and just south of Pfeiffer Big Sur State Park. Open daily 8 A.M.–6 P.M. Memorial Day through Labor Day; the rest of the year open daily 8 A.M.–4:30 P.M.

Nearest Campground: Pfeiffer Big Sur State Park (218 sites, $15). Reservations are recommended in the summer.

Additional Information:
www.parks.ca.gov/districts/monterey/ jpbsp.htm

EL SUR GRANDE

Hike 3—The Sandy Escape

Location	Molera Beach
Agency	Andrew Molera State Park
Highlights	Peace and quiet on the beach.
Distance	5.0 miles
Total Elevation Gain/Loss	200´/200´
Hiking Time	3–4 hours
Difficulty	★
Best Times	September through May
Optional Map	USGS 7.5-min *Big Sur*

For constantly being by the ocean, there is remarkably little coastal access from Highway 1 on the Big Sur coast. The jagged rocks and sheer cliffs that make the region so spectacular also make finding a beach, much less a secluded beach, a difficult proposition. Luckily there is Andrew Molera State Park and its 2-mile-long stretch of sand, whose farther end offers an opportunity to escape the crowds and commune peacefully with the sea.

The Hike explores the length of Molera Beach, traveling to its end before returning along the low bluffs. This is a tide-dependent hike and the beach is treacherous and impassable in places during high tides, making it necessary to walk along the bluffs during these times. Tide tables are usually posted on the information sign in the parking lot, or you can check at Big Sur Station (see Hike 2) before heading out. Those arriving around high tide should hike first along the bluffs and return along the beach closer to low tide. Due to the treacherous nature of ocean currents here, swimming is deemed unsafe. Be aware that the seasonal, starting footbridge across Big Sur River is removed after the first heavy winter rains, making it necessary to ford the swollen river during the winter months. Water is available at the trailhead.

To Reach the Trailhead, take Hwy. 1 south of Carmel for 22 miles to the park entrance and substantial parking lot. Approaching from the south, the turnoff is 4.2 miles north of the park entrance for Pfeiffer Big Sur State Park and is a hard, dog-leg left turn. There is a day-use fee of $4. It is possible to reach the trailhead by **public transportation** between Memorial Day and Labor Day on Monterey-Salinas Transit bus 22, which runs twice daily from downtown Monterey to Pfeiffer Big Sur State Park. Call (831) 899-2555 for current schedule and fare information, or go online at *mst.org*.

Description From the trailhead, cross Big Sur River on the narrow footbridge and bear right on Beach Trail. Paralleling but beyond sight of the river, you pass the Creamery, a former pasture slowly being replanted with native vegetation. Twisted sycamores, arroyo willows, black cottonwood, red alders, and a few redwoods line the river, and chest-high bush lupines dot the open meadow. Looking behind you to the east, a prominent ridge of the Santa Lucia Range is visible. Composed primarily of granite transported from the south along the San Andreas Fault, the mountain range owes much of its sheer topography to the erosion-resistant nature of its granitic rock. The Creamery is also an excellent area for birdlife—killdeer, black phoebes, and Cooper's hawks can often be spotted.

Continuing toward the beach, notice the incredibly grizzled redwood tree across the meadow on your left before you turn back toward the river. Then pass thick patches of poison oak and coffee berry, which is easily identified by the dark black berries that ripen in the fall. Driftwood shelters and other interesting constructs fill this first sandy area where you turn south and begin the beach walk.

The low bluffs along the beach expose the variegated hues of intensely deformed rocks. While part of the Franciscan Complex, they have been more heavily metamorphosed than similar exposures found farther north in California, as a result of the numerous northwest-trending faults associated with the San Andreas Fault, which slice apart the Big Sur region and intensely shear the adjacent rock. The rare mineral almondite is exposed in places, coloring the white sand purple where it has eroded onto the beach. Rounded granite stones are also present, washed down from the Santa Lucia Mountains.

Sea lions, seals, and even sea otters can sometimes be spotted offshore as you go (barefoot) up the beach. Crowds diminish and rocky points hem in secluded stretches of sand as you continue, eventually reaching the junction for Spring Trail, your access to the return route on the bluffs above.

Eighty feet of climbing up a narrow gully brings you to Bluffs Trail—go left back the direction you came. Coyote brush, poison hemlock, California poppies, and more lupine cover the open blufftops along the trail back toward the Creamery. At the bluffs' end, the trail intersects Ridge Trail—go left again, immediately dropping down to a wide

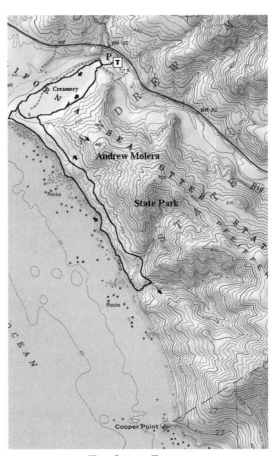

THE SANDY ESCAPE

dirt road. Bearing left here returns you to the Beach Trail. Turning right down the road takes you winding along the opposite side of the Creamery close to several large coast live oaks, before the road rejoins the Beach Trail at the footbridge over Big Sur River.

Nearest Visitor Center: Big Sur Station (see Hike 2).

Nearest Campground: Walk-in campsites are available here in a large meadow near the Big Sur River on a first-come, first-served basis ($4 per person, register at the entrance kiosk). The closest developed campground is in Pfeiffer Big Sur State Park (218 sites, $15). Reservations are recommended in the summer.

Hike 4—The Pinnacles

Location	High Peaks Trail
Agency	Pinnacles National Monument
Highlights	Naked monoliths of towering volcanic rock. Prairie falcons.
Distance	5.3 miles
Total Elevation Gain/Loss	1650´/1650´
Hiking Time	3–4 hours
Difficulty	★★★
Best Times	October through May
Optional Map	USGS 7.5-min *North Chalone Peak*

The story of the Pinnacles begins some 28 million years ago when the Pacific Tectonic Plate first makes contact with North America near present-day Los Angeles, and pushes an ancient, active, underwater volcanic ridge beneath the continent. Widespread geologic havoc follows and the first strands of the San Andreas Fault begin forming. Shortly after this collision, 23.5 million years ago, rising magma escapes onto the surface through one of the many newly formed fractures and creates a large, short-lived stratovolcano 24 miles long and roughly 8,000 feet high. Straddling the San Andreas Fault as it does, the volcano is

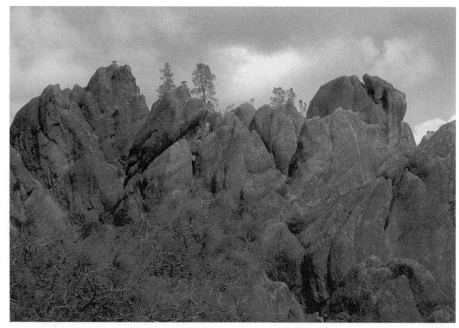

The Pinnacles

quickly ripped in two as lands west of the fault are pushed northwest. The western half of the volcano is tilted by associated splinter faults, protecting it from erosion until it is once again exposed at the surface. It weathers to form the spectacularly unique peaks of the Pinnacles, 195 miles away from its eroded rock counterpart in southern California.

While numerous volcanic rocks compose the Pinnacles, the two most common (and easily identifiable) are volcanic breccia, a mess of angular fragments welded together into the reddish rocks of the High Peaks, and flow-banded rhyolite, a fine-grained lava that preserves its original flow patterns. Several excellent sources of information on the local geology are available at the visitor center, including a guide to the Pinnacles Geological Trail, the first half of which is along this hike.

The Hike climbs from Bear Gulch Visitor Center along the Condor Gulch and High Peaks trails, winding through wild volcanic formations before dropping steeply back down to Bear Gulch Picnic Area. The best time to come is February. You have to time your visit to avoid winter storms, but the reward is early wildflowers, crystalline air, flowing streams, green hillsides and, most of all, solitude. The air, the water, and the green all remain from March through May—supplemented by a greater explosion of wildflowers—but the solitude vanishes, especially on weekends. An average of 200,000 people a year visit this small monument, and most of them come during this time. In the summer months temperatures are sizzling and average almost 100°F during the day—don't bother. The fall is mild but brown and dry. The park is day-use only and closes at sunset. Water is available at the trailhead.

To Reach the Trailhead, take Hwy. 25 south from Hollister for 32 miles to the posted turnoff for the Pinnacles on Hwy. 146. Approaching from the south, Hwy. 25 can be accessed from Hwy. 101 via Hwy. G13 at King City. Park in the visitor center parking lot, 4.8 miles past the turnoff. The trailhead is across the road. While it is also possible to approach the Pinnacles (but not this hike) from the west through Soledad, *there is no through connection on Hwy. 146.* There is an entrance fee of $5, valid for 7 days.

Description From the trailhead (0.0/1650), you begin climbing on the Condor Gulch Trail through large gray pines and deciduous blue oaks, quickly passing above a maintenance station. As you ascend, coast live oaks can be spotted in the riparian valley below. Toyon soon appears by the path, a shrub easily identified by its stiff, toothed, elliptical leaves and bright red berries, which first appear in December. At the first switchback, a rounded squat formation dubbed The Hippopotamus sits across the small gully. Looking like a stack of chips, Casino Rock is visible to the north. The trail then leads to an overlook where a small runnel of water gurgles down in season.

From the overlook, you leave the gulch behind and wrap around the ridge above you. Where the trail winds through open chaparral dominated by chamise, good views east of deeply furrowed San Benito Valley open up.

Views to the north appear as you intersect High Peaks Trail (1.7/2290)—go left. This is a good place to start looking for prairie falcons. Every year from January through June, roughly a dozen pairs of these raptors nest in the cliffs of the Pinnacles and can often be seen swooping between the peaks. They are readily identified by their pointed wings, narrow tails, quick wingbeats, and distinctive cries. Golden eagles also nest in this region and are occasionally spotted. Curving through massive boulders and outcrops, the trail then offers up views of the Balconies, a large, deeply sliced outcrop visible northwest.

Reaching a junction with Tunnel Trail (2.3/2480), continue straight on High Peaks Trail to begin an exciting section where bolted iron railings provide handholds for steep stairways, whose steps are mere scoops in the rock. Passage is tight beneath Condor Crags and descending those scoops is challenging; you soon reach a junction on the opposite side (3.0/2470) where an outhouse is conveniently situated.

Keeping left on High Peaks Trail, you begin the steep switchbacking descent to Bear Gulch. You pass the aptly named Anvil along a brief level section, before continuing down past large manzanitas to the junction with Rim Trail (4.5/1600). Descend left past Discovery Wall among handsome coast live oaks, and then go left again at the Moses Spring Trail junction (4.8/1550) to quickly reach Bear Gulch Picnic area. Cross the road and follow the easy path back to the visitor center.

Nearest Visitor Center: Bear Gulch Visitor Center, (831) 389-4485. Open daily 9 A.M.–5 P.M.

Nearest Campground: There are currently no campgrounds within the monument. Privately owned Pinnacles Campground is located immediately east of the monument on Hwy. 146. First-come, first-served. $7 per person per night (maximum of $28 per group).

Additional Information:
www.nps.gov/pinn

THE PINNACLES

Hike 5—The Invisible Canyon

Location	Fremont Peak
Agency	Fremont Peak State Park
Highlights	Superlative view of the entire Monterey Bay.
Distance	1.0 mile round trip
Total Elevation Gain/Loss	350´/350´
Hiking Time	1 hour
Difficulty	★
Best Times	After winter storms
Optional Map	USGS 7.5-min *San Juan Bautista*

Atop Fremont Peak on March 6, 1846, John C. Fremont defiantly raised the first American flag in California. Three days later, as he sat surrounded by Spanish forces threatening to attack, his flagpole blew down. Taking this as a bad omen, Fremont departed and left behind this unrivaled panorama of Monterey Bay.

The Hike is a quick and easy ascent of Fremont Peak (3169), a prominent summit located due east from the center of Monterey Bay. Unparalleled views are the reason to come here, making it critical to correctly time your visit. The air is cleanest and the grass greenest immediately following winter storms, but air quality rapidly declines without rain and will usually begin to deteriorate within 24 hours. Prepare for chilly and windy conditions during the winter months. Fog can completely obliterate the view during the summer. Crowds are minimal, especially in the winter. Water is available in the nearby campground.

To Reach the Trailhead, take Hwy. 156 east of Hwy. 101 for 3 miles to San Juan Bautista and head south on The Alameda (Hwy. G1). Approaching from the east, the turnoff is 8 miles past the Hwy. 156/25 junction. Immediately bear left on San Juan Canyon Rd. (Hwy. G1) at the complex four-way intersection and

proceed 10 miles to the upper parking lot at road's end. There is a $3 day-use fee.

Description: From the trailhead, proceed up the paved road signed AUTHORIZED VEHICLES ONLY. A single-track dirt trail quickly splits off across from a few, stout Coulter pines, passing through coyote brush punctuated by some valley oaks and small madrones. It wraps around the western slope where the antenna complex comes into view. A series of short switchbacks lead you to the rocky summit.

Savoring the view, ignore the antennas as you behold the curving expanse of Monterey Bay. Its southern arm is formed by the Monterey peninsula, visible beyond the city of Salinas. Its northern end contains south-facing Santa Cruz on its shores. Two main rivers drain into Monterey Bay: the longer Salinas River on the south, which flows 190 miles northwest through the broad Salinas Valley; and the Pajaro River on the north, which flows by Watsonville before entering the bay near its center. Between the two is Elkhorn Slough, a tidal embayment extending 7 miles inland, whose mouth is marked by the enormous 500-foot-high boiler stacks of the Moss Landing Power Plant. The slough is a haven for birdlife—the North American record for the most birds seen from a single spot in a single day (116) was set here in 1982. The broad alluvial plain around Monterey Bay is rich agricultural land and annually produces the country's largest crop of artichokes.

Immediately offshore of Elkhorn Slough is the beginning of Monterey Canyon, California's deepest submarine canyon. Twisting slightly southwest, it reaches a depth of 6,000 feet less than 15 miles from shore, almost twice the elevation of Fremont Peak 16 miles from the bay shore. To create so deep a submarine canyon requires erosive power far greater than that provided by the current rivers that flow into Monterey Bay. To explain its origin, theory holds that in the recent geologic past (up to 5 million years ago) a large amount of California drained through present-day Monterey Bay unhindered by any Coast Ranges,

carving a deep offshore canyon over the course of millions of years. As the San Andreas Fault system moved Monterey Bay north, the rising Coast Ranges limited its drainage basin to its current watershed. Cold water upwelling from March through September funnels nutrient-rich waters up Monterey Canyon, providing sustenance for the incredible diversity of sea life that makes Monterey Bay world-famous.

Nearest Visitor Center: No staffed visitor center. Call (831) 623-4255 for general information. There is also an observatory near the summit that offers public programs.

Nearest Campground: Fremont State Park Campground (25 sites, $7).

Additional Information:
www.parks.ca.gov/districts/monterey/ fpsp.htm

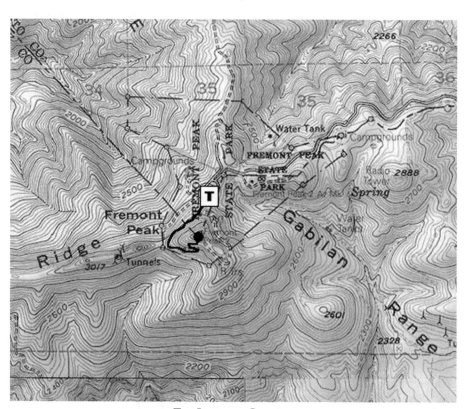

THE INVISIBLE CANYON

Hike 6—Redwoods Reborn

Location	Fall Creek
Agency	Henry Cowell Redwoods State Park
Highlights	Redwood forest. Fern mania.
Distance	6.5 miles
Total Elevation Gain/Loss	1300´/1300´
Hiking Time	4–6 hours
Difficulty	★★★
Best Times	Year-round
Optional Map	USGS 7.5-min *Felton*

Testament to Nature's resiliency, the second-growth redwoods of Henry Cowell State Park flourish above 15 of the 18 ferns found in Santa Cruz County. Burbling Fall Creek flows through it all, this silent forest of tranquility. All only 30 minutes from Santa Cruz.

Henry Cowell Redwoods State Park is divided into two sections, a smaller and more visited area along Hwy. 9, and a larger northern parcel known as the Fall Creek Unit. Almost the entire drainage of Fall Creek is protected within the upper unit, allowing the canyon to recover from the ravages of the lime industry. The bedrock beneath most of this hike is granite, formed approximately 100 million years ago near today's southern Sierra Nevada. Thrust north along the San Andreas Fault over the past 20 million or so years, the region was covered by the ocean for a very long period of time. Sand and silt settled underwater, forming thick layers over the granite. Millions of microscopic sea creatures died, their skeletal remains collecting on the bottom in thick pockets. Within the past five million years, changing geometry of the San Andreas Fault thrust the Santa Cruz Mountains above sea level, exposing the mudstone, sandstone, granite, and dead sea creatures (now limestone) on the surface. Limestone contains lime, which is relatively rare in the Bay Area but necessary for creating cement, making the limestone along Fall Creek a commercially valuable asset that was exploited from the early 1870s until 1919. In order to produce and ship the lime, tremendous amounts of wood were needed to cook the limestone and construct barrels. The surrounding old-growth redwoods did not last long. Today, the forest has been regenerating for more than 75 years and is apparently healing well, although the strangely quiet forest betrays the absence of animals slow to return to their altered habitats.

The Hike drops from Empire Grade Road into the canyon, follows Fall Creek for 1.5 miles upstream, and then returns steeply on recently constructed Big Ben Trail. The hike is cool, shaded, and pleasant year-round. You will likely see other people but crowds are seldom heavy. No water is available at the trailhead.

To Reach the Trailhead from Hwy. 9 at Felton, take Felton-Empire Rd. 3.6 miles west to Empire Grade and turn right. Proceed 1.1 miles to the signed gate that marks the trailhead on the right—it can be difficult to spot, so keep your eyes open. Park by the roadside but do not block the gate. It is also possible to reach the trailhead by **public trans-**

portation. Santa Cruz Transit bus 41 runs twice per morning weekdays only from Metro Center in Santa Cruz and stops directly across from the Sunlit Lane trailhead, returning twice in the afternoon. Call (831) 425-8600 for current schedule information or go online at *sctdc.com.*

Description Two trailheads lead into the park from Empire Grade and are located 0.2 mile apart along the road. The posted gate is the obvious entrance and initially follows a fire road. The smaller Sunlit Trail starts across from the bus stop, and can be identified only by a knee-high wooden trail post. Both paths soon intersect at a four-way junction (0.3/1940)—head toward Lost Empire Trail and the lime kiln area. The forest of the upper slopes is composed almost exclusively of tan oak, Douglas-fir, and

redwood with an unfortunate undergrowth of poison oak. Dropping slightly, you soon reach another junction at Big Ben (0.7/1850), the trail's only old-growth redwood.

The return trail is on the left but you bear right on Empire Grade Trail, a single-track trail heading downward. Madrone appear as you gradually descend the path into the canyon, crossing a pretty feeder stream at Lost Camp (1.4/1440) before making a long level traverse away from the plummeting stream. As the trail turns downward through deep gullies, granite rocks are much in evidence in the path. Approaching the bottom, you encounter numerous posted junctions—continue toward Fall Creek Trail at all of them. Once you reach Fall Creek Trail (3.2/820), head upstream and enjoy the crystalline

REDWOODS REBORN

water, gentle ferns, and soft moss. Staying near the creek, the trail passes an old barrel mill site complete with rusting remains and an informative sign. Pass the first Big Ben Trail junction on the right (4.6/1270) and continue straight for an additional 0.1 mile to follow Big Ben Trail as it crosses the stream and begins the climb out. Notches in the redwood stumps here mark the former location of springboards, planks wedged into the trunk that allowed lumbermen to cut the tree at a more advantageous place than the large base at ground level. It's a steady, switchbacking, calf-burning stint up Big Ben Trail to rejoin Big Ben at the earlier junction (6.0/1920).

Nearest Visitor Center: Henry Cowell Redwoods State Park Visitor Center, (831) 335-4598, located in the lower unit of the park by Hwy. 9. Open in summer daily 10 A.M.–4 P.M., winter weekdays 11 A.M.–3 P.M. and weekends 10 A.M.–4 P.M.

Nearest Campground: Henry Cowell Redwoods State Park Campground, located in the lower unit of the park (110 sites, $14–18 depending on season and day of the week). Reservations are recommended for weekends and summer. Campground closed December through February.

Additional Information:
www.parks.ca.gov/districts/santacruz/hcrsp418.htm

Hike 7—The Quiet Hills

Location	Little Coyote Creek
Agency	Henry W. Coe State Park
Highlights	Beautiful oak woodlands. The largest state park in Northern California.
Distance	5.2 miles
Total Elevation Gain/Loss	2300´/2300´
Hiking Time	4–5 hours
Difficulty	★★★
Best Times	February through May
Optional Map	USGS 7.5-min *Mount Sizer*

Here are gentle ridgetops, steep canyons, gurgling creeks, 700 different plants, 137 species of birds, a radiant profusion of spring wildflowers, and immortal words etched on the monument to Henry W. Coe—MAY THESE QUIET HILLS BRING PEACE TO THE SOULS OF THOSE WHO ARE SEEKING.

Henry W. Coe State Park is currently 81,000 acres, a vast expanse 126 miles square of rolling hills and deep valleys harboring a tremendous diversity of life. Common trees are blue oak, valley oak, gray pine, California bay, madrone, and California buckeye, with the occasional ridgetop stand of ponderosa pine. The shrubs of the park include coyote brush, blue elderberry, ocean spray, scrub oak, poison oak, and some of the largest manzanita specimens to be seen anywhere. Wildflowers abound from March through May. Visible wildlife are predominantly avian, although coyotes, bobcats, foxes, black-tailed deer, feral pigs, and mountain lions all live within the park and are occasionally spotted. Complete checklists are available at the visitor center.

The Hike is a general introduction to the park, dropping into the canyon of Little Coyote Creek on Fish Trail before making a ridgetop traverse back along Middle Ridge Trail and Hobbs Road. While the hike can be done year-round,

spring is the time to come as hillsides are carpeted green, wildflowers bloom, and temperatures are most ideal. For being so close to the Bay Area, crowds are minimal, especially on weekdays. Water is available at the trailhead.

To Reach the Trailhead, take Hwy. 101 to Morgan Hill and take the East Dunne Avenue exit. Follow East Dunne Ave. east for 11 miles to the visitor center parking lot at the road's end. After leaving the residential area of Morgan Hill, the road is a narrow twisting ascent—RVs and trailers are not recommended. There is a $5 day-use fee.

Description: From the parking lot (0.0/2690), the hike begins on Corral Trail and crosses a small stream before heading southeast above the sheer gully of Soda Springs Creek. You soon reach a posted junction (0.5/2510) where three trails head southeast toward Manzanita Point. Bear left on Fish Trail, immediately crossing Manzanita Point Rd. and encountering a three-way junction—continue straight on Fish Trail.

Now descending into the Little Coyote Creek drainage, the trail parallels a mossy seasonal trickle lined with California bay and ferns before crossing it and remaining on the level as the creeklet plummets downward. From here, it is a gradually descending traverse through open woodlands of blue and valley oak mixed with gray pine, until a series of steep switchbacks near the bottom bring you to Little Coyote Creek (1.6/2080). Easily rockhopped (except after winter storms when it may have to be forded), the creek is too small for swimming. A short climb brings you out of the valley to the junction with Middle Ridge Trail (2.2/2400)—go left.

After you reach its highest point, the trail drops quickly before continuing slightly below the ridgeline to reach the posted junction for Frog Lake (3.3/2850)—go left. Immediately after this junction, a nicer spur loop splits right, rejoining the main trail shortly before small, unexciting, and unpotable Frog Lake.

Past Frog Lake, the trail quickly intersects Hobbs Rd. (3.8/2450)—go left again. Crossing the upper stretch of Little Coyote Creek, the trail reaches yet another junction. The narrower Flat Frog Trail bears left, offering a longer but more level return to the earlier junction at Manzanita Point Rd. This description continues on Hobbs Rd., as it begins a section of steep and sustained climbing into ponderosa pine forest, common throughout California but unusual so close to the Bay Area. Near the top of the climb, you reach another junction (4.6/2940)—bear right on the Monument Trail. Two short side trips split off from Monument Trail, and both are worthwhile. The monument to Henry W. Coe honors the man whose family ranched these lands from roughly 1900 to 1953 and is 0.1 mile east of Monument Trail near Hobbs Rd. A delightful bench is 0.2 mile west of Monument Trail and offers good vistas south

of the Santa Clara Valley. Back on Monument Trail, awesome final views of Soda Springs Canyon can be had as the trail descends on open slopes to rejoin the paved road near the visitor center by the ranger residence.

Nearest Visitor Center: Park visitor center, (408) 779-2728. Open Friday through Sunday 8 A.M.–4 P.M., sporadically Monday through Thursday.

Backpacking Information: Backcountry camping is allowed in designated sites scattered throughout the park. No campfires are permitted. Sites along or close to this hike are on Hobbs Rd. and Manzanita Point Rd.

Nearest Campground: Headquarters Campground, located below the visitor center (20 sites, $8).

Additional Information: *www.coepark.parks.ca.gov*

THE QUIET HILLS

Hike 8—Sweet Sunol

Location	Indian Joe Creek & Little Yosemite
Agency	Sunol Regional Wilderness
Highlights	A hidden oasis behind Mission Peak.
Distance	5.0 miles
Total Elevation Gain/Loss	1450´/1450´
Hiking Time	3–5 hours
Difficulty	★★
Best Times	February through May
Optional Map	USGS 7.5-min *La Costa Valley*

Less than 15 miles away, the feverish heart of Silicon Valley drives the world at Net speed. Yet shielded from view behind landmark Mission Peak, beyond the hustle and rush of the cyber-world, peaceful Sunol Wilderness offers escape in beautiful rolling woodlands.

The Hike explores the multifaceted character of Sunol Wilderness, passing along a small creek, walking open hillsides, and pausing at substantial Alameda Creek as it rushes through a scenic section dubbed "Little Yosemite." The hike is open year-round but spring is the time to come as hillsides are carpeted green, wildflowers bloom, and temperatures are most ideal. Cows are usually seen as they graze throughout the park,

Sweet Sunol

creating a pleasant manicured parkland full of cowpie minefields. Crowds around Little Yosemite can be heavy, especially on weekends, but the rest of the trails are more peaceful. Water is available at the trailhead.

To Reach the Trailhead, take Hwy. 680 east of Fremont to the Calaveras Rd. exit and proceed south on Calaveras Rd. for 4.3 miles to Geary Rd. Turn left on Geary Rd., reaching the visitor center parking lot and trailhead in 1.9 miles. There is a day-use fee of $4.

Description: From the visitor center (0.0/400), begin on the paved path for Indian Joe Nature Trail, passing behind the interpretive center before crossing Alameda Creek on a solid, year-round bridge. Once across, head upstream through a riparian alley of willows and sycamore and cross Indian Joe Creek. From its opposite bank, turn uphill on single-track Indian Joe Creek Trail and continue straight through the metal gate as Indian Joe Nature Trail splits left. You are now in the world of cow shit.

Named for "Indian Joe" Wilson, a worker and resident on the Geary Ranch that once operated here, Indian Joe Creek is an excellent place to look for salamanders and newts. The California newt, rare California tiger salamander, California slender salamander (or "worm salamander"), and yellow-eyed salamander all inhabit the park. The California newt, like all newts, passes the first year of life in the water as a larva complete with gills and a long fin. After transforming into adult form, newts leave their watery world behind and strike forth to live in damp holes and crevices in the hillsides. After achieving sexual maturity, newts make an annual migration to breed in their pond or creek of birth, utilizing a newt navigational sense—for which science provides no explanation—to travel cross-country for up to 5 miles. The slender and yellow-eyed salamanders are lungless and breathe through their moist skin, in sum-

mer months burrowing deep in the damp, underground environment they require to breathe. Amphibian numbers are declining worldwide and there is concern about the population in Sunol Wilderness. The park appreciates any reports of amphibian sightings.

Crossing back and forth over the creek before briefly winding above it, the trail passes valley oaks, coast live oaks, and more sycamores. With their broad leaves, sycamore trees can lose up to 50 gallons of water per day and grow only where such large volumes are available. Here they are found only directly in the creekbed. Once the trail rejoins the creek one trail splits left but you continue straight, passing an impressive maze of large boulders before reaching a junction with Cave Rock Rd. (1.5/1150)—go right.

Now climbing a broad fire road through open fields flush with bovine, the trail offers increasingly good views south of Alameda Creek drainage, the largest watershed in the East Bay. Flowing into the Bay by Coyote Hills (Hike 9), Alameda Creek still sustains a winter run of steelhead. Continue straight at the two junctions with Eagle View Trail, making a few gentle switchbacks before cresting the ridge by Cerro Este Overlook Trail (2.4/1780). West, the east slope of Mission Peak hides most of the Bay from view, but Mt. Tamalpais, downtown San Francisco, and landmark Sutro Tower peek out northwest in the distance. North, the summit of Mt. Diablo (Hike 10) is identifiable beyond the cities of Danville and Walnut Creek.

Calaveras Reservoir is prominent in the south as you begin the long steady descent on Cerro Este Road to Little Yosemite, passing two junctions for McCorkle Trail along the way. Poison oak increasingly lines the path near the intersection with the main thoroughfare of Camp Ohlone Rd. by Little Yosemite (3.7/450). With a rushing river coursing through a small gorge over boulders blue and green, Little Yosemite is a pretty sight. From here, it is a level walk near Alameda Creek to rejoin the park road at the upper parking lot (4.6/420). Watch for gray pine, California buckeye, and the reappearance of coast live oak and California bay along this final section. Walk the road to return to the visitor center.

Nearest Visitor Center: Park visitor center (925) 862-2601. Open weekends 9:30 A.M.–4:30 P.M.

Nearest Campground: Sunol Wilderness has four campsites that can be reserved by calling (510) 636-1684. While drop-ins are accommodated if there is space, sites are usually booked during the summer ($11).

Additional Information:
www.ebparks.org/parks/sunol.htm

Sweet Sunol

Hike 9—Bayside

Location	Coyote Hills
Agency	Coyote Hills Regional Park
Highlights	Shorebird paradise.
Distance	2.5 miles
Total Elevation Gain/Loss	400´/400´
Hiking Time	1–2 hours
Difficulty	★
Best Times	December through May
Optional Map	USGS 7.5-min *San Leandro*

A grassy swell in the flatlands, Coyote Hills exist almost in the center of south San Francisco Bay. Protected marshlands enhance the unique perspective and offer a rich assortment of wildlife.

For thousands of years, the Ohlone Indians occupied the region around Coyote Hills, harvesting oysters, clams, mussels, cockles, and abalone from the extensive Bay mudflats; salmon, seals, seal lions, sea otters, and sturgeon from the water; and deer, elk, antelope, and rabbit from the surrounding hills. Using tule reeds from the vast marshlands, they constructed small boats for paddling in the bay. We know all this because four substantial *middens* still exist in Coyote Hills Regional Park. Middens—also referred to as shell mounds— are large piles of accumulated debris, the "kitchen wastes" of the Ohlone. Shells, bones, trinkets, and other discarded materials forming these large piles have shed a great deal of light on the Ohlone lifestyle.

With the arrival of the Spanish, it all came to an end. Disease and the mission system decimated the Indian population, and by the 19th Century salt evaporation ponds and ranch lands began to surround Coyote Hills, all but eliminating the vast marshlands. Having passed through various owners, the ranch land that included Coyote Hills and a large remaining segment of marsh was purchased by the East Bay Regional Park District in 1967. Today it provides an excellent opportunity to imagine the Bay as it was before the Europeans came.

Although certainly reduced from pre-European times, wildlife still abounds in this ecological oasis. At least 210 species of birds have been spotted in the park, including a variety of herons, egrets, owls, pheasants, hawks, and shorebirds. More than 30 different mammals also exist in the park, mostly small rodents hunted by foxes, weasels, and raptors.

The Hike connects several short segments of trail to form a loop, passing first along the marsh before returning via Red Hill (291). Expansive hilltop views can only be enjoyed immediately after a winter storm has cleansed the thick South Bay air; move fast—air quality begins to deteriorate within 24 hours. The hills are velvety green from January through May, turning brown in summer and fall when the skies fill with haze. Water is available at the trailhead.

To Reach the Trailhead, take Hwy. 84 to the east side of the Dumbarton Bridge and exit at Paseo Padre Parkway. Head north on Paseo Padre for 1 mile and turn left onto Patterson Ranch Rd., following it for 1.4 miles to the visitor center at road's end. There is a $4 day-use fee. The park opens at 8 A.M. and closes at sunset.

Description: From the visitor center parking lot, go through the gate and take the paved Bayview Trail, skirting the edge of the marsh partly shaded by small willow and sycamore trees. A chittering of birds and croaking of frogs keeps you company. The trail passes a few Monterey pine before reaching the junction for Lizard Rock Trail at the far end of the marsh—go right toward the red rock outcrop. This outcrop is Franciscan chert, formed from the silica-rich skeletons of microscopic sea creatures that collected on the ocean floor over millions of years. All of Coyote Hills is composed of this chert, which gains its red color from trace amounts of iron. Highly resistant to erosion, chert has withstood the elements while the surrounding area eroded and became covered with thick layers of mud and silt washed down from the hills. In a sea of mud Coyote Hills is an isolated island of bedrock.

Stay by the marsh and loop east around the small hill before returning to Bayview Trail, passing a many-branched coast live oak along the way. Continuing on the paved path, you soon reach a junction where another paved trail splits right for the Alameda Creek Trail. Here you go left up dirt Red Hill Trail, climbing steeply to the top of the first hill before dropping down to a junction with Nike Trail, named for the

NIKE missile site that was situated on these hills between 1955 and 1959 to protect America from Communist invasion. Continuing straight, the trail ascends Red Hill, high point of the park, where your best views are had. Descending Red Hill, return to the visitor center by bearing left on Soap Root Trail and left again on wide Quail Trail.

Nearest Visitor Center: Coyote Hills Visitor Center, (510) 795-9385. Open Tuesday through Sunday 9:30 A.M.–5 P.M.

Nearest Campground: Sunol Wilderness (see Hike 8).

BAYSIDE

Hike 10—The Ultimate View

Location	Mt. Diablo Summit
Agency	Mt. Diablo State Park
Highlights	Viewpoint for much of Northern California.
Distance	0.7 mile
Total Elevation Gain/Loss	100′/100′
Hiking Time	1 hour
Difficulty	★
Best Times	After storms
Optional Map	*Trail Map of Mount Diablo State Park,* Mount Diablo Interpretive Association

Dominating the landscape, Mt. Diablo offers vistas from the Sierra Nevada to the Golden Gate in an all-encompassing sweep of Northern California. There is no other view like it.

Surrounded by encroaching development and connected to no greater mountain range, Mt. Diablo is an oasis of both plant and animal life. Besides a variety of wildlife—and particularly birdlife—several plant species occur on the mountain that can be found nowhere else. Due to variations in elevation and precipitation, a variety of ecosystems are found here, and several can be explored on this short hike.

The Hike follows the Fire Interpretive Trail, an easy loop around the summit of Mt. Diablo (3849) offering spectacular vistas in every compass direction. An interpretive brochure and informative signs enhance the experience. The optimal time to come is immediately following a spring or winter storm when the air is cleanest, the views most far-reaching, and the landscape carpeted a vibrant green. Even then, a good breeze is necessary to blow away all lingering and newly forming clouds, which can hover around the mountain. Strong easterly winds during the spring can also push the haze away. While the hike is open year-round, haze and heat are thick throughout summer and fall. Water is available at the trailhead.

To Reach the Trailhead, take the Ygnacio Valley Rd. off-ramp from Hwy. 680 in Walnut Creek and proceed 3.5 miles east on Ygnacio Valley Rd. to Oak Grove Rd. Turn right on Oak Grove Rd. and then turn left onto North Gate Rd. in 1 mile. You reach a junction with Mt. Diablo Scenic Rd. at park headquarters 7.4 miles later; take Summit Rd. 4.4 miles farther to the summit. Park in the large lot where the lanes divide near the top. It is also possible to approach from the south by taking Diablo Rd. from Hwy. 680 in Danville east for 3 miles to Mt. Diablo Scenic Rd. Turn left and proceed up the narrow, twisting road for 6 miles to the junction with Summit Rd., on which you continue 4.4 miles to the summit. There is a day-use fee of $5.

Description Be sure to pick up an interpretive brochure at the visitor center before you start. Beginning by the picnic tables across the road from the parking lot, the first half of the hike is paved and passes through a small sample of the oak woodland plant community, offering exceptional views north of distant Snow Mountain (Hike 34) and Mt. St. Helena (Hike 32), northeast of Sierra Buttes (Hike

73), besides the nearby spur of Diablo, Eagle Peak (Hike 11). Mt. Shasta would be visible 240 miles away were it not blocked by the curvature of the Earth. The rocks around you are greenstone and chert, the uppermost layers of what is known as an *ophiolite suite*, a group of rocks and minerals found close together wherever ancient sea floor is exposed.

The sea floor is composed of five layers. The bottom three form a surface that is essentially a solid piece of the Earth's crust. The upper two layers are deposited underwater on this surface. At tectonic spreading ridges, liquid basalt is squeezed out onto the sea floor, piling up in distinctively shaped pillow basalts, which compose the first of the two upper layers. These are in turn covered by sediment settling from the ocean. Primarily made up of the microscopic skeletons of tiny sea creatures, this silica-rich upper layer takes millions of years to accumulate, gradually forming thin layers mixed with small bits of sand and mud. Altered by pressure and temperature, these two upper layers eventually become greenstone and chert. The Mt. Diablo Ophiolite, as it is called, has been so heavily deformed and tilted that the sequence no longer lies flat. While its upper layers are visible at the summit, its lower layers are exposed northwest at the Lone Star Quarry, where diabase, a constituent rock of the lower sequence, is utilized for roadbeds and foundations. Exactly how this entire piece of 165-million-year-old sea floor became emplaced in the young sediments ringing Mt. Diablo remains a mystery.

As you hike into chaparral on the drier east slope of the mountain where the path becomes

dirt, the peaks of Yosemite National Park (Hikes 83-86) can be identified. Let the gospel flow from atop Devil's Pulpit, a large outcropping of chert with a mildly precarious scramble to the top. Beyond it, the trail curves onto the south side of the mountain, where grassland replaces the chaparral ecosystem on this sunniest side of the summit. Coyote Hills (Hike 9) can be spotted to the southwest by the Bay. The trail ends back by the parking lot.

Nearest Visitor Center: Summit Visitor Center, (925) 837-6119, constructed on the actual summit of the mountain. Open from March through October Wednesday through Sunday 11 A.M.– 5 P.M., and from November through February Wednesday through Sunday 10 A.M.–4 P.M. For general information also try calling (925) 837-2525.

Nearest Campground: Juniper Campground, located along Summit Rd. ($13–16 depending on season). Also, Junction Campground by park headquarters, and Live Oak Campground on Mt. Diablo Scenic Rd./South Gate Rd. Reservations are recommended for weekends.

Additional Information: *www.mdia.org*

The Ultimate View

Hike 11—Eagle Eye

Location	Eagle Peak
Agency	Mt. Diablo State Park
Highlights	Flowers, oaks, and a secluded summit.
Distance	4.0 miles
Total Elevation Gain/Loss	1800′/1800′
Hiking Time	3–4 hours
Difficulty	★★★
Best Times	February through May
Optional Map	*Trail Map of Mount Diablo State Park,* Mount Diablo Interpretive Association

From a sea of rippling grassland rises Eagle Peak, a little-visited summit below the ramparts of Mt. Diablo.

The Hike climbs to the summit of Eagle Peak (2369) from the northern boundary of Mt. Diablo State Park, ascending on Mitchell Rock Trail before returning via the Eagle Peak and Coulter Pine trails. While the hike can be done year-round, spring is the time to come as the land is carpeted green, wildflowers bloom, and temperatures are most ideal. Sections of the trail are exposed, making sun protection crucial most of the year. Ticks and poison oak are of particular concern in the brush along much of the route. Crowds are minimal. Water is available at the trailhead.

To Reach the Trailhead, take the Ygnacio Valley Rd. off-ramp from Hwy. 680 in Walnut Creek and proceed 8 miles east on Ygnacio Valley Rd. to Clayton Rd. Turn right and in 1 mile turn right again on Mitchell Canyon Rd., proceeding 2 miles to the lot at the road's end. There is a day-use fee of $5.

Description: From the parking lot (0.0/640), begin by the fire gate and information sign and start up Mitchell Canyon Rd., bearing left onto Mitchell Rock Trail at the immediate junction. Stay on the wide trail as you pass two junctions for Bruce Lee Trail before turning right on single-track Mitchell Rock Trail (just past the second Bruce Lee intersection). In season, abundant wildflowers liven the ground here and throughout the hike—look for California poppy, yarrow, paintbrush, lupine, iris, orange bush monkey flower, yerba santa, blue dicks, Ithuriel's spear, and the endemic Mt. Diablo fairy lantern.

As you climb upward into thick forest, note the increasing number of pine trees. Two pines are found in this area, both producing massive cones with sharp hooks on the scales. Gray pine is the more common, abounding throughout California's foothills and easily identified by its wispy character. Its upper half, often drooping slightly to one side, tends to fork into a multitude of small branches with no clear center trunk. Its long grayish needles come in groups of three and give the tree its name. Coulter pine, on the other hand, is straight, stout, and considerably less common than gray pine, occurring only in the Coast Ranges from Mt. Diablo south. They are at the northernmost limit of their range here and can be identified by their single trunk, long stiff needles (also in groups of three), stouter appearance, and gargantuan cones. Coulter pine cones are the largest known, giant loaves 12–14" long that easily weigh several pounds.

As you climb steadily, your views north of the creeping edge of suburbia continue to improve until you reach an open rock platform (0.6/1080). Directly across Mitchell Canyon, noisy Lone Star Quarry digs up diabase for use in roadbeds and foundations. Continuing up the trail, you ascend to a small saddle below Twin Peaks. As you traverse below Twin Peaks to attain the ridge, the Sacramento River delta appears to the north and the broad expanse of the Great Central Valley peeks out east over the hills. An eagle eye can discern the confluence of the San Joaquin and Sacramento rivers. Once on the ridgeline, views open up of the Mt. Diablo massif—both North Peak (3557) and the summit (3849) are visible. From Twin Peaks (1.5/ 1733), Eagle Peak is clearly seen up the ridge.

Descending briefly, the trail passes a junction for Eagle Peak Trail (your return route) and then makes a steep, brushy, view-rich climb up the ridgeline to just below the summit, where a series of final switchbacks bring you to the top (2.3/2369). Bear right on Eagle Peak Trail on your downhill return from the summit to take a much steeper and more direct route to the bottom than Mitchell Rock Trail. Dropping above Back Creek canyon, the trail cuts sharply back before passing over a scree gully below Twin Peaks. As you continue to descend, an increase in pines and poison oak marks the approaching junction

with the Coulter Pine Trail (3.4/780). Bear left and enjoy the gentle ramble through flowers and oaks and rippling grass that returns you to the Mitchell Rock Trail and your trailhead.

Nearest Visitor Center: Mitchell Canyon Ranger Station, (925) 837-2525, located near the end of Mitchell Canyon Rd. Open weekends 8 A.M.–2 P.M. For general information call (925) 837-2525.

Nearest Campground: There are no park campgrounds accessible from the north side of Mt. Diablo State Park. Please see Hike 10 for information on the three campgrounds in the park.

Additional Information: *www.mdia.org*

EAGLE EYE

Hike 12—East Bay Escape

Location	Wildcat Peak
Agency	Tilden Regional Park
Highlights	East Bay escape. Outstanding views of the Bay Area.
Distance	7.0 miles
Total Elevation Gain/Loss	1000´/1000´
Hiking Time	3–5 hours
Difficulty	★★
Best Times	Year-round
Optional Map	USGS 7.5-min *Richmond*

A surprising world hides behind the East Bay Hills. Rolling hills, soaring raptors, and superlative views of the Bay Area highlight a peaceful oasis of Nature.

The Hike runs through Tilden and Wildcat Canyon regional parks, passing along Wildcat Creek before returning via San Pablo Ridge and Wildcat Peak (1280). The excellent views from the open ridgetop are best in the morning and after storms. While the hike can be done year-round, the trails become thick with mud during the winter rainy season. As they have since European settlement of the region, cows graze on the open hillsides. People are common, especially along popular San Pablo Ridge, but quiet glades can usually be found. Water is available at the trailhead.

To Reach the Trailhead, take the Buchanan St. off-ramp from I-80 in Berkeley, and proceed east on Marin Ave. for 2 miles. Climb Marin above Marin Circle on the East Bay's steepest road, and turn left at the first stop sign onto Spruce St. Follow it to Grizzly Peak Blvd. Cross the intersection and take Canon Dr. steeply downhill to the visitor center and parking lot in Tilden Nature Center.

It is also possible to reach the trailhead by **public transportation.** AC Transit bus 67 runs Monday through Friday every 20 minutes from the El Cerrito, North Berkeley, and Berkeley BART stations to the intersection of Spruce St. and Grizzly Peak Blvd. From the intersection, walk down Canon Rd. to the trailhead as described above. On weekends and holidays, bus 67 runs hourly from the Berkeley BART station and will drop you directly at the trailhead. Call (510) 817-1717 for current schedule and fare information.

Description From the trailhead (0.0/530), strike north from a small patch of redwood trees on wide Wildcat Creek Trail. Willow, California bay, coast live oak, coyote brush, California buckeye, poison oak, and introduced French broom line the trail as it parallels Wildcat Creek. Passing diminutive Jewel Lake, the trail soon crosses into Wildcat Regional Park. A wire fence lines the path below increasingly open hillsides. After nearly 2 miles of easy walking, you reach a gated junction for the Havey Canyon and Conlon trails (2.3/490)—on your right immediately before reaching Rifle Range Road. Go through the gate and continue straight toward Havey Canyon. The trail climbs a lush, riparian valley flush with ferns, snowberry, and some unusually massive California bay before breaking out onto open slopes dotted with coyote brush. While cows are a common sight, more exciting are the raptors often seen overhead: red-tailed hawks, easily identified by their namesake tail feathers; and northern harriers, spotted by the distinctive white patch of feathers on their rump. As the trail curves north, distant Mt. Tamalpais (Hike 26) becomes visible to the west. Soon, you go through another gate to

reach paved Nimitz Way atop San Pablo Ridge (3.8/950)—bear right (south).

Views along the ridge are far-reaching, stretching from Vallejo in the north to Mt. Diablo (Hike 10) in the east. The East Bay Hills' highest peaks rise from the ridge to the south, and San Pablo Reservoir lies below you. You reach another junction near Wildcat Peak

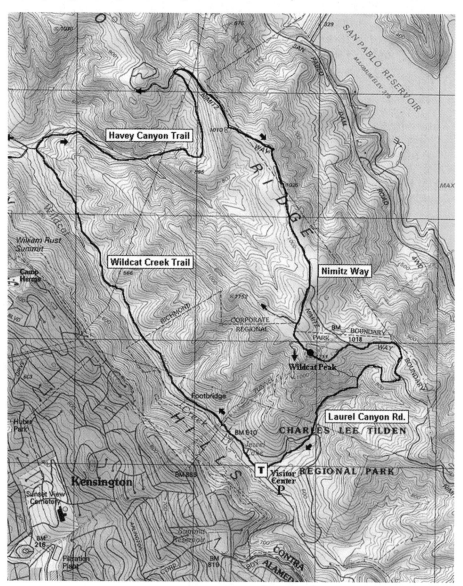

East Bay Escape

(4.8/1140)—leave the pavement and go straight up the rocky trail. After passing a few Monterey pine and Monterey cypress, you swing right along the wide path to descend the Conlon Trail. At this point, leave the trail to find a bench with incredible views of the Golden Gate (Hike 23) and central Bay Area. From the bench, bear left on a faint, barbed-wire-lined path, and cross through the fence at a small gap to continue up to Wildcat Peak's summit (5.4/1280). A stone platform crowns the summit and explains the purpose of the nearby Rotary Peace Grove. Savor the amazing views before dropping down to explore the grove of bushy giant sequoia, seemingly healthy despite being far removed from their native Sierra Nevada habitat.

To return to the trailhead, follow Peak Trail as it descends east from the summit, and take the single-track trail branching right to quickly reach Laurel Canyon Rd.—below. Alternatively, you can continue on Peak Trail to rejoin Nimitz Way—bear right and then right again upon reaching Laurel Canyon Rd.

Laurel Canyon is within the Tilden Nature Study Area, a designated area for protection of Tilden's unique flora and fauna. A maze of trails winds through it, each marked with a symbol. Laurel Canyon Rd. is the widest and easiest route, but any number of trail combinations will return you to the trailhead (7.0/530)—just keep bearing downhill.

Nearest Visitor Center: The Environmental Education Center and Visitor Center, (510) 525-2233, located at the trailhead. Open Tuesday through Sunday 10 A.M.–5 P.M.

Nearest Campground: There are two group campgrounds in the Tilden Nature Study Area. Reservations are required and can be made by calling (510) 636-1684.

Additional Information: *www.ebparks.org/parks/tilden.htm*

East Bay escape

Hike 13—Get Big

Location	Berry Creek Falls
Agency	Big Basin Redwoods State Park
Highlights	Continuous old-growth redwood forest. Waterfalls.
Distance	9.0 miles
Total Elevation Gain/Loss	3200´/3200´
Hiking Time	6–8 hours
Difficulty	★★★★
Best Times	Year-round
Optional Map	USGS 7.5-min *Big Basin, Franklin Point*

With a continuous forest primeval, untainted by saw, and laced with gurgling streams, Big Basin is a green blaze of life. Yes, the park is popular and the waterfalls are a common destination. And yes, it's worth it.

Established in 1902, Big Basin was the first state park created to protect a substantial piece of the rapidly diminishing old-growth redwood forest in the Santa Cruz Mountains. The 3,800 acres initially set aside as parkland were the very first to protect coast redwoods—anywhere! The park holdings have since expanded and the total park area now exceeds 19,000 acres, stretching from the Pacific Ocean at the mouth of Waddell Creek to the heart of the Santa Cruz Mountains. The old-growth redwood forest is extensive—the southernmost existing today—and is unmatched in total area for hundreds of miles up the coast.

The Hike is an all-day adventure loop through substantial redwood forest to three waterfalls: Silver Falls, Golden Falls, and photogenic Berry Creek Falls. Fog may be present in the summer and rains might fall heavy in the winter but there is no bad time to come here. Just be prepared for some very wet trail conditions if you arrive after a winter storm, and be ready for mud year-round. No matter what day you come, other people

will be on the trail. Weekend crowds can be especially thick. A fall, winter, or spring weekday is the best bet for some solitude. Water is available at the trailhead.

To Reach the Trailhead, take Hwy. 236 west from one of its two junctions with Hwy. 9. Approaching from the north on Skyline Blvd. (Hwy. 35), the turnoff is 5.8 miles south of the junction with Hwy. 9. From this turnoff, Hwy. 236 is a one-lane twister that reaches the visitor center in 8 miles—RVs and trailers are not recommended. Approaching from the south, the turnoff from Hwy. 9 is in Boulder Creek. This more easily driven section of Hwy. 236 reaches the visitor center in 9 miles. Park in the large lot across from the visitor center. There is a day-use fee of $6.

Description: Beneath some particularly large redwoods, take broad Redwood Trail from the trailhead (0.0/990) beyond the restrooms and across Opal Creek to your junction with the Skyline-to-the-Sea Trail. Your return trail joins from the right but you head left, passing some large Douglas-fir and many tan oak, whose toothed leaves wave everywhere. Continue toward Berry Creek Falls at the next junction and begin a steady climb out of the East Waddell Creek drainage. As you crest into the

West Waddell Creek drainage (0.7/ 1320), a sign warns of the strenuous hiking ahead.

As you pass a connector to Sunset Trail, your trail drops rapidly down to Kelly Creek. The hike passes through dense stands of large redwoods, encrusted green by the moist environment, before reaching Timms Creek Trail (2.4/ 560), another shortcut to Sunset Trail. Continuing, you descend to reach the junction with Berry Creek Falls Trail (3.8/350). Turn right toward the falls, leaving the Skyline-to-the-Sea Trail that continues to the ocean, less than 6 miles away.

Unless a recent winter storm has swollen the waters, Berry Creek Falls are thin and drop in small cascades that mist the surrounding greenery. Passing near the bottom of the waterfall, the trail then climbs left above the falls, and crosses Berry Creek. The muddy track stays close to the water and soon reaches Silver Falls, a small cascade falling over exposed sedimentary rock representative of the Santa Cruz Mountain geology.

The bedrock of the Santa Cruz Mountains is granite formed some 100 million years ago near the location of today's southern Sierra Nevada. When the San Andreas Fault became active, this piece of land began moving slowly northwest, becoming submerged beneath the sea as it went. Sand and mud settled from the ocean on this underwater surface, forming thick layers of loosely consolidated sandstone and mudstone. Within the past four million years, a change in the geometry of the San Andreas Fault thrust these layers above ground, folding them into the Santa Cruz Mountains and exposing the muddy layers to your boots. These loosely consolidated rocks create the huge landslide problems associated with this area today.

After climbing above Silver Falls, you soon reach Golden Falls and its series of three distinct cascades. Wooden steps and the odd switchback lead past this final waterfall to the junction with Sunset Trail (4.7/850). Sunset Trail Camp is 100 yards straight ahead, but you turn right to begin the return journey.

GET BIG

Crossing Berry Creek on a solid wooden bridge, the trail then weaves slowly over a small divide between West Waddell and Berry creeks. Fleeting views of both drainages open up before the trail descends to the Timms Creek Trail junction (5.9/680). A long undulating traverse from here along the Sunset Trail returns you to the earlier junction with the Skyline-to-the-Sea Trail. Go left on the short Redwood Trail to the trailhead.

Nearest Visitor Center: Park visitor center, (831) 338-8860. Open daily 8:30 A.M.–4 P.M. (extended hours during the summer months).

Backpacking Information: Backcountry camping in Big Basin Sate Park is allowed only at designated trail camps.

Sunset Trail Camp is the only option on this hike, located above the waterfalls. Reservations are required and can be made by calling (831) 338-8861 Tuesday through Sunday between 10 A.M. and 5 P.M. There is a $5 reservation fee and each site costs $10 per night for up to 6 people. No campfires are allowed.

Nearest Campground: There are 4 park campgrounds: Huckleberry (58 sites), Blooms Creek (54 sites), Sempervirens (32 sites), and Wastahi (27 sites). Blooms Creek is closest to the trailhead but all are nearby. Sites cost from $14 to $18 depending on season and day of the week. Reservations are essential during the summer months.

Additional Information:
www.members.aol.com/bbrsp/index.htm

Hike 14—The Grove

Location	Peters Creek Grove
Agency	Portola Redwoods State Park
Highlights	A grove of gargantuan old-growth redwoods.
Distance	12.4 miles round trip
Total Elevation Gain/Loss	2250´/2250´
Hiking Time	6–8 hours
Difficulty	★★★★
Best Times	Year-round
Optional Map	USGS 7.5-min *Mindego Hill*

In the Santa Cruz Mountains, few old-growth redwoods remain that can rival the size of those on the North Coast. Yet, these massive specimens on Peters Creek await you in a distant secluded grove accessible only by trail.

The Hike is an all-day trip to the redwood grove on Peters Creek, passing through thick and unchanging forest to get there. Fog may be present in the summer and rains might fall heavy in the winter but there is no bad time to come here. Those seeking solitude should avoid the summer months; consider coming during the winter when the campground is closed. Water is available near the trailhead at the visitor center and campground.

To Reach the Trailhead, take Hwy. 35 to the turnoff for Alpine Rd., located 6 miles north of the junction with Hwy. 9, and 7 miles south of the junction with Hwy. 84. Head south on Alpine Rd. and in 2.5 miles bear left on Price Ave. Continue another 3.4 miles to the small parking lot on the right just past the campground entrance. There is a day-use fee of $6.

Description: Beginning across the road on posted Slate Creek Trail (0.0/430), your hike passes redwoods, canyon live oak, and the ubiquitous tan oak before almost immediately hitting a

junction. While a large Douglas-fir, which toppled in February '00 due to heart rot, lies trailside and Old Tree Trail continues straight, you bear left toward Slate Creek Trail Camp. The single-track trail immediately climbs among large Douglas-fir. Continuing uphill past a junction where a spur trail from the campground joins (0.5/670), you pass a pleasant bench in the Bolton Memorial Grove. Several quick switchbacks lead to a more level traverse, where California bay enter the mix of trees. Continue on Slate Creek Trail where Summit Trail joins it (1.3/930); Summit provides an alternate route back to the park road for the return trip. From here it's a long traverse to Slate Creek Trail Camp (2.5/1000) and the junction for Peters Creek on Bear Creek Trail.

Bravely pass the CAUTION sign on Bear Creek Trail and begin the STRENUOUS 7-MILE ROUND TRIP HIKE FROM THIS POINT. Winding along Bear Creek, you may notice the big leaf maple, hazel, and decaying car by the creek before you break out into an opening thick with poison oak. A huge, moss-draped coast live oak is on the right past this clearing near the high point of the hike (1450). The trail then passes through thick Douglas-fir forest and begins the descent into the Peters Creek drainage. A brief view of the valley is had along the ridge where a few California buckeye appear, but the steady drop is mostly uneventful—until the redwoods reappear. From the junction at the bottom for the Peters Creek Loop (5.0/740), either direction is good but going left first saves the fattest trees for the very end. The loop trail crosses Peters Creek twice, which may be necessary to ford after winter storms. The enormous specimens upstream approach 10' in diameter and exhibit striking similarity to their even larger cousins, the giant sequoia. They owe their size to the almost ideal growing conditions and constant water supply found so close to the creek. Savor them and then return the way you came.

Nearest Visitor Center: Park visitor center, (650) 948-9098. Open April through October daily 9 A.M.–6 P.M. (extended hours on the weekends). Open November through March Friday through Sunday 9 A.M.–6 P.M. (sporadic hours Monday through Thursday).

Backpacking Information: Backcountry camping is allowed only at Slate Creek Trail Camp, located roughly halfway to Peters Creek (6 sites, $10, creek water only). No campfires are allowed. Reservations are not required but can be made by calling the visitor center and are recommended for weekends and holidays. The trail camp is closed December through February.

Nearest Campground: Park campground (53 sites, $14–18). Reservations recommended during the summer, especially on weekends and holidays.

The Grove

Hike 15—Purisima

Location	Purisima Creek Redwoods Open Space Preserve
Agency	Midpeninsula Regional Open Space District
Highlights	A secluded redwood forest in a small canyon. Rising above it along an open ridgetop.
Distance	7.0 miles
Total Elevation Gain/Loss	1200´/1200´
Hiking Time	3–5 hours
Difficulty	★★★
Best Times	Year-round
Optional Map	USGS 7.5-min *Woodside*

Just south of Half Moon Bay, Purisima Creek slices quickly and deeply to the sea, with the northernmost redwood forest on the Peninsula in its protected headwaters. So close to the urban mania yet hidden well enough to receive only light use, Purisima is a perfect place to quickly, easily, and totally get away from it all.

The rugged character of Purisima Creek canyon proved challenging to early logging efforts. While readily accessible from the coast, the sheer walls at the creek's headwaters made shipping lumber directly east to the Bay Area difficult. Despite the uncooperative topography, virtually all of the old-growth redwoods had been cut by the early 1900s, and seven different mills operated along Purisima Creek over the years. Today the forest has rebounded, with impressive second-growth redwoods now lining Purisima Creek. While no old-growth redwoods can be found along the trails, a few ancient trees are reputed to exist in the most inaccessible corners of the preserve.

The Hike follows Purisima Creek upstream through a substantial second-growth redwood forest before returning along Harkins Ridge. The open ridgetop

offers excellent views of the valley, visible from mountain to sea. Fog may be thick in the summer and rains might fall heavily in the winter, but there is no bad time to come here. While the main approach to the preserve is from Hwy. 35, this hike begins from the lower boundary, accessible only from the coast. Crowds are consequently light, although you will definitely see other people on the weekends. No water is available at the trailhead.

To Reach the Trailhead, on Hwy. 1 drive 4.6 miles south of the intersection with Hwy. 92 in Half Moon Bay to Verde Rd. Turn left (east) and continue straight on Purisima Creek Rd. for 0.3 mile where Verde Rd. curves right. The small parking lot is 3.6 miles farther at the road's deepest penetration into the valley. It is also possible to reach the trailhead on longer and twistier Higgins-Purisima Rd., which joins Hwy. 1 next to the new Half Moon Bay fire station, 1.3 miles south of the Hwy. 92 intersection.

Description: From the parking lot (0.0/420), head up the wide path to quickly reach an information sign, where a bathroom is located and free maps are usually available. Your return trail crosses the creek on the left, but the hike continues straight on Purisima Creek Trail. As you go upstream, blackberry, hazel, thimbleberry, stinging nettle, poison oak, dogwood, deer fern, sword fern, five-finger fern, and bracken fern cover the surrounding slopes beneath the overhanging redwood trees. In addition to the redwoods, trees on this trail include the moss-coated trunks of alder, tan oak, and big leaf maple. Remain on Purisima Creek Trail as you pass the junctions for Borden Hatch Mills Trail and Grabtown Gulch Trail, slowly gaining elevation on the gentle gradient until the trail switchbacks and reaches the junction with Soda Gulch Trail (2.3/1040)—go left.

Briefly joining the Bay Area Ridge Trail as you ascend on Soda Gulch Trail, the now single-track path initially winds around a small stream gully. Look for the good-sized Douglas-fir above the trail immediately before crossing the small stream, easily identified by their rougher, unfurrowed bark so distinct from that of the redwoods. Continuing, a few tantalizing glimpses of upper Purisima Canyon can be had as the vegetation changes into that of the drier, sunnier upper slopes. Tan oak is still found here, but is now mixed with coast live oak and California bay. After traversing around substantial Soda Gulch, the trail suddenly bursts out into open fields of coyote brush and poison oak. Views are at their best here, as virtually the entire drainage of Purisima Creek can be seen curving west to the ocean.

Turning away from this excellent viewpoint, the trail climbs four quick switchbacks to reach the wide road of Harkins Ridge Trail (4.9/1540)—go left. As you descend along the ridgetop, Higgins Creek drainage is briefly visible to the north. Your views are obscured when the trail reenters thick vegetation, descending on four, long, lazy switchbacks to Purisima Creek and the earlier junction.

Nearest Visitor Center: No visitor center. For more information call the Midpeninsula Regional Open Space District at (650) 691-1200.

Nearest Campground: Half Moon Bay State Beach Campground is closest, located just west of town in southern Half Moon Bay (54 sites, $16). Reservations are recommended for weekends. Also consider the campgrounds at Portola Redwoods State Park (see Hike 14) and San Mateo County Memorial Park, located on Pescadero Rd. near Hwy. 84.

Additional Information:
www.openspace.org/PURISIMA.html

PURISIMA

Hike 16—Mavericks

Location	Pillar Point
Agency	City of Half Moon Bay
Highlights	The largest wave on the west coast.
Distance	1.0 mile round trip
Total Elevation Gain/Loss	50′/50′
Hiking Time	1 hour
Difficulty	★
Best Times	Big winter swells
Optional Map	USGS 7.5-min *Half Moon Bay*

A half mile offshore lies a jagged reef. Waves approaching it travel through a deep underwater canyon, jacking upward into towering walls of water as they encounter the sudden shallows of the submerged shelf. Each wave breaks, falling over on itself in an exploding cauldron of whitewater, pushing its seething foam through a harrowing set of exposed rocks. This is Mavericks, the largest wave on the West Coast, playground for the world's best surfers.

During the 1980s, Mavericks was the exclusive domain of Jeff Clark, a Half Moon Bay local who first surfed the epic wave. By the early '90s other locals had joined him, surfing the huge waves on custom-made surfboards 10–11′ long. By 1994 word had spread and the world's premier big-wave surfers began to congregate at Mavericks. During the winter of '94–95, Mavericks demonstrated its ferocity by claiming its first (and to date, only) victim. Mark Foo, an experienced big-wave rider from Hawaii, drowned at Mavericks after wiping out on take-off. As the '90s progressed, the publicity surrounding Mavericks increased. The K2 Big Wave Challenge offered $50,000 to the surfer photographed riding the largest wave of the '97–98 winter season. Although the contest was eventually won on a wave at Todos los Santos in Baja, the spotlight was on Mavericks. Over the following two seasons, Quiksilver sponsored two big-wave surfing contests at Mavericks, starting a trend that seems likely to continue.

The Hike is a short and easy stroll to Pillar Point, skirting a saltwater marsh near Pillar Point Harbor to reach the best vantage point for observing the big waves. Mavericks only breaks when the swell is huge, an event that occurs just a handful of times each year during the winter months. Generated by large storms in the Pacific, these swells can usually be predicted a day or so before they reach California. Those wishing to see the monster waves must keep an eye on current ocean conditions in order to time their visit correctly. *Stormsurf.com* is the source currently recommended for this information. The waves break far offshore, requiring a telescope or good pair of binoculars for observation. If Mavericks is breaking, crowds will be thick. If not, this hike is a pleasant stroll with few people. No water is available at the trailhead.

To Reach the Trailhead, take Hwy. 1 to the stoplight at Capistrano Rd. in El Granada, located 5 miles north of Half Moon Bay. Go west on Capistrano Rd., left on Prospect, and continue straight through Princeton-by-the-Sea on Har-

MAVERICKS

vard. Turn right on West Side Dr. and take it to the dirt parking lot on the left. If Mavericks is breaking, the lot fills rapidly and vehicles stretch out along West Side Dr. The road leading to the top of Pillar Point belongs to the Air Force and is off-limits.

Description: From the parking lot, follow the wide path as it skirts Pillar Point Marsh, a fertile area of wetlands where almost one fifth of all North American bird species have been identified. Stinging nettle and coyote brush grow from the steep bluff of Pillar Point, whose summit has served various uses over the years: ranch land, artichoke field, underground bunker, instrumentation site for the Navy Pacific Missile Range, rocket launchsite for the Air Force Western Test Range, and now the northernmost instrumentation site of the Western Space and Missile Center located at Vandenberg Air Force Base (Vanderwerf 1995).

When you reach the end of the broad path by the start of the breakwater, a sign warns of EXTREMELY HAZARDOUS WAVES. Heed the warnings! If Mavericks is breaking the ocean will be rough, dangerous, and capable of washing careless individuals out to sea. Rogue waves can crest the main breakwater, pouring across the small concrete wall adjacent to the bluff, and sweeping people onto the rocks behind. Climb up along the bluff edge for the best views of Mavericks.

Nearest Campground: Half Moon Bay State Beach Campground, located just west of town in southern Half Moon Bay (54 sites, $16). Reservations are recommended for weekends.

Additional Information:
www.mavsurfer.com

Pillar Point Harbor Breakwater during big swell

Hike 17—Mountain Next Door

Location	Montara Mountain
Agency	San Pedro Valley County Park
Highlights	A dominating mountain overlooked. Montara Beach.
Distance	6.3 miles one way
Total Elevation Gain/Loss	1650´/1650´
Hiking Time	4–6 hours
Difficulty	★★★
Best Times	Spring and Fall
Optional Map	USGS 7.5-min *Montara Mountain*

Montara Mountain is a solid block of granite towering over Pacifica, a landmark peak forgotten by the Bay Area. Views are tremendous. Montara Beach is an idyllic stretch of sand—hemmed by bluffs, washed by the soothing waves of the Pacific Ocean.

The Hike climbs over Montara Mountain (1813) from San Pedro Valley Park in Pacifica to reach Montara Beach, a one-way journey that necessitates two cars or the use of public transportation to return to the trailhead (see below). Fog envelops the mountain during the summer, obscuring views and making for a cold day at the beach. Winter views between storms can be spectacularly clear, but strong winds are often a problem on the exposed mountain. Bring a warm sweater and windbreaker year-round. Water is available at the trailhead.

To Reach the Trailhead, take Hwy. 1 south from San Francisco to Linda Mar Blvd. in Pacifica and turn left (east)—the intersection is located at the southernmost stoplight in Pacifica. Proceed 1.6 miles to Oddstad Blvd. and turn right. The entrance is immediately on your left. Park in the Trout Farm Picnic Area lot to the right of the visitor center. There is a $4 day-use fee. Since the gate closes at dusk, those anticipating a post-sunset

return should park outside the entrance on the street. To reach Montara Beach, take Hwy. 1 south of Linda Mar Blvd. for 4 miles and park by the northern end of the beach.

To reach the trailhead by **public transportation,** plan your hike on a weekday. Take BART to Daly City and SamTrans bus 110 to the Linda Mar Shopping Center (weekday frequency every 30–60 minutes). Transfer to SamTrans bus 14 and get off at Terra Nova Blvd. and Oddstadt Blvd. (weekday frequency every 30–60 minutes, no weekend service). Walk the few blocks east on Oddstadt to the park entrance. Returning to the trailhead from Montara Beach, take SamTrans bus 294 north to the Linda Mar Shopping Center. The bus stop is at the south end of Montara Beach, located at the intersection of Hwy. 1 and 8th St. (weekday frequency every 90 minutes). Transfer and return as described above. Call SamTrans at 1-800-660-4287 for a current schedule or go online at *samtrans.com*.

Description: The trail begins in the Trout Farm Picnic Area lot by the restrooms (0.0/220) and follows Montara Mountain Trail for the first half of the hike. Both poison oak and stinging nettle grow nearby and are a hazard throughout the day. Ticks are common in the brush as well—stay on the trail! The trail reaches an immediate fork as you begin—bear right and continue on Montara Mtn. Trail. To the left is Brooks Falls Trail, an alternate route that rejoins Montara Mtn. Trail in 0.8 mile. Crossing a road, the trail begins switchbacking through dense eucalyptus before breaking out onto increasingly open slopes.

The vegetation of Montara Mtn. is primarily coastal scrub composed of coyote brush, manzanita, and other low-lying brush highlighted with a seasonal display of wildflowers. Iris, lupine, buttercup, wild radish, monkey flower, California poppy, and horse nettle are but a few of the varieties found here. Coast live oak, California bay, and Monterey cypress grow in more sheltered locations. Raptors—especially red-tailed hawks—can often be seen overhead hunting for unlucky rodents. Quail, bobcat, gray fox, and deer roam the hillsides. The rarely seen mountain lion is known to live here as well.

Passing a bench with a good view north of nearby Sweeney Ridge (Hike 18), the trail continues its steady ascent. The towers of the Golden Gate Bridge (Hike 23) and the headlands of distant Point Reyes National Seashore (Hike 28) can be picked out north-northwest on clear days. The view becomes ever more expansive as the trail gets rockier on the steep upper flanks of the mountain. A steep, switchbacking climb brings you to the ridge and an intersection with the broad road leading to the summit (1.7/1460). To head directly to Montara Beach, bear right and follow the road 0.5 mile to the junction with Old San Pedro Road, a wide trail that drops down the southern flanks of Montara Mtn. To make the recommended trip to the summit, bear left and follow the gradual trail 1.0 mile to the top.

The rocks of Montara Mtn. are granite and can be found exposed in places along the upper sections of trail. Formed approximately 80 million years ago in Southern California, the granite has since been forced hundreds of miles north by the San Andreas Fault system. You can trace this fault as it travels underwater northwest from Mussel Rock (located just offshore north of the Pacifica Pier) and continues through the low gap between Point Reyes National Seashore and Mt. Tamalpais. Lands west of the fault, including Montara Mtn. and all of Pacifica, are currently moving north at an average rate of 1–2" per year. Over the millenia, the exact position of the San Andreas Fault has shifted in response to various geologic forces, and the San Andreas Fault once ran along the base of Montara Mtn. on what is known today as the Pilarcitos Fault. During this period, the rocks along the fault were crushed into sediment; this easily eroded away to form San Pedro Valley after the San Andreas Fault shifted to its present course. Ancient movement along Pilarcitos Fault brought the rocks of Montara Mtn. and landmark Pedro Point into contact with those found north of San Pedro Valley. Beyond their current proximity to each other, the two rock groups are totally unrelated.

From its junction with Montara Mtn. Trail, Old San Pedro Road drops west through McNee Ranch State Park on an easy gradient all the way to Hwy. 1. Prior to the construction of Hwy. 1 along Devils Slide, this was the only way to drive south of Montara Mtn. Bits of old pavement are still identifiable in the roadbed. As you descend past several confusing junctions into the Martini Creek drainage, follow the most obvious road to reach Hwy. 1 near a large yellow gate. Just across the road is the beach.

Nearest Visitor Center: San Pedro County Park Visitor Center, (650) 355-8289. Open weekends 10 A.M.–4 P.M.

Nearest Campground: Nothing close. Try farther south on the Peninsula (see Hikes 13–16).

Additional Information:
www.eparks.net/parks/sanphome.htm

MOUNTAIN NEXT DOOR

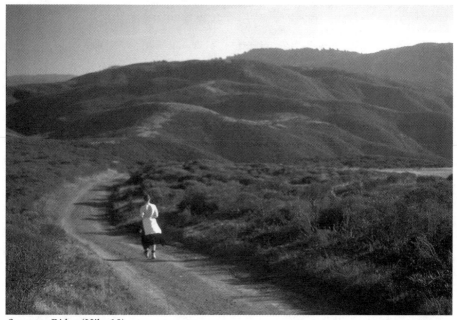

Sweeney Ridge (Hike 18)

Hike 18—Discovery

Location	Sweeney Ridge
Agency	Golden Gate National Recreation Area
Highlights	November 4, 1769.
Distance	4.8 miles round trip
Total Elevation Gain/Loss	1000´/1000´
Hiking Time	3–4 hours
Difficulty	★★
Best Times	September through May
Optional Map	USGS 7.5-min *Montara Mountain*

On November 4, 1769, Juan Crespí sighted San Francisco Bay from atop Sweeney Ridge. A member of the expedition sent north by the Spanish government to found missions at San Diego and Monterey, he had journeyed overland from San Diego through absolute terra incognita, recording a California barely imaginable today.

The Hike climbs Sweeney Ridge from Pacifica, roughly approximating the route traveled by Juan Crespí the day the expedition sighted San Francisco Bay. While easier access points exist for Sweeney Ridge, the history told below is best enjoyed by approaching from the Pacific side. Summer months are foggy in Pacifica, chilling the air and obscuring views for days on end. Weather is best in the fall, views are clearest after winter storms, and wildflowers explode March through May. The ridge is open and exposed, making a good windbreaker worthwhile year-round. Crowds will be minimal beyond Shelldance Nursery. No water is available at the trailhead.

To Reach the Trailhead, take Hwy. 1 south from San Francisco to the first stoplight in Pacifica, and make a U-turn to go north. In 0.3 mile turn right to Shelldance Nursery (accessible only from the northbound direction). Be ready for the sharp turn—it appears

quickly and traffic moves fast around you. Proceed up the hill toward the nursery and park by the SWEENEY RIDGE sign. Approaching from the south, look for the Vallemar/Reina del Mar stoplight—the turnoff is 0.3 mile ahead.

The trailhead is also accessible by **public transportation.** From Daly City BART, SamTrans bus 110 runs to Pacifica at least once per hour Monday through Saturday, with reduced hours Sundays and holidays. Return service goes well into the evening weekdays but ends by 6 P.M. on weekends. Ask to be let off at Reina del Mar. Cross Hwy. 1 and walk up the road toward Shelldance Nursery (see above). Call 1-800-660-4287 for a current schedule or go online at *samtrans.com*.

Description: Follow the dirt road adjacent to the signed trailhead (0.0/220), cross through the gate, and climb the wide trail as it steeply ascends the ridgeline. When Father Juan Crespí was here, his journey had begun more than six months earlier.

In early 1769 a "sacred expedition" (Paddison 1999) set forth from Baja California to establish two settlements in little explored Alta California. To be located at San Diego and Monterey, these missions would strengthen Spain's tenuous hold on California, just as

Britain and Russia had begun to eye it for their own. Initially composed of three ships and two overland parties traveling separately to a rendezvous in San Diego, the expedition rapidly dwindled to a small band of 60 men striking north from San Diego in search of Monterey Bay. Led by Captain Juan Gaspar de Portolá, 50-year-old governor of Baja California, the party included an adventurous 58-year-old missionary named Juan Crespí. After a long overland journey, the expedition reached the latitude of Monterey Bay, but didn't recognize "the best port that could be desired" here, as explorer Sebastián Vizcaíno had described it in 1602 (Paddison 1999). They continued north into the Santa Cruz Mountains.

Crespí spoke of "a large mountain range covered with a tree very like the pine in its leaf, save that this is not over two fingers long. The heartwood is red, very handsome wood, handsomer than cedar. There are great numbers of this tree here, of all sizes of thickness, most of them exceedingly high and straight like so many candles. What a pleasure to see this blessing of timber." (Paddison 1999) Old-growth redwood forest covered the Santa Cruz Mountains, a forest unscarred by mankind.

As the expedition proceeded along the coast just north of Waddell Creek, Crespí encountered the native people of the area in "a large village of very well behaved good heathens, who greeted us with loud cheers and rejoiced greatly at our coming. These heathens presented us with a great many large black- and white-colored *tamales*. They brought two or three bags of the wild tobacco they use, and our people took all they wanted of it. One old heathen man came up smoking upon a large and well-carved Indian pipe made of hard stone. They all go naked and bare-headed, and all of them are well-featured, stout, and bearded." (Paddison 1999) Between 150,000 and 250,000 native people inhabited the area now composing California.

The expedition continued north along the coast until November 3, when "the scouts who had been sent out came back from their exploring, firing off their guns as they arrived; and on reaching camp reported that they had come upon a great estuary or very broad arm of the sea extending many leagues inland." (Paddison 1999) San Francisco Bay had been discovered.

Surely excited, Crespí and the expedition began climbing Sweeney Ridge on November 4. Montara Mountain could be seen to the south with its westernmost arm dipping into the sea at Point San Pedro. To the west the jagged incisors of the Farallon Islands protruded out of the Pacific. But the towers of the Golden Gate Bridge could not be seen to the north, houses did not fill the valleys of Pacifica, and Highway 1 did not wind along the coast below. California's dense coastal fog and treacherous shoreline had prevented discovery of San Francisco Bay for more than two centuries. Early European explorers had failed to spot the Golden Gate through the fog, and later commercial vessels steered west of the Farallones to avoid the dangerous bottom near shore. But then Crespí was there, staring east across San Francisco Bay.

Once on the ridgetop (1.2/1030), you go right on Sweeney Ridge Trail, passing an abandoned NIKE-missile command center (1.7/1200) from the 1950s, before reaching the Discovery Site on a paved trail (2.0/1250). Those feeling energetic can continue 1.4 miles south along Sweeney Ridge to the boundary of the off-limits Peninsula Watershed.

While you stay on the ridge, Crespí descended the slopes "down upon a large plain, five or six leagues in extent, all grown over with white-oaks—large and small—and some live-oaks. We saw three or four smokes within these woods from heathen villages, of which the scouts say there are many. The soldiers report that down next to the large estuary there are many lakes and little inlets with countless fowl, ducks, geese, cranes, and others. Very large bears have been seen, and here where the camp was set up I saw two fresh droppings of these beasts, full of acorns." (Paddison 1999) Wetlands ringed the Bay, grizzly bears roamed the hills, and 10–20,000 native people called it home. Crespí did not see the world of Silicon Valley, the San Mateo Bridge, or the sea of asphalt. He saw a California that is today only a dream within these pages. Return the way you came.

Nearest Visitor Center: The GGNRA and city of Pacifica run an excellent visitor center, (650) 355-4122, located 1 mile south of Shelldance Nursery at 225 Rockaway Beach. Open Monday through Friday 9 A.M.–5 P.M., weekends 10 A.M.– 4:30 P.M.

Nearest Campground: Nothing close. Please see Hikes 13–16 for ideas.

Additional Information:
www.nps.gov/goga

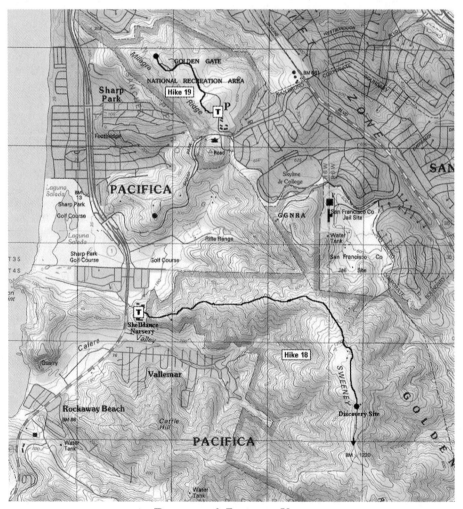

Discovery & Farallon View

Hike 19—Farallon View

Location	Milagra Ridge
Agency	Golden Gate National Recreation Area
Highlights	The Farallon Islands.
Distance	1.5 miles round trip
Total Elevation Gain/Loss	250′/250′
Hiking Time	1–2 hours
Difficulty	★
Best Times	September through May
Optional Map	USGS 7.5-min *San Francisco South*

Thirty miles offshore, the jagged rocks of the Farallon Islands protrude from the Pacific Ocean expanse. Less than a mile from the ocean, hidden Milagra Ridge rises 700 feet above the sea, making it one of the best locations to view these remote outposts of California.

The Farallon Islands are a linear series of small rocky islets stretching 8 miles northwest from the principal island cluster. With a summit 348′ high, the largest and most commonly sighted member of the group is Southeast Farallon, located at the far southern end of the chain. Eight miles northwest, a smaller group of rocky pillars known as the North Farallones jut from the water, ranging in elevation from 78 to 112 feet. Between the two groups is the lonely pinnacle of Middle Farallon, a single rock 50′ wide standing 22′ above the sea. *Farallon,* which means in Spanish "rocky promontory rising from the ocean," was a generic appellation that over the course of time became exclusively associated with these islands.

The rock of the Farallon Islands is granite rifted from the southern Sierra Nevada and transported several hundred miles northwest through the actions of the San Andreas Fault. Between the islands and the mainland stretches a large shelf no more than 200

feet below the surface. Immediately beyond the islands, the continental shelf ends and the ocean bottom plummets to over a mile deep.

On August 3, 1579, Sir Francis Drake anchored the *Golden Hinde* off the Farallon Islands and—with his crew—set the first European footprints on their rocky soil. During the early 19th Century, New England merchants were involved in a lucrative shipping trade between Boston, the West Coast, and China. Hundreds of thousands of furs were harvested along California's coast by these traders, decimating the vast populations of fur seals then found around the Farallones. By 1834, the annual yield of fur seals had dwindled to 60 and the species was all but exterminated.

Next came the Russians. Seeking provisions for their recently established settlement of Fort Ross on the present-day Sonoma coast, they established an outpost on the islands that was permanently staffed from 1817 until the early 1830s. Sea lions, elephant seals, and other wildlife were hunted and shipped to Fort Ross. Abandoned in 1838, this remote station on the Farallon Islands marked the southernmost limit of Russian expansion in North America.

Following the discovery of gold in California, the Farallones became the site for a much-needed lighthouse. Constructed atop the summit of Southeast Farallon, the light went into operation in 1855. Over the following 117 years, the lighthouse was staffed and cared for by a long line of lighthouse keepers and their assistants. Often living with their families in a few lonely houses at the base of the peak, they were responsible for maintaining the light, foghorn, and related equipment until the lighthouse became fully automated in 1972. Today the lighthouse still perches on the narrow summit, flashing brightly at regular 15-second intervals.

During the early decades of San Francisco, a lack of poultry led to an acute egg shortage. As early as 1849, the harvesting of murre eggs from the Farallon Islands helped satisfy the demand. Double the size of a chicken egg, the common murre egg was evidently quite palatable, although the white remained transparent after frying and the yolk had a bright orange-red hue. In the mid-19th Century, hundreds of thousands of murres nested on the Farallones, laying countless eggs in precarious rocky roosts, which were collected by daring men climbing on the cliffs. Egging continued until 1896 when an ever-dwindling supply and increasing public pressure brought operations to a halt.

During the 20th Century, Southeast Farallon was used for several military radio and radar installations. In 1909 Theodore Roosevelt created the Farallon Reservation, a wildlife preserve protecting the North Farallones. In 1969 the southeast island group was included in the renamed Farallon National Wildlife Refuge. All of this is today a part of the vast Gulf of the Farallones National Marine Sanctuary, 948 square nautical miles of protected ocean stretching from Bodega Bay to well south of the Farallon Islands. The only remaining human inhabitants on Southeast Farallon are a few members of the Point Reyes Bird Observatory assigned to safeguard and monitor the recovering wildlife. Since 1969, elephant seals once exterminated from the islands have returned to breed, and the diminishing murre population has rebounded from a record low of 6,000 nesting birds to well over 100,000 today. Great white sharks up to 18 feet in length prey on the increasing numbers of marine mammals, and are a common underwater denizen of the Farallon Islands (White 1995).

The Hike winds along the open hilltops of Milagra Ridge, offering views of Pacifica and the distant Farallon Islands. In order to see the Farallones, you will need a day with good visibility and no fog. Winter and spring provide the best opportunities, with air quality generally best immediately following storms and when strong easterly winds blow. Summer months bring fog, which almost always sits offshore, obscuring the islands. A telescope or strong pair of binoculars are useful. Crowds are generally light, especially on weekdays. No water is available at the trailhead.

To Reach the Trailhead, take Westborough Dr. west from its exit on I-280 in South San Francisco. You steeply ascend the ridge to Skyline Dr. (Hwy. 35). Cross Skyline Dr. and continue 0.5 mile to the intersection with College Dr. Turn right and go 0.2 mile past a housing complex to the gate at the road's end. Parking is limited—if there are no spaces available, the next closest parking is almost a mile away at Skyline College, located at the opposite end of College Dr. Approaching from Hwy. 1, take the Sharp Park off-ramp and drive 1.3 miles east up Sharp Park Dr. to College Dr. Turn left and continue as described above. While reaching the trailhead by **public transportation** is challenging, SamTrans bus 40 does run regularly between Pacific Manor Shopping Center in north Pacifica and Tanforan Shopping Center in South San Francisco, stopping at nearby Skyline College along the way. Call 1-800-660-4287 for current schedule and connection information, or go online at *samtrans.com*.

Description: From the trailhead climb the stairway, passing a buried water tank. The trail winds through coyote brush and seasonal wildflowers—California poppies, paintbrush, clover, and checkerbloom are a few of the more common. The trail crests out at a vista point providing a good Farallon view. Southeast Farallon is located almost due west at 276°, and the North Farallones can be picked out on exceptionally clear days at 284°. Much of Pacifica is laid out beneath you and Montara Mtn. (Hike 17) dominates the southern skyline.

From here, the trail descends from its highest point and traverses among a maze of paths northwest along the ridgetop, providing good views north of Mt. Tamalpais (Hike 26) and northeast of upper San Bruno Mtn. (Hike 21). Passing a '50s NIKE missile launchsite, the trail terminates at an old WW II 6"-gun platform, where old military bunkers are buried in the hillside. Return the way you came.

Nearest Visitor Center: Rockaway Beach in Pacifica (see Hike 18).

Nearest Campground: Nothing close. See Hikes 13–16 for ideas.

Additional Information: *www.nps.gov/goga*

★ *See map on page 62.*

Hike 20—The Fault

Location	Phillip Burton Memorial Beach
Agency	Golden Gate National Recreation Area
Highlights	The San Andreas Fault. Fossils on a forgotten beach.
Distance	3.5 miles one way
Total Elevation Gain/Loss	50´/50´
Hiking Time	2–3 hours
Difficulty	★
Best Times	September through May
Optional Map	USGS 7.5-min *San Francisco South*

After covering 500 miles overland, the San Andreas Fault dives northwest from the bluffs of Daly City into the Pacific Ocean. North of this tectonic landmark, a beach of surprising seclusion runs for more than three miles below cliffs of mud, sand, and fossils.

Approximately two million years ago, the geography of the Bay Area differed radically. The Point Reyes Peninsula sat directly west of today's Golden Gate, partially enclosing a shallow basin between itself and the mainland. Sediments poured in from the surrounding land masses, filling the basin with thick layers of sand, mud, and gravel. In all, a deep reservoir of sediment more than a mile thick was deposited. Layers formed during periods of shallow water include thick beds of fossils—crushed shells make up the bulk of the material, but entire preserved sand dollars and clams can also be found. Within the past 300,000 years, changing geometry along the San Andreas Fault lifted the entire basin and tilted its beds gently north to expose it as today's Merced Formation. A small piece of the northern basin remained attached to the southeast corner of the Point Reyes Peninsula as it was wrenched into its current position; it is now exposed in the bluffs east of Bolinas (Konigsmark 1998).

The Hike follows the beach north from Mussel Rock in north Pacifica to Fort Funston in San Francisco. **WARNING:** This trip can become dangerous during high tides, when big waves can wash to the base of the bluffs and suck people out to sea. **Do not venture onto the beach if you see waves reaching the bluffs.** No tide tables are posted at the trailhead—check in advance. The hike can be made into a round trip by returning along the beach to the trailhead. Otherwise, car arrangements must be worked out for the return to Pacifica. For those unable to do the full hike, the general flavor and experience of the locale can be had in a short 1-mile round trip from the trailhead. While the hike can be done year-round, fog is thick in the summer and makes for a cold, low-visibility day at the beach. Crowds are light compared to other area beaches. No water is available at the trailhead.

To Reach the Trailhead from San Francisco, follow Hwy. 1 south, take the first Pacifica exit at Manor Dr., and turn right on Palmetto Dr. Go 0.7 mile and turn left on Westline Dr. Bear left toward the Mussel Rock Transfer Station (the dump), left again as the road forks right to the dump, and park in the large lot at the road's end. To reach Fort Funston, take Skyline Dr. (Hwy. 35) 4 miles north from Hwy. 1 in north Pacifica—the parking lot is on the left. Approaching Fort Funston from San Francisco, follow Skyline Dr. 0.7 mile south of the Great Highway.

Description: From the parking lot by Mussel Rock, walk through the opening in the fence and descend along roads leading down toward the beach. Looking above you to the west, notice the loose, unconsolidated slopes along the bluffs—the result of many landslides. The bluffs above the landslide area recede at a rate of up to 3 feet per year, undercutting houses that should never have been built or purchased in the first place. The edges of the landslide mark the rough boundaries of the San Andreas Fault Zone, an area approximately a half mile wide. The loose slopes mask any actual fault trace in the hillside, but it is definitely there—the great 1906 San Francisco earthquake had its epicenter immediately inland from this location.

Walking north on the beach, notice the northward tilt of the layers in the bluffs. Deposited sequentially, these layers represent a chronology of the former basin environment; they become progressively younger as you go north. Fossil beds can be identified by the white, linear exposures of crushed shells contained in a matrix of mudstone. The views north include most of the Marin coast, and Point Bonita (Hike 24) can be picked out across the Golden Gate on clear days. Fort Funston can be identified near the northern end of the bluffs as they drop in elevation. Turning south, Montara Mtn. (Hike 17) forms the skyline closest to the sea, plunging into the ocean at landmark Pedro Point.

Continuing north, you pass the deep gash that Woods Gulch makes in the bluffs. Because saturated slopes increase the risk of landslides and accelerate erosion, draining this threatened area is an attempt to slow the imminent destruction of its cliffside homes. The number of people increases as you approach the

path that leads up to the viewing platform and parking lot at Fort Funston. A former military reservation developed at the turn of the century, Fort Funston is now part of the Golden Gate National Recreation Area. It's a popular site for hang gliders and parasailors between March and October, when strong west winds rise over the blufftop.

Nearest Visitor Center: Fort Funston Visitor Center, (415) 239-2366, located near the parking lot. Open weekends noon–4 P.M.

Nearest Campground: Nothing close. See Hikes 13–16 for options on the Peninsula, and Hikes 24-26 for possibilities in Marin County.

THE FAULT

Hike 21—Peak over the Peninsula

Location	Ridge Trail
Agency	San Bruno Mountain State and County Park
Highlights	An island of Nature in a sea of humanity.
Distance	4.9 miles round trip
Total Elevation Gain/Loss	700′/700′
Hiking Time	2–3 hours
Difficulty	★★
Best Times	After storms
Optional Map	USGS 7.5-min *San Francisco South*

Four cities lap at the base of San Bruno Mountain, encircling it with the concrete bustle of the 21st Century. Yet it stands, protected, an oasis of rare plant life, the hunting ground for dozens of soaring raptors, one of the premier viewpoints in the Bay Area.

Viewed from nearby freeways, San Bruno Mountain seems barren and almost lifeless. Yet this landmark ridge preserves a large native plant community akin to what once covered all the hills of San Francisco. Isolated as it is from surrounding mountain ranges, San Bruno harbors several species of plants found almost nowhere else today. At present, 14 species of rare or endangered plants exist on the mountain. In addition, four rare species of butterflies flutter over the slopes, including the endangered San Bruno elfin and Mission blue. Non-endangered rodents scurry through the thick brush, prey for dozens of raptors.

As the tide of development reached the base of the mountain in the 1960s, efforts began to protect this unique natural feature and its native habitats. In 1978 the state purchased the core of the new park, and in 1982 the Habitat Conservation Plan was established with developers, allowing construction on some of the surrounding native habitat

in exchange for funding to preserve and protect the ecosystem within the park. This unusual plan created the San Bruno Mountain Habitat Conservation Trust Fund, used to eradicate encroaching non-native species such as eucalyptus, and reestablish endangered, existing native plants.

The Hike follows the spine of San Bruno Mountain (1314) from the central ridgetop parking lot to the eastern end above Hwy. 101, an easy hike with incredible views. The trail is entirely exposed to the elements. Wind is common and fog can envelop the mountain from May through September, so be prepared. Views are best immediately following a winter storm, hazing up rapidly in the days that follow. A camera with a telephoto lens and binoculars are best for capturing the expansive vistas. Despite the millions of people residing and working around the mountain, the trails are lightly traveled—especially on weekdays. No water is available at the trailhead.

To Reach the Trailhead: It is possible to approach from both I-280 and Hwy. 101. From 101, take the Bayshore Blvd. exit and turn west on Guadalupe Canyon Pkwy., reaching the park entrance (on the north side of the road) in 1.5 miles. Approaching on I-280 from the north, take the Eastmoor Ave. exit, turn left on Sullivan Rd., then quickly left again on San Pedro Rd. to cross the freeway. As you continue on San Pedro Rd., it becomes first East Market St. and then Guadalupe Canyon Pkwy. before reaching the park entrance. Approaching on I-280 from the south, take the Mission St. exit, turn left on Junipero Serra Blvd., right on San Pedro Rd., and proceed as described above. From the parking lot at the park entrance, drive underneath Guadalupe Canyon Pkwy. and up Radio Rd. to the summit parking lot. There is a day-use fee of $4.

Description: The trail begins at the east end of the parking lot, following a disused dirt road on an undulating route to East Peak. Yarrow, wild strawberry, poison oak, and other small plants hide among the skeletal fingers of the ubiquitous coyote brush. San Francisco International Airport is less than 5 miles away and continuously fills the skies with aircraft. Raptors soar in the more immediate air. The more common include:

red-tailed hawk, easily identified by the distinctive cry and orange-red tail; northern harrier, spotted by the large white patch on the rump; and American kestrel—the smallest raptor—identified by its small size, bandit black eye stripes, and constant tail twitching while in flight. While East Peak seems close throughout the hike, it takes longer to get there than you think. Where the slopes plummet down to Hwy. 101, you've arrived. Return the way you came, pondering this dramatic contrast between urban mania and Mother Nature.

Nearest Visitor Center: No visitor center. For general information, call San Mateo County Parks and Recreation Division at (415) 363-4020.

Nearest Campground: Nothing close. See Hikes 13–16 for options on the Peninsula and Hikes 24–26 for possibilities in Marin County.

Additional Information:
www.eparks.net/parks/SBMtHome.htm

PEAK OVER THE PENINSULA

Hike 22—Urban Wild

Location   San Francisco's Pacific Shore
Agency   Golden Gate National Recreation Area
Highlights   The wild, scenic, historic Pacific margin of San Francisco.
Distance   5.5 miles one way
Total Elevation Gain/Loss   500´/500´
Hiking Time   5–7 hours
Difficulty   ★★
Best Times   September through May
Optional Map   USGS 7.5-min *Point Bonita, San Francisco North*

Here is the power of the Pacific, breaking upon storied shores too rugged for development, punctuated by wild geologic exposures, immediate to the densest collection of humanity in California. Wander the urban wild of San Francisco.

The Hike follows San Francisco's Pacific shore from Ocean Beach to the Golden Gate Bridge, an all-day adventure completely accessible by public transportation. Cool ocean breezes make a warm sweater and/or windbreaker critical year-round. Avoid the summer months when fog envelops the Pacific shore, lowering the temperature and obscuring the spectacular views. A shuttle by bus or car is required to return to Ocean Beach at the end of the day. While no water is available at the trailhead, sources are plentiful along the way.

WARNING: There is no safe swimming anywhere along this hike. The Pacific Ocean in San Francisco is dangerous, currents are strong, and waves can be powerful. People have been swept out to sea and drowned. Precarious cliffs are also a hazard. Respect the ocean and heed all warning signs. Do not become the next tragedy.

To Reach the Trailhead, head to the north end of Ocean Beach at the western edge of Golden Gate Park and park in one of the large lots adjacent to the beach. Approaching from the Golden Gate Bridge, take Hwy. 1 south, turn right on Kennedy Dr. and, when Kennedy Dr. ends, turn right again on Martin Luther King Jr. Dr. to reach the ocean. Approaching from the south on I-280, take the Hwy. 1/19th Ave. exit, go north on 19th Ave. to Kennedy Dr., turn left, and proceed as described above. Approaching from the Bay Bridge, take the Fell St. exit, go west on Fell St. to Golden Gate Park, bear right on John F. Kennedy Dr., follow it through the park, and continue as described above.

The northern end of this hike is in the large tourist parking lot at the southern end of the Golden Gate Bridge, located immediately east of the toll plaza. **Public Transportation** for this hike is provided by Muni bus 38 (service along Geary Blvd. to Point Lobos) and bus 28 (service from the Golden Gate Bridge with a stop at Geary Blvd.). Call (415) 673-MUNI for current schedule information or go online at *ci.sf.ca.uf/muni.*

Description: From the parking lot at Ocean Beach, drop down a stairwell to the open sand. Four miles long, Ocean Beach is the largest beach in the Bay Area and stretches from Fort Funston to the Cliff House, visible on the rocks immediately north. The Richmond and Sunset districts east of the beach were built upon a vast field of sand dunes, which covered most of northwest San Francisco and was once the fourth largest dune complex in California. All this sand originated between ten and fifteen thousand years ago during the last Ice Age, when sea level was approximately 200 feet lower, San Francisco Bay was dry land, and the shoreline was roughly 20 miles west of its current location—you could have walked to the Farallon Islands! Instead of dropping its sediment in the Bay as it does today, the Sacramento River flowed beyond the Golden Gate, depositing sand in a broad alluvial fan that was blown onshore by prevailing northwesterly winds to form Ocean Beach and the vast dune fields.

After enjoying Ocean Beach, walk north toward the Cliff House, head up stairway 4, cross the Esplanade to the corner of Balboa and La Playa, and climb the stairs toward Sutro Heights. As is true throughout this hike, numerous use paths diverge in all directions as you proceed. Continue generally north through eucalyptus and Monterey cypress to reach the top of Sutro Heights, where an open area of grass and unusual trees can be found. The tall, straight-trunked trees sporting strange wandlike foliage here are monkey puzzle trees, a type of araucaria native to Chile and Argentina.

To understand the history of Sutro Heights and its surrounding landmarks requires a brief biography of Adolph Sutro. A native of Prussia, Sutro emigrated to California in 1850, and in 1869 began constructing a tunnel designed to access and ventilate the rich mines of Nevada's Comstock Lode. Completed in 1878, the Sutro Tunnel was a huge financial success, earning Sutro a tidy fortune when he sold his shares in 1879. Returning to San Francisco, he acquired vast amounts of real estate for the future structures of Sutro Heights, the Cliff House, and the Sutro Baths. At one point, he owned one eleventh of all city

land! Over the next 20 years Sutro helped build San Francisco, even serving as mayor from 1895 to 1897. After his death in 1898, the sights and wonders he created slowly fell into disrepair, leaving little but memories and the photographs so well-preserved by the National Park Service today.

Acquired by Sutro in 1881, Sutro Heights was an open blufftop with little vegetation. With the help of 11 full-time gardeners, he transformed it into an exotic plant and flower garden with a substantial greenhouse. A popular tourist destination while in operation, the structure was torn down in 1939. South from the large viewing platform, you can see the long stretch of Ocean Beach and distant Montara Mountain (Hike 17) terminating in the ocean at Point San Pedro. The Farallon Islands west and Point Reyes northwest are visible on clear days.

From Sutro Heights, head down to the Cliff House parking lot—the dirt path splits north from the paved trail by the small gazebo. Cross Point Lobos Ave. and make the quick side trip down to the Cliff House, and the outstanding GGNRA visitor center on the lower deck. The current Cliff House is the third structure occupying this precarious site. The first was an unassuming structure known as Seal Rock House, purchased by Sutro in 1881, that catered to San Francisco's elite. Destroyed by fire in 1894, Seal Rock House was replaced by the opulent Victorian Cliff House, an eight-story marvel styled after a French chateau, which survived the 1906 earthquake only to be destroyed by fire in 1907. Constructed in 1909 by Sutro's daughter, the third and current Cliff House is a less-exciting neoclassic building. Seal Rocks sit immediately offshore from the Cliff House, named for the California and Steller's sea lions (once considered seals) that have historically used the rocks as a safe haven, barking boisterously into the wind. Today, Seal

Rocks are much quieter as most of the sea lions seem to be congregating near Fisherman's Wharf at Pier 39.

From the Cliff House, walk back up Point Lobos Ave. and head down to the ruins of Sutro Baths. Opened to the public in 1896, the Sutro Baths complex covered more than three acres and was enclosed by 100,000 square feet of glass. In addition to one freshwater pool, 1.685 million gallons of sea water filled six separate saltwater swimming tanks that could be flushed in less than an hour by the incoming tides. There were 9 springboards, 7 toboggan slides, 3 trapezes, 1 high dive, 30 swinging rings, 20,000 bathing suits, 40,000 towels, 500 private dressing rooms, a 5,300-seat amphitheater, 3 restaurants, natural history exhibits, art galleries, and a jungle of exotic plants. Up to 1,600 bathers could swim at once, the main room had a capacity of 15,000, and more than 25,000 people could visit in a single day. Following Sutro's death, the baths slowly fell into disrepair; they were destroyed by fire in 1966. Today the trail leads past the remaining foundation to a large concrete platform, which was the site of two-gun Battery Lobos during WW II.

The trail continues uphill north of Sutro Baths, rejoining the broad Coastal Trail via several use paths. Bear left on the Coastal Trail, the former roadbed of the Ferries and Cliff House Railroad. Continue north where a wide trail joins from the right; you will soon see the entire Golden Gate Bridge (Hike 23) through the surrounding Monterey cypress. As the large building of the Veterans Administration Hospital appears south over the bluffs above you, look left for one of the unposted trails leading down to the ocean at Lands End. A small promontory offering views of a San Francisco coastline as wild as any in California, Lands End is a side trip not to be missed.

Now heading east along the main trail, you have incredible views past off-limits Painted Rock Cliff before reaching the immaculate greens of Lincoln Golf Course. At El Camino del Mar, go left (east) down the sidewalk, bearing left at all intersections to reach the posted access for China Beach (via a hard left leading to parking above the small sandy beach). From this intersection, continue on Sea Cliff Dr. to its eastern end, where a path leads down to Baker Beach. Alternatively, you can follow the larger thoroughfare of El Camino del Mar a short distance to Bowley St., and turn left to reach the beach.

Named for a prominent San Francisco lawyer killed in the Civil War, Baker Beach was the site of San Francisco's only shark attack, a fatal incident that occurred in 1959. Walk north along the beach toward its clothing-optional section, and make the sandy, exhausting ascent up the stairway to Lincoln Ave. Turn left and walk along Lincoln Ave for approximately 50 yards to a trail heading left for Battery Crosby, one of 22 coastal batteries constructed in and around the Presidio. The majority of these—including Crosby—were built and manned between 1895 and 1945 as a defense against potential invasion. From here, a maze of trails wind north on the bluffs above the ocean. While the main trail continues along Lincoln Blvd., it is possible to follow any number of the use paths—just keep heading north.

The distinctive green bluffs here are composed of serpentine, an unusual rock that produces soils inhospitable to most plants. Consequently, unique ecosystems have developed on serpentine outcrops around the state, which harbor many rare and endangered species found nowhere else. Please respect the signs and fences along this section—they are designed to protect and rehabilitate this rare San Francisco ecosystem. The heavily sheared, landslide-prone bluffs here can be closely examined by scrambling down to the secluded rocky shoreline at their base, an exciting side trip.

Continuing north past Batteries West (armed with 12 cannons; operational 1873–1898), Godfrey (3 guns, 1896–1943), Boutelle (2 guns, 1898–1917), Marcus Miller (3 guns, 1899–1920), and Cranston (2 guns, 1898–1943), the maze of trails meet at a paved path that leads underneath the Golden Gate Bridge to the large parking lot and tourist center by the toll plaza.

Nearest Visitor Center: Cliff House Visitor Center, (415) 556-8642. Open daily 10 A.M.–5 P.M.

Nearest Campground: The Marin Headlands (see Hike 24).

Additional Information:
www.nps.gov/goga

URBAN WILD, THE GOLDEN GATE, & *QUE BONITA*

Hike 23—The Golden Gate

Location	Golden Gate Bridge
Agency	Golden Gate National Recreation Area
Highlights	The bridge. The view. The experience.
Distance	2.4 miles round trip
Total Elevation Gain/Loss	60´/60´
Hiking Time	1–2 hours
Difficulty	★
Best Times	September through May
Optional Map	USGS 7.5-min *San Francisco North*

A graceful sweep of perfection, the Golden Gate Bridge is the defining landmark of Northern California. It is a marvel of human ingenuity that spanned an impossible gap across a violent strait, an engineering masterpiece famous the world over.

The Hike covers the length of the Golden Gate Bridge and explores its location, history, and construction. While the round-trip hike can be completed from either end, the description below begins from the south. It is usually cold and windy on the bridge with summer months bringing dense fog to the mix, obscuring the incredible views and making the rest of the year preferable for a visit. A warm sweater and windbreaker are recommended items year-round. Tourists are thick on the bridge and the wide diversity of countries represented is entertaining. The bridge is closed to pedestrians between 9 P.M. and 5 A.M. Water is available at the trailhead.

To Reach the Trailhead, take Hwy. 101 to the southern end of the bridge and park in the main tourist lot immediately east of the toll plaza. To reach the trailhead by **public transportation**, take MUNI bus 28 or 29. Call (415) 673-MUNI for current schedule information or go online at *ci.sf.ca.uf/muni.*

Description: The hike begins by the statue of Joseph Strauss, chief engineer of the Golden Gate Bridge from inception to completion. An engineer whose college graduation thesis was a bridge design for spanning the 50-mile-wide Bering Strait between Alaska and Russia, Strauss was a man of intense vision, purpose, and ingenuity. By the time construction began in early 1933, he had completed more than 400 bridges around the world and was considered by many to be the only man capable of realizing such an ambitious project. It would be his final and greatest work.

From here, head to the bridge itself, passing the rotunda gift shop to get to the east sidewalk near a barrage of signs and regulations. As you begin walking across the bridge, contemplate the fury beneath your feet. The Sacramento River drains more than 59,000 square miles (40% of the entire state), pouring into shallow San Francisco Bay from the northeast. The Bay has only one outlet—The Golden Gate—a narrow 1-mile-wide channel to the sea that is affected twice daily by the changing tides. During incoming tides, the rising waters pour into the Bay and impound the freshwater brought in by the Sacramento River. As the tides reverse, an unbelievable volume of water rushes out the narrow entrance. Every 12 hours, the Bay disgorges one sixth of its entire volume through the Golden Gate at a rate of roughly 2.3 million gallons per second. Moving at a speed of between 4.5 and 7.5 knots, the average flow is seven times that of the Mississippi River! Add to that powerful winds capable of reaching 60 miles per hour and the fury of Nature here is readily apparent.

Savor the views as you walk toward the south tower. Southeast, Coit Tower and downtown San Francisco are apparent, connected to the East Bay via the Bay Bridge. Looking east across the Bay, the summit of Mt. Diablo (Hike 10) can be seen crowning the East Bay Hills, and downtown Berkeley is visible beyond nearby Alcatraz Island. Northeast is substantial Angel Island and the Tiburon Peninsula. While views west are somewhat obscured by the far railings, the jagged spit of Point Bonita (Hike 24) juts from the north. Fort Point is directly beneath you, a pre-Civil War fort built during the 1850s to safeguard America's

newfound western possession. In designing the bridge, Strauss recognized that preservation of this important historical landmark was imperative; he built the distinctive rainbow arches above to frame it visually. The many emergency phones along the sidewalk are to help prevent potential suicides—to date more than 1,000 people have leapt to their deaths from the bridge.

Reaching the south tower, look up its fluted form. Tapering as it rises to its peak of 746' above sea level, this tower proved to be one of the greatest engineering challenges of the bridge. Its concrete foundation pier sits more than 1,100 feet offshore on a sloping underwater ledge between 60 and 80 feet deep, fully in the brunt of waves and tidal current. To build it required construction of a precarious trestle from shore to site, building fenders around the pier site, blasting a foundation hole to a level depth of 100' below sea level, extending the fenders from surface to bottom, and then dewatering the entire thing. The

The Golden Gate Bridge

trestle and fenders were destroyed by waves during early construction and had to be rebuilt prior to pouring the concrete. The north pier foundation proved much less difficult; it was built close to shore on a flat, shallow ledge located a mere 20 feet below the surface.

The massive steel towers sit on top of these concrete piers, each constructed of 43 million pounds of steel designed to support 85 million pounds of dead weight. Surprisingly, they are not solid, constructed instead of hollow cells 42" square by 35' high, which allow each tower to move laterally up to 13" and to bend 18" toward the channel and 22" toward the shore, as the cables expand and contract with the temperature. In driving the 600,000 rivets required to put each tower together, workers had to scramble inside and through the honeycombed boxes. Remarkably, the entire south tower was constructed in a scant 101 days.

The distance between the two towers is 4,200' and as you walk it, admire the catenary curve of the two main bridge cables. These huge cables measure 36.5" in diameter, are 7,650' long, and each weigh 7,125 tons. They attach to the earth at four, massive, concrete anchors buried 12 stories deep in the ground and capable of each withstanding 63 million pounds of pull. Essentially spun in place, each cable is composed of 27,000 strands of thin wire, which were individually strung from anchorage to tower to tower to anchorage and back again. 80,000 miles of this pencil-thin wire were used, enough to wrap around the equator three times.

The Golden Gate Bridge is a suspension bridge. That is, the roadway is suspended from cables supported by towers. Once the cables were complete, construction of the 90'-wide roadway began. Strauss was farsighted enough to build a bridge six lanes wide, a width considered somewhat excessive at the time— the traffic around you today probably would have surprised him. Construction began from both towers simultaneously and the roadway was joined in November 1936. Paving the roadway followed; it resulted in the main fatalities of the construction process. An innovative safety net had been rigged beneath the expanding and precarious roadway, saving fallen men from plummeting to their death. (Those so saved by the net formed a small "Halfway to Hell" club.) Unfortunately, in February 1937 a platform supporting a work crew detached, ripping through the net and killing 10 men. An earlier crane accident had claimed the bridge's first victim, making a final count of 11 fatalities. Yet, construction proceeded and on May 27, 1937, the $35 million bridge opened to the public amid great fanfare. Joseph Strauss died the following year. (Cassady 1986) Continue to the viewing platform at the north end of the bridge and admire this masterpiece before returning.

Nearest Visitor Center: Nothing at the bridge itself. Try the William P. Mott Visitor Center, (415) 561-4323, located by the main parade grounds in The Presidio. Open daily 9 A.M.–5 P.M.

Nearest Campground: Marin Headlands (see Hike 25).

Additional Information: *www.nps.gov/goga*

★ *See map on page 73.*

Hike 24—*Que Bonita*

Location	Point Bonita Lighthouse
Agency	Golden Gate National Recreation Area
Highlights	The jaws of the Golden Gate. The legacy of "wickies" and "surfmen."
Distance	1.0 mile round trip
Total Elevation Gain/Loss	50´/50´
Hiking Time	1 hour
Difficulty	★
Best Times	September through May
Optional Map	USGS 7.5-min *Point Bonita*

Take a short stroll to the farthest edge of the Bay Area. Perched on a naked fin of rock jutting into the ocean, Point Bonita Lighthouse is a lonely sentinel with extraordinary views.

The Hike follows an easy paved path through a tunnel and over a unique suspension bridge to the lighthouse. Unfortunately, the lighthouse path is only open Saturday through Monday from 12:30 to 3:30 P.M.; otherwise, it is closed at the tunnel. While the hike to the tunnel is pleasant, it cannot rival the full lighthouse experience. Prepare for wind—lots of wind—as Point Bonita is always blustery. Timing is important—fog blankets the point for days on end during the summer months, making the rest of the year better for a visit. The lighthouse may be closed if wave and weather conditions are too severe.

To Reach the Trailhead, take Hwy. 101 to the Alexander Avenue exit, the first off-ramp north of the Golden Gate Bridge. Following signs to the Marin Headlands, quickly turn left to pass through the one-lane tunnel. A mile past the tunnel turn left onto McCullough Rd., follow it uphill, and then turn right onto spectacular Conzelman Rd., which becomes a narrow one-lane road that drops precipitously to a T-junction by a

YMCA. Go left and park in the posted Point Bonita lot. **Public transportation** to nearby Battery Alexander is available from San Francisco on Sundays and holidays aboard MUNI bus 76, which departs once an hour from downtown. For current schedule information, call (415) 673-MUNI or go online at *ci.sf.ca.uf/muni*.

Description: From the parking area, follow the paved path below a stand of Monterey Cypress. Dropping toward the tunnel, you reach an informative placard detailing the story of the Point Bonita Lifesaving Station and the "surfmen" who manned it. According to a 1908 San Francisco Chronicle article describing the surfmen, "Every man enlisted in this daring work must have had at least three years of experience as a sailor. He must be an expert boatman and physically perfect. He is not allowed to drink while in uniform, and to be caught intoxicated means immediate dismissal. As a matter of course he must be courageous. The discipline is very strict."

As you approach the tunnel, the first views north open up and Point Reyes and Bolinas are visible beyond the pounding surf. The shark fin of rock through which the tunnel passes is composed of pillow basalt, a rock highly resistant to erosion. It is formed on the ocean bottom when liquid magma is extruded from the sea floor. As the molten rock encounters seawater, its outer shell is instantly cooled to form a distinctive pillow shape. Liquid magma remains inside, however, and as it is squeezed out again another pillow is formed on top, creating large stacks of these distinctive formations.

Before you enter the tunnel, notice the odd, large-leafed plants clinging to cracks in the rock. These are feral cabbages, escaped from the gardens of past lighthouse keepers and now uniquely adapted to survive the hostile environment of Point

QUE BONITA

Bonita. On the other side of the tunnel, railings protect you from the drop to the rocks below. When you reach the suspension bridge, please observe the five person limit.

When Point Bonita Lighthouse opened in 1855, it was the third lighthouse constructed on the West Coast, built in response to the more than 300 ships that had run aground near the Golden Gate during the Gold Rush period. The original Fresnel Lens, constructed in France, was capable of bending 70% of radiant light onto a horizontal plane. Its original light was the flame on an oil-fed wick, tended by resident lighthouse keepers known as "wickies." Incredibly, the same lens is still in use today, sending a beam of light visible for 18 miles. In 1980 the lighthouse was the last to become automated, and today a single 1,000-watt bulb provides the light. The lighthouse building is

open to the public but the light itself is off-limits.

Nearest Visitor Center: Marin Headlands Visitor Center, (415) 331-1540, located 1 mile from Point Bonita on Bunker Rd. in Rodeo Valley. Open daily 9:30 A.M.–4:30 P.M.

Nearest Campground: Group campgrounds in the Marin Headlands include Kirby Cove (4 sites, open April through October) and Battery Alexander (1 site, open year-round). The fee for each is $20. There is also an easily accessible, free, walk-in campground at Bicentennial near Battery Wallace (3 sites, maximum 2 people per site, open year-round). Reservations are required for all campsites in the Marin Headlands and can be made up to 90 days in advance by calling the visitor center. Permits must be picked up at the visitor center during open hours.

Additional Information:
www.nps.gov/goga

Hike 25—Head Out

Location	Marin Headlands
Agency	Golden Gate National Recreation Area
Highlights	A blufftop ramble with terrific sea views.
Distance	4.7 miles
Total Elevation Gain/Loss	1300´/1300´
Hiking Time	2–3 hours
Difficulty	★★
Best Times	September through May
Optional Map	USGS 7.5-min *Point Bonita*

A remarkable patch of wild, the Marin Headlands are close to the dense humanity of San Francisco, yet removed in a way that transcends the mere physical separation of the Golden Gate.

The Headlands owe their preservation to their former use as ranches and to the military presence that existed here for more than 100 years. Active gun batteries once lined the bluffs north of the Golden Gate and numerous dairy ranches operated in the inland valleys, monopolizing huge amounts of real estate and preventing development until 1960, when entrepreneurs purchased land in the Marin Headlands to create a bedroom community known as Marincello. A ground swell of opposition prevented

Marin Headlands

this tragedy and in 1972 the area became protected as a national park, saving the land for its plant and animal denizens.

Most of the hilly terrain is covered by low coastal scrub. Coyote brush, poison oak, blackberry, and thimbleberry make dense thickets along trails highlighted seasonally with wildflowers—lupine, paintbrush, columbine, monkey flower, shooting stars, and California poppy are common. Rabbits and other small rodents scurry through the undergrowth, hunted by the ever-vigilant raptors that soar overhead. Seven different birds of prey are found in the headlands, congregating in large numbers during September and October as they migrate south. Other birds add color and song to the landscape, including snowy egrets, great blue herons, and yellow-rumped warblers. Deer and bobcats wander the hills, best spotted at dusk or in the early morning. The Pacific Ocean is seldom out of sight beyond the steep bluffs and the spouts of migrating gray whales can be seen occasionally during winter and spring.

The Hike approaches the Marin Headlands from the north at Muir Beach and provides a good survey of the Headlands experience, passing first along rocky bluffs above Pirates Cove before returning via open ridgetops offering good views into deep coastal valleys. Fog is generally thick from June through August, tapering off in September. Temperatures are generally cool year-round and the wind can spring up at any time—bring a sweater. Crowds are heavy in the Marin Headlands, especially on the weekends, and Muir Beach is no exception. Water is available at the trailhead.

To Reach the Trailhead, take Hwy. 1 to the turnoff for Muir Beach, located where Hwy. 1 first reaches the coast north of the Golden Gate, roughly halfway between Stinson Beach and the Hwy. 101/1 split in Marin City. The large parking lot is at the end of Pacific Way.

Description: The trail begins at the south end of the lot (0.0/10) and immediately crosses Redwood Creek. Originating on the southern slopes of Mt. Tamalpais, Redwood Creek flows south through Muir Woods before turning west to enter the ocean here. Winter rains swell the creek and allow it to break through the beach sandbar, permitting steelhead trout and silver and coho salmon to migrate upstream and breed. Across the creek, you reach the junction for the Coastal Trail—go left, briefly paralleling the creek before turning right where Green Gulch Trail splits left. Coyote brush dominates the surrounding slopes as the trail climbs to the bluff's edge and ascends steeply to reach another junction (0.8/520)—go right on single-track, hikers-only Pirates Cove Trail. By now, expansive views have opened up. North, Muir Beach and the summit ridge of Mt. Tamalpais (Hike 26) dominate. Turning south, Pt. Bonita (Hike 24) and its suspension bridge jut out on the north side of the Golden Gate, beyond which is the Pacific coastline of San Francisco (Hike 22) —Lands End and Ocean Beach are both discernible. The Farallon Islands are visible west-southwest 25 miles offshore.

It's an undulating traverse above the ocean on Pirates Cove Trail, with at least one spot where the rocky shore can be accessed. A steep climb near the end leads to Coyote Ridge and a major intersection with two fire roads (2.3/570)—go left, up the ridge. As you wind along the ridgetop, views of undeveloped Tennessee Valley below you south are a highlight. Tennessee Valley cuts centrally through the headlands down to Tennessee Beach. The namesake steamer *S.S. Tennessee* wrecked there in 1853. Downtown San Francisco peeps out between a saddle southwest where the trail reaches another major junction. The route along Coyote Ridge heads right, but you continue straight, dropping steadily to return to Muir Beach.

Nearest Visitor Center: The Marin Headlands Visitor Center (see Hike 24).

Backpacking Information: Backcountry camping is allowed only at two designated primitive campgrounds: Haypress and Hawkcamp. Haypress is closest to this hike and is located in Tennessee Valley (5 sites). Hawkcamp is more remote, located near the ridge dividing Gerbode and Tennessee valleys (3 sites). While the sites are free, reservations are required and can be made up to 90 days in advance by calling the visitor center. Permits must be picked up at the visitor center during open hours. No campfires are allowed.

Nearest Campground: Mt. Tamalpais State Park (see Hike 26).

Additional Information: *www.nps.gov/goga*

HEAD OUT

Hike 26—Tam

Location	Mt. Tamalpais
Agency	Marin Municipal Water District
Highlights	Premier views of the Bay Area. A summit challenge.
Distance	6.0 miles
Total Elevation Gain/Loss	1900´/1900´
Hiking Time	4–6 hours
Difficulty	★★★
Best Times	Year-round
Optional Map	USGS 7.5-min *San Rafael*

Visible throughout the Bay Area, the long spine of Mt. Tamalpais constantly beckons the hiker with a few recreational hours to spare. Read on for an excellent taste of all the mountain has to offer.

The Hike climbs steeply from Mountain Home Inn on Panoramic Highway directly to the summit of Mt. Tamalpais (2571), before looping around the mountain's eastern flanks to return to the trailhead. With a maze of trails crisscrossing the mountain, the hike utilizes the following ones in this order: Gravity Car Grade, Old Railroad Grade, Vic Haun, Temelpa, Verna Dunshee, Eldridge Grade, Wheeler, and Hoo-Koo-E-Koo. The hike can be done year-round, with spring and fall offering the most idyllic weather. The stunning views are clearest following winter storms. Summer fog can be thick in the area, but even then views tend to remain dramatic. Water is available at the trailhead.

To Reach the Trailhead from Hwy. 101 in Marin City, take Hwy. 1 northwest toward Stinson Beach and bear right on Panoramic Highway at the posted **Y**-junction. Remain on Panoramic Highway for 5 miles following the ridgetop, and park in the lot across from Mountain Home Inn (at the edge of Mt. Tamalpais State Park). If the lot is full, go down the small paved road across the

highway and park at the side where it turns to dirt.

You have to go on a weekend or holiday to reach the trailhead by **public transportation,** when Golden Gate Transit bus 63 runs to the trailhead. Service ends early (around 6 P.M.). For the current schedule and connection information, call (415) 923-2000 or go online at *goldengate.org.*

Description: From the trailhead (0.0/930), Muir Woods' deep watershed is visible southwest below you and the summit towers due north above you. The trail begins across the highway on a small paved road that immediately brings you to a fork by a watershed boundary sign—bear right. Now on a dirt road, the trail soon crosses a gate. Beyond the gate, Douglas-fir, madrone, coast live oak, toyon, and tan oak all appear along the broad trail, as do abundant second-growth redwood trees. Tantalizing views of San Francisco and the Bay Area open up intermittently as you proceed, soon reaching an area where several wide roads intersect (0.8/1100)—continue left toward East Peak on Old Railroad Grade.

For the next 0.3 mile, you are walking on the old roadbed utilized by steam trains of the Mount Tamalpais and Muir Woods Railway between 1896 and 1930.

While in operation, "the crookedest railroad in the world" journeyed 8.25 miles from Mill Valley to the summit on an estimated 281 curves. After making two of those curves, the roadbed reaches a posted junction with the wide Hoo-Koo-E-Koo Trail (1.4/1200), which heads east while Old Railroad Grade curves back west. Between these two wide paths, directly at the junction, the unposted single-track Vic Haun Trail strikes almost directly uphill—take it!

Vic Haun Trail immediately begins climbing through a tunnel of manzanita and small redwoods before breaking out onto more open slopes with increasingly excellent views south. Large chinquapin bushes appear occasionally by the trail before it traverses east, crossing a small stream thick with California bay. When you reach the Temelpa Trail, your path continues steeply upward via numerous switchbacks to the paved Verna Dunshee Trail, which encircles the summit (2.3/2320). Go either left or right; either way gets you to the parking lot at the crowded summit. The fire lookout above you marks the top and is easily accessible by a popular and partially boardwalked trail.

The summit and spine of Mt. Tam are composed of an unusual erosion-resistant tourmaline, formed by a reaction when sandstone becomes permeated with boron-rich water. Exposures are plentiful as you make the final push to the lookout. From the top you can see the heart of the Bay Area.

Back down at the parking lot, walk a short distance down the main paved road to find the posted gate for Eldridge

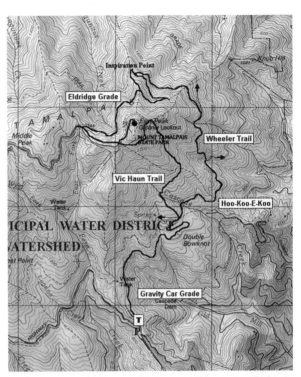

TAM

Grade on the right. Drop down the wide rocky trail, noting the change in vegetation. California bay and madrone are common, joined by California nutmeg trees with pointy fir-like needles. Winding below the summit, the trail reaches an obvious spur on the left due north from the peak. This is a steep, single-track shortcut to Inspiration Point that bypasses a long switchback on Eldridge Grade. From Inspiration Point (4.0/1880), continue descending east on Eldridge Grade until you reach a posted junction (4.6/1580) at a large switchback—continue straight on single-track Wheeler Trail.

Wheeler Trail is steep, descending rapidly through thick, young redwood forest and huckleberry bushes to reach the wide Hoo-Koo-E-Koo Trail (5.0/1110). Turn right and stay on Hoo-Koo-E-Koo Trail until you rejoin the Old Railroad Grade (5.7/1200).

Nearest Visitor Center: Summit Visitor Center, located by the summit parking lot. Open summer weekends 10 A.M.–5:30 P.M.; winter weekends noon–4 P.M. Also try Pantoll Ranger Station, (415) 388-2070, located 2.6 miles west of the trailhead on Panoramic Highway. Open in summer daily 8:30 A.M.–7 P.M., winter daily 10:30 A.M.–5:30 P.M.

Nearest Campground: Pantoll Campground, located by Pantoll Ranger Station. 16 first-come, first-served sites that require a short 100-yard walk-in. Sites ($12–16) usually fill by late afternoon. Also Steep Ravine Environmental Campground, located on a marine terrace 1 mile south of Stinson Beach on Hwy. 1. 10 rustic cabins ($30/night) and 6 primitive campsites ($7–13) are available. Reservations are essential and can be made 10 days to seven months in advance by calling 1-800-444-7275 or going online at *reserveamerica.com*.

Additional Information:
www.parks.ca.gov/districts/marin/ mtsp239.htm

Looking south from the flanks of Mt. Tamalpais

Hike 27—The Birds

Location	Bolinas Lagoon Preserve
Agency	Audubon Canyon Ranch
Highlights	Developing avian awareness at a major heronry.
Distance	2.3 miles
Total Elevation Gain/Loss	700´/700´
Hiking Time	2–3 hours
Difficulty	★★
Best Times	Weekends April through July
Optional Map	USGS 7.5-min *Bolinas*

With more than 100 pairs of great egrets, great blue herons, and snowy egrets nesting in a perfectly visible treetop community, the Audubon Canyon Ranch is a terrific draw. Add Bolinas Lagoon, a shallow mudflat alive with more than 60 species of birds, and an impressive oak forest, and the allure becomes difficult to resist.

In Bolinas Lagoon Preserve, three small canyons cut down to the edge of a large, shallow mudflat and protect a rich array of life regenerating from past human influences. Logged to build 19th Century San Francisco and once used for dairy ranching, the landscape is recovering well. More than 90 species of birds can be sighted here, amphibians crawl its moist creekbeds, and steelhead trout once again swim its streams. The herons and egrets arrive by March, choose mates after elaborate courtship rituals, and then raise their young for 12 weeks in the heronry. Located in the upper canopy of a few redwood trees in lower Picher Canyon, the site provides shelter and ready access to the fish and crustaceans found in Bolinas Lagoon. From mid-June through mid-July volunteers keep careful track of the nesting pairs, follow the development of the chicks, and then watch the entire community gradually disperse.

The Hike is a circuit around Picher Canyon on Griffin Trail, passing the overlooks of Bolinas Lagoon and the heronry early on. Telescopes are provided and friendly docents enrich the experience, making this one of the best sites in California to learn about birds. The preserve is only open to the public from mid-March until mid-July on Saturdays, Sundays, and holidays from 10 A.M. until 4 P.M. While April and May are the most eventful months in the heronry, a powerful telephoto lens is necessary to capture the scene on film. Crowds tend to concentrate at the overlooks, leaving the trails surprisingly empty. Water is available at the trailhead.

To Reach the Trailhead, drive 3 miles north of Stinson Beach on Hwy. 1—the posted turnoff has an OPEN sign hanging if you've come at the right time. Volunteers usually greet you and tell you where to park. While there is no entrance fee, donations are strongly encouraged and help support Audubon Canyon Ranch, a private non-profit managing this and two other nature preserves in Marin and Sonoma counties.

Reaching the trailhead by **public transportation** is challenging but possible. Golden Gate Transit bus 63 goes to Audubon Canyon Ranch on Saturdays, Sundays, and holidays, leaving Marin

City in the morning and returning mid-afternoon. Call (415) 455-2000 for current schedule information or go online at *goldengate.org*.

Description: Pick up a free map of the preserve from the visitor center before walking briefly back down the entrance road to the start of Griffin Trail (0.0/10). The wide trail immediately starts climbing through California buckeye, live oak, and California bay to reach the first overlook. Depending on tides, Bolinas Lagoon may be filled with shallow water or exposed as fractal-patterned mudflats. Birdlife is always abundant, and the Audubon's interpretive panels and telescopes are lots of fun.

Past the lagoon overlook, the trail forks—bear right toward the next overlook. Climbing through dense foliage, you soon reach another fork—bear right again and climb the short spur to Henderson Overlook (0.3/200). Note the sign: QUIET—BIRDS NESTING. White splotches in the green canopy, enlarged and defined by powerful telescopes here, compose the heronry below you to the east. Learn all you can of these beautiful birds before returning to the main trail.

Back on Griffin Trail, you ascend the ridge. Look for redwood trees providing excellent examples of basal sprouting. Once cut, a redwood tree immediately sprouts a series of saplings from its root system, forming a roughly concentric circle around the stump known as a "fairy ring." Some rings here include more than a dozen trees. Where Zumie's Loop splits left at the junction near the top (0.8/720), keep right on the Griffin Trail. After cresting out, the trail swings right and crosses the lush creek gully; then it continues on a level traverse through a dense alder thicket. The path gradually descends through a thick forest of redwood and Douglas-fir to an open ridgetop before beginning its steep descent to the trailhead.

Views of Stinson Beach, Bolinas Lagoon, and Olema Valley open up as you descend. The San Andreas Fault underlies these landmarks, and fault movement in the Olema Valley during the 1906 earthquake was more than 12 feet in places. One earth fissure reportedly swallowed an entire cow—except for the legs left protruding upward from the ground! The trail descends the ridgeline steeply to the visitor center, passing beneath some very impressive coast live oaks at the end.

Nearest Visitor Center: Audubon Canyon Ranch visitor center and bookstore, (415) 868-9244, located among the old ranch buildings. Open when the preserve is open.

Nearest Campground: Privately owned Olema Campground or Samuel P. Taylor State Park (see Hike 29). Also try Mt. Tamalpais State Park (see Hike 26).

Additional Information: *www.egret.org*

THE BIRDS

Hike 28—Sea Spray

Location	Alamere Falls
Agency	Point Reyes National Seashore
Highlights	Mind-bending geology. Ocean vistas. A beachside waterfall.
Distance	8.5 miles round trip
Total Elevation Gain/Loss	900´/900´
Hiking Time	5–7 hours
Difficulty	★★
Best Times	September through May
Optional Map	USGS 7.5-min *Bolinas, Double Point*

Alamere Falls is an easily accessible yet remote destination, where a small stream tumbles directly over coastal bluffs onto a sandy beach. The oceanside cliffs, Double Point view, and inviting freshwater lakes along the trail are all expressions of the unique geology of southern Point Reyes National Seashore.

The Hike follows the Coast Trail from Palomarin trailhead to Alamere Falls, a fairly long dayhike that can be extended to an overnight trip by continuing 1.5 miles past Alamere Falls to Wildcat Camp. Fog is common in the summer months and should be avoided. Swimming and fishing are possible in freshwater Bass Lake halfway to the falls, but ocean frolicking is not recommended due to the strong rip currents, undertow, and frigid water. This is not an isolated hike—especially on the weekends—and you can expect to see other people on the trail and at the waterfall. Poison oak, stinging nettle, and ticks are common hazards in the brush. No water is available at the trailhead and there are no reliable sources before Alamere Falls.

To Reach the Trailhead, take Hwy. 1 north from Stinson Beach for 4.4 miles to the northern edge of Bolinas Lagoon and turn left onto the Olema-Bolinas Rd. The turnoff is not posted so keep your eye out. In 1.2 miles the road reaches a T-junction—go left, continuing on Olema-Bolinas Rd. for another 0.6 mile before turning right again on Mesa Rd. Follow Mesa Rd. 4.6 miles to the parking lot at the road's end, passing a Coast Guard radar station and the Point Reyes Bird Observatory along the way. The last 1.3 miles are unpaved.

Description From the trailhead (0.0/280), the wide path immediately enters a thick eucalyptus grove where wild cucumber vines twine and a few enormous trees dominate—one huge Hydralike specimen is by far the largest eucalyptus of this book. Good views south open up next as the trail winds along open blufftops, and the Farallon Islands are visible southwest on a clear day. The trail turns inland, crossing two small creek gullies choked with brush, horsetail, watercress, monkey flower, and ferns before resuming ocean views. At the third significant creek gully, the trail continues inland, climbing over a small divide to the Lake Ranch Trail (2.2/570) junction. Continuing ahead on the Coast Trail, you meander through a dense forest of Douglas-fir, the conifer common throughout this hike. The trail passes several swampy ponds full of lily pads before Bass Lake comes into view. Gradually descending along its northern shore, the path leads to a short spur trail and an open space excellent for a break on hot days. Beyond the lake, the trail soon passes a junction for unexciting Crystal Lake before traversing above beautiful Pelican Lake. Point Reyes and the long curving arc of beach and coastal bluffs appear north.

Descending, you reach a spur junction on your left (4.0/290) immediately after views north are hidden by coastal bluffs. This small trail leads 0.3 mile to the top of Pelican Hill (380) and the north end of Double Point, a spectacular,

recommended side trip. Besides far-reaching views south and north from the summit, the inaccessible cove beach below is often filled with hundreds of hauled-out seals. This is also a good vantage point to contemplate the geologic forces that created this landscape.

The rock of this area is called the Monterey shale, a sequence of sedimentary layers up to 8,000 feet thick that were deposited on top of the granite bedrock of Point Reyes National Seashore over the past 20 million years. In the region around Double Point, this shale has become involved in a huge landslide nearly four miles long and at

SEA SPRAY

least a mile wide. As this huge block of land slips slowly toward the sea, depressions are formed that fill with freshwater lakes such as Pelican and Bass lakes. (Galloway 1977)

Immediately past the junction for Pelican Hill, another unposted spur trail splits left. This overgrown and brushy path leads down to Alamere Falls, unseen until the very end, where some scrambling is required to reach the stream and its series of cascades. Some more challenging scrambling will take you down to the beach via a rocky chute. The bluffs are impressive, and the tilted, exposed layers of Monterey shale are spectacular south of the falls.

Those heading to Wildcat Camp can either return to the main trail and continue via scenic Ocean Lake Loop Trail, or walk north up the beach from Alamere Falls for approximately 1 mile. Be aware that hiking north on the beach can be dangerous at high tide and should not be done during these times.

Nearest Visitor Center: Bear Valley Visitor Center, (415) 663-1092, located on Bear Valley Rd. just west of Olema, 8 miles north of the turnoff for the Olema-Bolinas Rd. Open weekdays 9 A.M.–5 P.M., weekends and holidays 8 A.M.–5 P.M.

Backpacking Information: Backcountry camping in Point Reyes National Seashore is by permit only and is confined to four, designated, backcountry campgrounds. No wood fires are allowed. Wildcat Camp, an open blufftop meadow with ocean views and nearby beach access, is closest to this hike (7 sites). Glen Camp is another, more distant possibility, located 8 miles northwest of Palomarin trailhead in an inland, wooded valley (12 sites). Camping permits cost $10 per night and must be picked up at the Bear Valley Visitor Center (after-hours pickup is possible). Reservations are strongly recommended and can be made up to three months in advance by calling (415) 663-8054 between 9 A.M. and 2 P.M., Monday through Friday. Fax reservations at (415) 663-1597. For a recorded message of camping availability for the next three months, call (415) 663-1092, ext. 400.

Nearest Campground: There are no drive-in campgrounds within Point Reyes National Seashore. The closest are either in Mt. Tamalpais State Park (see Hike 26) or near Olema (see Hike 29).

Additional Information: *www.nps.gov/pore*

Hike 29—Cold Tomales

Location	Tomales Point
Agency	Point Reyes National Seashore
Highlights	Prairie blufftops above pounding surf. A herd of tule elk.
Distance	9.0 miles round trip
Total Elevation Gain/Loss	1300´/1300´
Hiking Time	4–5 hours
Difficulty	★★★
Best Times	September through May
Optional Map	USGS 7.5-min *Tomales*

Here is a hike of sweeping coastal views along an elevated, granite peninsula, covered by an open grassland famous for its wildflowers and tule elk.

The Point Reyes Peninsula is a migrant piece of land. Its deepest bedrock is granite, formed in southern California approximately 100 million years ago. When the San Andreas Fault became active 28 million years ago, pieces of North America located west of the emergent fault began slowly migrating north at a rate of 2–3 centimeters per year, traveling hundreds of miles over the ensuing millenia. The granite of Point Reyes Peninsula was one of these pieces, and became covered by thick, waterborne sediments while submerged beneath the sea for almost 10 million years on its journey north. Roughly four million years ago, a slight change in the geometry of the San Andreas Fault system increased compression between the rocks on either side of the fault, pushing Point Reyes Peninsula—and most of the Coast Ranges—above sea level. Erosion then began stripping away the overlying sediment, once again exposing the erosion-resistant granite on today's Inverness Ridge and the bluffs of Point Reyes itself. Today, Tomales Point is a solid piece of granite battered by the seas into sheer cliffs of solid rock, a striking con-

trast to the loose slopes found most places on the California coast.

The Hike goes to land's end at Tomales Point from historic Pierce Point Ranch, a chilly trip that is almost always rainy, windy, foggy, or some combination of the three. The trail is entirely exposed and offers no shelter from the elements, making a good sweater and windbreaker crucial year-round items. Fog is consistent during the summer months, obscuring views and making a visit at some other time more desirable. While you will almost surely see other people, crowds are generally light. No water is available at the trailhead or anywhere en route.

To Reach the Trailhead, take Sir Francis Drake Blvd. west from Point Reyes Station on Hwy. 1 for 6.1 miles to the turnoff for Pierce Point Rd. Bear right on Pierce Point Rd. where Sir Francis Drake Blvd. curves left, and proceed 8.5 miles to the parking lot by the white buildings of historic Pierce Point Ranch.

Description: The trail begins from the west side of the parking lot by an informative sign, and for most of its length the hike follows an old lane—now a broad and friendly path—to the former site of lower Pierce Point Ranch. Passing between the still operational buildings of upper Pierce Point Ranch and a linear windbreak of Monterey cypress, the wide trail shortly breaks out into open fields of bush lupine and coyote brush where wild cucumber wraps its tendrils through the brush. Raptors—especially red-tailed hawks—are a common sight as they soar over the open fields, hunting for small prey. As you continue on the undulating route, keep an eye out for the herd of tule elk that wanders these bluffs, reintroduced in 1978 by the National Park Service. Numbering in the hundreds, these impressive creatures are a memorable and photogenic sight.

To the east the San Andreas Fault underlies Tomales Bay, a trough formed when the rocks along the fault were ground into easily eroded sediment. The fault continues northwest toward Bodega Head (Hike 30), the small peninsula immediately north of Tomales Point. Similar to Point Reyes Peninsula, Bodega Head is another piece of granite covered by sediment, separated from the mainland by the San Andreas Fault, and slowly moving northwest. Northeast, the highest peak visible is Mt. St. Helena (Hike 32). Looking south, the long sandy stretch of Point Reyes Beach terminates at rocky Point Reyes itself.

A long undulating traverse more than 300 feet above the breaking waves eventually leads to a steady descent that ends in a grove of trees, the former site of lower Pierce Point Ranch. From here, the trail gets sandier and less distinct as it passes through fields thick with irises, climbing first before dropping down to the precipitous granite cliffs of Tomales Point itself. Bird Rock, located just offshore to the west, is a rookery for numerous seabirds and a major pupping area for harbor seals. Great white sharks are commonly sighted in the waters around Tomales Point and have attacked divers in the past. You can get close, but the ocean remains out of reach less than 30 feet below. Be respectful of the dangerous cliffs as you explore the point. Return the way you came.

Nearest Visitor Center: Bear Valley Visitor Center (see Hike 28).

Nearest Campground: There are no drive-in campgrounds within Point Reyes National Seashore. The closest campground is privately owned Olema Ranch Campground, located in Olema on Hwy. 1 (200 sites, $18–20). Also try the campground in Samuel P. Taylor State Park, located 6 miles east of Hwy. 1 on Sir Francis Drake Blvd. (60 sites, $16). Reservations are recommended for Samuel P. Taylor April through October.

Additional Information:
www.nps.gov/pore

Cold Tomales

Hike 30—Barefoot in the Sand

Location	Bodega Dunes
Agency	Sonoma Coast State Beach
Highlights	Dune fields. Barefoot beach hiking.
Distance	2.2 miles
Total Elevation Gain/Loss	50′/50′
Hiking Time	1–2 hours
Difficulty	★
Best Times	Year-round
Optional Map	USGS 7.5-min *Bodega Head*

A chunk of granite spearheading the tectonic migration northwest, Bodega Head is backed by massive sand dunes and the longest beach on the Sonoma County coast. The fun of hiking barefoot is enhanced by distant views north up the rugged coastline.

The Hike explores the world of Bodega Dunes and the geology of Mussel Pt. before returning along Salmon Creek Beach. The entire hike is on loose sand that makes walking arduous but shoes unnecessary. Fog is common during the summer months, eliminating views and chilling the air. Fall offers the most consistent weather, winter the clearest views (between storms), and spring a profusion of flowering bush lupine. Crowds are heaviest in the summer months, dwindling to only the local surfers in the winter. Monarch butterflies overwinter in the park campground, making December and January an exciting time to visit. No water is available at the trailhead.

To Reach the Trailhead, take Hwy. 1 north from the town of Bodega Bay for 6 miles—the posted turnoff is on the west side of the highway. Approaching from the north, the turnoff is 8 miles south of the Hwy. 1/116 junction. Past the entrance station, turn right on Beach Rd. and follow it to the substantial parking lot and picnic area at the road's end. There is a day-use fee of $5.

Description: The trail begins at the gate by the parking lot entrance and immediately enters dune world. As is evident from the beginning, paths crisscross the dunes throughout this hike. The actual trail is generally obvious and parallels the beach behind the front line of dunes—please try to stay on this main trail in order to prevent erosion of the fragile environment.

The trail initially parallels a line of scrubby Monterey cypress and conspicuous flecks of white are everywhere in the sand around them. These are shell fragments, part of a *midden* used by the native inhabitants of the area prior to European settlement. Regularly harvesting shellfish from the ocean for food, the Coast Miwok would deposit the accumulated shell debris in large piles, an ancient "kitchen sink" they also filled with discarded bones, artifacts, and tools. Built up over hundreds of years, they are now covered by drifting sand, the scattered fragments on the surface their only indication.

As you continue through the dune fields, you are gradually surrounded by a world of sand, bush lupine, and beach grass. The larger dunes here approach 150 feet in elevation, somewhat stabilized by the European beach grass planted after cattle grazing had dangerously denuded existing native vegetation. Foxes, weasels, and black-tailed deer roam the dunes. Northern harriers and red-tailed hawks scan the ground below for the mice, voles, and jack rabbits that scurry through the undergrowth.

Although several trails split left back to the campground, continue to parallel the hidden beach at all junctions. Posted Jackrabbit and Scrub Jay spur trails on your right head to the beach, providing quicker access for those unexcited about continuing through the dunes. The last beach access point is located at the posted junction for Westshore Regional Park—bear right toward the ocean.

Once on the broad beach, views of the coastline north open up dramatically. Between you and the north end of Salmon Creek Beach, the San Andreas Fault slices underground and travels just offshore before briefly touching land again 15 miles north near Fort Ross. A keen eye can pick out Goat Rock and the mouth of the Russian River 9 miles up the coast.

Continue south along the beach to its terminus at Mussel Point, which is also the northern end of Bodega Head. A surprising outcrop of granite is exposed beneath a thin layer of sandstone here. Bodega Head is the northernmost exposure of the Salinian Block, a large piece of granite bedrock torn from southern California and thrust northwest by actions of the San Andreas Fault. Significant in size, the Salinian Block stretches from here out to the Farallon Islands and south down the entire California coast, but its granite heart is exposed in few places. At the north edge of the Salinian Block, the rocks at Mussel Point are the northernmost outcrop of granite on the California coast.

Closed for ecological study, Mussel Point's bluffs are unfortunately off-limits. Return along the beach, enjoying the views north, and reach the parking lot via the obvious wooden platform and walkway.

Nearest Visitor Center: No visitor center in the park. Call (707) 875-3493 for general information. Try park headquarters, located 0.7 mile north of the park turnoff on Hwy. 1. Also try the visitor center along Hwy. 1 in Jenner. Open weekends 10 A.M.–4 P.M.

Nearest Campground: Bodega Dunes Campground (97 sites, $16). The monarch butterflies congregate in the upper loop during December and January.

BAREFOOT IN THE SAND

Hike 31—Jack London

Location	Wolf House
Agency	Jack London State Historic Park
Highlights	Jack London. His life. His place.
Distance	1.0 mile round trip
Total Elevation Gain/Loss	200´/200´
Hiking Time	1–2 hours
Difficulty	★
Best Times	Year-round
Optional Map	USGS 7.5-min *Glen Ellen*

A native son of California, Jack London was a man of great adventure, whose epic tales still inspire us today.

The Hike is a short stroll to Wolf House, Jack London's dream home that burned to its foundation shortly before completion in 1913. Along the way are his grave site and a museum chronicling the remarkable story of the famous author's life. The day-use-only park is open in summer 9:30 A.M.–7 P.M., but closes in winter at 5 P.M. Crowds are minimal on weekdays. Water is available at the trailhead.

To Reach the Trailhead, drive 6 miles north of Sonoma on Hwy. 12, turn left (west) on Arnold Dr., and proceed 0.9 mile to London Ranch Rd. Turn right and go 1.3 miles to the park entrance. Park in the main paved lot on the left. There is a $6 entrance fee.

Description: The paved path begins at the east end of the main parking lot, quickly reaching the House of Happy Walls in about 100 yards. Built by Jack London's widow Charmian between 1919 and 1926, the building is a striking assemblage utilizing stone walls and Spanish tiles; it now houses an impressive collection of Jack London's books and possessions. Donated to the state in 1959, the building and surrounding 40 acres compose the core of today's state

park, which now includes more than 800 acres of memory-laden trails.

From here the path briefly descends through a forest of young Douglas-fir, madrone, and California buckeye. Warning signs indicate the threat of poison oak and rattlesnakes along the trail— also check for ticks if you go tromping through the brush. At the paved service road, go left, soon reaching the junction for Jack London's grave site. A short side trip leads you to a large rock beneath which his ashes lie. A habitual drinker, London died in 1916 at age 40 of gastrointestinal uremic poisoning. Many believe it was suicide.

Back on the main trail, you soon reach Wolf House. While large structural remains of the building are all that is left, the architect's drawings are strategically placed to help you visualize the home that almost became reality. Nearly complete, it burned on the night of August 22, 1913 and crushed London's long-cherished dream. The source of the fire remains unknown. Wolf House was never rebuilt. Enjoy a reflective stroll of life, ambition, and meaning among the ruins and young redwoods before returning.

Nearest Visitor Center: House of Happy Walls, (707) 938-5216. Open daily 10 A.M.–5 P.M.

Nearest Campground: Sugarloaf Ridge State Park Campground, located at the end of Adobe Canyon Rd.—the turnoff is on Hwy. 12 four miles north of Arnold Rd. (49 sites, $15–16). Reservations are recommended in the summer.
Additional Information:
www.parks.sonoma.net/jlpark.html

JACK LONDON

Hike 32—Robert Louis Stevenson

Location	Table Rock
Agency	Robert Louis Stevenson State Park
Highlights	Distant views. Dead-drop cliffs. Riding The Rhino.
Distance	4.4 miles round trip
Total Elevation Gain/Loss	1400´/1400´
Hiking Time	3 hours
Difficulty	★★★
Best Times	Year-round
Optional Map	USGS 7.5-min *Detert Reservoir*

Overlooking Calistoga Valley, beneath dominant Mt. St. Helena, on the lip of sheer volcanic cliffs, the view from Table Rock is something to remember.

The Hike travels to Table Rock, an unusual volcanic formation within a delightful pocket of hidden wilderness. Much of the hike is exposed, making sun protection imperative most of the year. Because the cliff edge is unprotected and a fall would be fatal, this is not a good location for children. Robert Louis Stevenson State Park is little known and has few amenities. No water is available at the trailhead.

To Reach the Trailhead, take sinuous Hwy. 29 north from Calistoga for 7 miles to the divide below Mt. St. Helena. Park in the lot east of the road exactly at the divide. Approaching from the north, take Hwy. 29 south from the Hwy. 29/53 junction in Lower Lake for 22 miles to the divide.

Description: From the posted trailhead (0.0/2300) the trail gently climbs among Douglas-fir, tan oak, madrone, ponderosa pine, California bay, and black oak, while you get increasingly better views of Mt. St. Helena (4343). In the summer of 1880, author Robert Louis Stevenson spent a month-long, cash-strapped honeymoon squatting in an old cabin on the slopes of Mt. St. Helena,

penciling notes later incorporated into his novels. *The Silverado Squatters* and *Treasure Island* both include descriptions of the surrounding landscape.

As the trail winds briefly along northern slopes, views north down Collayomi Valley appear and Snow Mountain (Hike 34) can be seen capping the skyline beyond the valley's end. You'll see wispy gray pines and get ever more distant views beyond Mt. St. Helena as the trail traverses back around to the southern exposure.

After a very brief climb, the trail reaches a junction (0.7/2550)—go right toward Table Rock. As the trail begins to descend, tantalizing views south transform into sweeping panoramas at "Devils Sofa," an exposure of large, rounded, volcanic boulders. Napa Valley's rich tapestry trends southeast toward the distant massif of Mt. Diablo (Hike 10). Looking east on a clear day, the Sierra Nevada can be seen beyond linear Blue Ridge. West, the sea is just beyond the farthest visible hills.

From here, the trail descends among thick chaparral before climbing to regain the open slopes and reach the posted junction (2.0/2350) for nearby Table Rock, a short 0.2 mile away. Fantastical formations will delight as you walk toward the cliff edge. Look for The

Rhino (*see* Frontispiece). Thrill to a hair-raising view down a vertical cliff face. Contemplate the geology as you savor the view.

Over the past 28 million years, the ever-shifting geometry between the Pacific and North American tectonic plates has created a vast system of faults, associated with the greater San Andreas Fault system. These faults have ripped apart this region and formed the distinctive linear valleys and ridges visible here. Between 13 and 2.7 million years ago, some large fissures created by this activity allowed liquid magma to rise to the surface and spill across the landscape, covering it with thick layers of volcanic rock. Over time, erosion weathered the hardened basalt to form the sheer cliffs below you. Return the way you came.

Nearest Visitor Center: No park visitor center. For general information, call (707) 942-4575.

Nearest Campground: Bothe-Napa Valley State Park Campground, located 5 miles north of St. Helena on Hwy. 29 ($15–20).

Robert Louis Stevenson

Hike 33—Cached

Location	Cache Creek
Agency	BLM Clear Lake Resource Area
Highlights	Oak woodland. Bald eagles. Tule elk.
Distance	3.5 miles round trip
Total Elevation Gain/Loss	1000´/1000´
Hiking Time	3 hours
Difficulty	★★
Best Times	December through April
Optional Map	USGS 7.5-min *Lower Lake*

Gnarled oaks twist skyward in a rolling landscape flushed green by winter rains. Cache Creek ripples through placid pools, a herd of tule elk wanders the area, and a population of bald eagles winters here. Come for a taste of the low-lying foothills ringing the Great Central Valley.

The Hike follows Redbud Trail over a low divide to Baton Flat on Cache Creek, sampling what the area has to offer. While the hike is open year-round, summer months are scorching and fall is extremely dry with brown vegetation. Winter rains usually begin in December, coinciding with the arrival of the first bald eagles. Because the protected area along the Cache Creek corridor—55,000 acres—is substantial, most wildlife may be in deeper than this hike goes. To maximize your chances for sightings, consider an overnight trip farther along Redbud Trail; keep in mind the trail is closed beyond this hike April through June and Cache Creek can be difficult to ford after heavy storms (no bridge is provided). Crowds are minimal, especially on weekdays. Be aware that hunting is allowed in the area—both deer and elk are hunted from mid-September through October. Fishing is allowed in Cache Creek. No water is available at the trailhead.

To Reach the Trailhead, take Hwy. 20 east from the Hwy. 53/20 intersection near Clear Lake for 6 miles. The turnoff is just west of the Cache Creek highway crossing. Approaching from the east on Hwy. 20, the turnoff is 6.4 miles past the junction with Walker Ridge Rd.

Description: From the lot (0.0/980), the hike begins along a gravel road, which crosses a meadow to reach a wash gully. Veer right where the trail enters the trees and begin looking for the two types of oak that exist here: valley oak and blue oak. Blue oak is the most drought-resistant oak and can be identified by its smaller (1–3″) leaves that have wavy margins and shallow lobes. Adapting to the intense heat and dry conditions found in California at low elevations, the blue oak reinforces its leaves with cellulose, and drops them entirely in times of severe drought. Found on drier hillsides, they develop a bluish cast in the late summer and fall. Valley oak is deciduous and can be identified by its larger leaves (2–4″) that are deeply lobed. Requiring more water than blue oak, it is found along valley bottoms. Among the oak are gray pines, wispy trees that generate substantial cones.

As you slowly climb above North Fork Cache Creek, keep an eye out for elk tracks and the animals that made them. The sandstone badlands across the river contain sediments deposited over the past 5 million years, when sea-level fluctuations submerged this low-lying region for long periods and coated it with thick layers of sand and mud. More recent tectonic compression has molded it into these rolling foothills. As you crest the ridge (1.0/1450), the drainage of Cache Creek opens up.

Cache Creek drains Clear Lake, a large body of water formed within the past few thousand years when a large landslide dammed the headwaters of Cold Creek and blocked the westward flow of water into the Russian River drainage. Water impounding behind the new barrier filled the level valleys, creating an enormous lake. It found an outlet east in Cache Creek, draining into the Sacramento River.

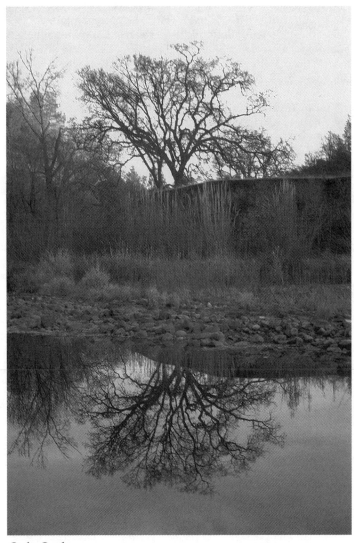

Cache Creek

As you descend toward Cache Creek, note on the opposite south slope the continued presence of gray pine but the total absence of oak. This is due to the nutrient-poor serpentine soil found there. Oaks are unable to survive in such deficient soils but gray pines continue to thrive.

A gradual, occasionally switchbacking descent brings you to the banks of Cache Creek near a delightful swimming hole at Baton Flat. A few campsites are located on both banks and the creek is fun to explore in both directions. Although this hike ends here, Redbud Trail continues for many miles, reaching more-isolated Wilson Valley approximately 3 miles farther. Return the way you came.

Nearest Visitor Center: No visitor center nearby. The area is managed joint-ly by the BLM in Ukiah, (707) 468-4000; and the California Department of Fish and Game in Yountville, (707) 944-5500.

Backpacking Information: Back-country camping is only allowed beyond Baton Flat (at the end of the described hike) and a campfire permit is required. Cache Creek can be impassable after heavy winter storms since no bridge is provided. Campfires are allowed only in designated sites during certain times of the year, and are prohibited when fire danger becomes extreme. Call the BLM office for current information.

Nearest Campground: Nothing close. Try Clear Lake State Park on its south shore near Kelseyville or Snow Mountain Wilderness (see Hike 34).

Additional Information:
www.ca.blm.gov/ukiah/index.html

CACHED

Hike 34—Wallow in It

Location	Snow Mountain Wilderness
Agency	Mendocino National Forest
Highlights	Stony Creek gorge. Coast Range excitement.
Distance	0.5 mile round trip
Total Elevation Gain/Loss	100´/100´
Hiking Time	1 hour (or less)
Difficulty	★★
Best Times	Spring and Fall
Optional Map	USGS 7.5-min *Saint John Mountain; Foot and Horse Trails of Mendocino National Forest,* Forest Service Map available free at Stonyford Ranger Station

A land of surprising topography deeply incised by Stony Creek Gorge, Snow Mountain Wilderness admits you to a secret wonder of the Coast Ranges.

The Hike is a short bushwhack uphill to a spectacular overlook and provides a quick introduction to the possibilities of the area. There is no trail to the overlook and the brush is thick in spots—long pants and a long-sleeve shirt are advisable for protection against scratches and ticks. Those interested in a longer hike can follow Bear Wallow Trail for up to 6 miles from the parking area. The trail includes good views of the gorge and access to fishable Bear Wallow Creek but you must return along the same path, making this up to a 12-mile round trip. While winters are cold and snow is possible, warm sunny days do occur. Summer temperatures are sweltering and not recommended. Crowds will be very sparse. No water is available at the trailhead.

To Reach the Trailhead, take I-5 to the Maxwell off-ramp, located 8 miles north of the Hwy. 20/I-5 intersection. Follow Maxwell-Sites Rd. 5 miles east to Sites and turn right onto Lodega-Sites Rd. Follow it for 7.6 miles as it turns into Lodega-Stonyford Rd. and reaches the turnoff for Fouts Spring Rd. by Stonyford Ranger Station, located 0.3 mile north of Stonyford General Store. Follow Fouts Springs Rd. (Hwy. 43A) east for 7.8 miles to Forest Service Road 18N03 and go right, quickly passing Fouts Springs and South Fork Campgrounds. Follow FS Rd. 18N03 for 2.3 miles, as it turns to dirt and reaches the junction with FS Rd. 18N06 (posted as FS Rd. 8W19), 0.2 mile past North Fork Campground. Go left toward St. John Mountain—the trailhead is located 4.1 miles up the road on the left side.

Description: From the trailhead (0.0/3750) look west down the road. The highest point on the ridge above the curve is your destination. Leaving the road at a convenient spot, climb upward through canyon live oak, California bay, and gray pine toward the promontory, scrambling through thicker brush near the top. Having achieved the viewpoint, Stony Creek Gorge (carved by Middle Fork Stony Creek) can be observed in all its rocky depth; in contrast, the significant rise of East Snow Mountain (7056) looms across the canyon.

The geology of the region is complicated—a confused assemblage of metavolcanic rocks beside the Coast

Range Ophiolite. Approximately 140 million years ago, a major subduction trench formed along the edge of prehistoric California. Current geologic theory holds that east of this trench a large piece of the sea floor was broken off and attached to California, forming the bottommost layer of a basin that was subsequently covered with miles of sediment washed in from nearby mountains. Over the eras, this huge basin filled in to become today's Great Central Valley. Tectonic compression has since exposed the edge of that bottommost layer—the Coast Range Ophiolite—at the surface as a nearly continuous band along the eastern edge of the Coast Ranges, marking the eastern limit of the ancient subduction zone. A piece of it forms the northern slopes of upper Stony Creek Gorge and outcrops are common north and south of here. Snow Mountain itself is composed of some of the first rocks stuffed into the developing subduction zone, of volcanic origin but heavily metamorphosed during the subduction process.

Looking east on a clear day, the Sierra Nevada can be spotted beyond the Central Valley's Sutter Buttes. Those up for an exciting adventure can bushwhack through the seemingly impenetrable brush below you to the south, and explore along the ridge above lower Stony Creek Gorge for some distance. Those not up for intense bushwhacking should return the way they came.

Nearest Visitor Center: Stonyford Ranger Station, (530) 963-3128. Open Monday through Saturday 9 A.M. –NOON and 1–4:30 P.M.

Backpacking Information: Backpacking is permitted along Bear Wallow Trail. A valid campfire permit is required.

Nearest Campground: Of the 3 campgrounds passed on the way in, North Fork Campground is closest (free, river water only).

Additional Information:
www.r5.fs.fed.us/mendocino

Wallow in It

Hike 35—Great Central Valley

Location	Gray Lodge Wildlife Area
Agency	U.S. Fish and Wildlife Service
Highlights	Valley wetlands. Wildlife galore. Sutter Buttes.
Distance	1.0 mile
Total Elevation Gain/Loss	20´/20´
Hiking Time	1–2 hours
Difficulty	★
Best Times	Year-round
Optional Map	USGS 7.5-min *Pennington*

California's greatest natural resource, the Great Central Valley produces more than a quarter of the nation's agricultural output. Before settlement, it was a world of extensive wetlands and woodlands that supported grizzly bears, elk herds, and millions upon millions of birds. Today its remaining rich diversity is compressed into small pockets of protected land, which still provide habitat for millions of resident and migrant birds. Gray Lodge Wildlife Area is one of these pockets, a wildlife delight in the shadow of Sutter Buttes.

Birdlife varies by season. The Pacific Flyway, one of North America's principal migratory routes, passes directly over much of California. Approximately 30 percent of the waterfowl population utilizing this route winters in the Central Valley, filling available wetlands with an estimated 3 million ducks and 750,000 geese. These migrants begin to arrive in the fall, peaking in population between December and February. As they depart in the spring, shorebirds move in to feed at the mudflats and year-round residents such as herons and egrets begin their breeding season. During the hot summer months, ducklings are endearing, and many small birds arrive to feast on the plentiful insects. Animal life is also abundant—otters, beavers, coyotes, rab-

bits, deer, turtles, and lizards all live in the preserve. Overhead, raptors—especially northern harriers—are a common year-round sight, and the occasional bald eagle can be spotted during the winter months.

The Hike follows an easy circuit through the refuge and offers good opportunities for viewing wildlife. Binoculars are a must. While the hike can be done year-round, the unpleasantly hot summer months necessitate a visit during the early morning or evening hours. The preserve is a popular destination for birders but receives relatively light use overall, especially on weekdays. No water is available at the trailhead.

To Reach the Trailhead, take Hwy. 99 north for 9 miles from the Hwy. 20/99 junction in Yuba City to Pennington Rd. in the town of Live Oak. Go west on Pennington Rd. for 9 miles, turning north at the junction with North Butte Rd. The posted turnoff for the preserve is on Rutherford Rd., which reaches an outstanding bird display case near the refuge headquarters in 2 miles. The trailhead lot is just past this by the open-air information kiosk. There is a $2.50 day-use fee per person (waived for holders of a current California hunting or fishing license).

Description: While the hike can be completed in either direction, this description begins on the paved trail by the handicapped parking spaces and goes counterclockwise. The trail quickly reaches a short spur trail on the left to the first of two viewing platforms, on a small dirt hill camouflaged with reeds for more discrete viewing. The paved road continues, reaching its terminus at a large wooden platform looking north, which offers a free, high-powered telescope for your viewing pleasure. The sea of wetlands is without visible end, a limitless expanse of brown, gray, and green. Willows are the dominant tree in the area, thriving in places of abundant water supply. Grasses are thick and a wide variety can be found in the preserve, including sprangletop, smartweed, and joint grass.

Continue your loop on the unpaved trail, curving left (west) just before the second platform and offering some of the best views south of nearby Sutter Buttes. Just over 10 miles in diameter with a maximum elevation of 2,117 feet, Sutter Buttes are the remains of an extinct volcano. Active in recent geologic time, their formation began with an intrusion of subsurface magma that lifted the overlying sediments from the valley floor. Between 1.6 and 1.3 million years ago Sutter Buttes underwent a period of greater activity, erupting lava directly onto the surface and forming the craggy domes of the core. Inactive today, Sutter Buttes remain a baffling mystery for geologists: it is unclear why this volcano developed as the single topographic feature of the Central Valley.

Reaching the dirt loop road of the preserve, cross it and continue on the narrow trail, passing a large thicket of bamboo adjacent to the road. Slowly looping south and then east, the trail widens again before rejoining the trailhead lot on its south side.

Nearest Visitor Center: No staffed visitor center. For general information call (530) 846-3315.

Nearest Campground: Colusa Sacramento River State Recreation Area Campground, located just north of Colusa by the Sacramento River (14 sites, $10).

Additional Information:
www.r1.fws.gov/sacnwrc

Hike 36—Coastal Greenbelt

Location	Fern Canyon
Agency	Van Damme State Park
Highlights	The lushness of a small coastal river canyon.
Distance	5.0 miles round trip
Total Elevation Gain/Loss	200´/200´
Hiking Time	2–3 hours
Difficulty	★
Best Times	Year-round
Optional Map	USGS 7.5-min *Mendocino, Mathison Peak*

With its gurgling alley of green in a verdant canyon, Van Damme State Park provides an easy sampling of the lush ecosystem found just inland from the coast. The highlight is Fern Canyon, a small gorge 400´ deep that shelters Little River and a lush, regenerating redwood forest. A diminutive coastal river barely 5 miles long, Little River provides critical habitat for coho salmon, steelhead, and a variety of other wildlife. Logged during the late 19th Century, the forest has since rebounded to impressive dimensions with only gigantic decaying stumps to remind us of the past.

Logging began here on October 15, 1864, in response to the heavy demand for lumber in the burgeoning city of San Francisco. By 1865, more than three dozen schooners were hauling wood from Little River to San Francisco; activity continued unabated for the next 30 years. The redwoods were cut by burly men perched on wide planks known as "springboards," placed approximately 6 feet above the base of a tree. This allowed loggers to fell a tree at a narrower, more easily hewn point. Once cut, logs were floated down-river to be stored and milled near the river mouth. Bull teams, wagons, and a tramway moved trees from the more difficult locations, and skid roads were constructed to

access ever farther up-canyon. By 1893 all profitable timber had been cut and the mills closed for good. The Jackson History Trail explores past milling operations in the park with the help of an excellent interpretive brochure, available at the visitor center or entrance station.

The Hike follows wide and level Fern Canyon Scenic Trail along Little River, an easy hike that can be extended significantly by adding the 3.5-mile Pygmy Forest loop at the hike's up-canyon terminus. The sun seldom shines in narrow Fern Canyon, making it cool and damp year-round with winter months colder and wetter than the rest. Fog does not detract from this hike—if anything, it enhances the experience—making it an excellent option for fogbound summer days. The very popular trail does not offer solitude, particularly during summer months. Water is available at the trailhead.

To Reach the Trailhead, drive 3 miles south of Mendocino on Hwy. 1 to the park entrance. Follow the park road to its end behind the campground. There is a $5 day-use fee.

Description: From the trailhead, go through the gate and get an interpretive brochure. It explains the coho salmon life cycle with the help of metal fish markers spaced periodically along the hike. As you begin down the wide paved path, note the lush growth around you. Moss, fern, horsetail, huckleberry, stinging nettle, poison oak, thimbleberry, and the seasonal displays of tiger lily, columbine, and iris cover the ground and cut banks. Tan oak and Douglas-fir join second-growth redwood to form the dense canopy overhead.

The trail follows a road constructed during the 1880s to provide up-canyon logging access, which was improved by the CCC during the 1930s with the construction of several bridges. As you pass Fish 3, large redwood stumps begin to appear by the trail—look for springboard notches near the tops. Scan the river as you proceed and you may be lucky enough to spot a Pacific giant salamander. Largest of all terrestrial salamanders, they achieve lengths of up to 12" and can be identified by their mottled, purplish-brown backs and pale yellow underbellies. Living in moist places where they can breathe through their skins, they consume everything from insects to fish to frogs to snakes to other salamanders, lunging to grab their prey with sharp, blade-like teeth.

Once cut, a redwood tree immediately sprouts a series of genetically identical saplings from its root system, in time forming a roughly concentric circle of mature trees around the stump known as a "fairy ring." Several good examples of this basal sprouting can be spotted as you continue up-canyon—check around Fish 9. After passing 10 environmental campsites, the trail soon reaches the end of the Fern Canyon Scenic Trail in a large clearing.

Those wishing to continue their hike to the Pygmy Forest can begin the 3.5-mile loop here. Begin the loop on the trail section to the left, a single track that delves deeper into the canyon. The return stretch is along the wide fire road to your right. Unless you are passionate about ecology, the Pygmy Forest is not as exciting as it sounds. If you don't wish to go farther, return the way you came.

Nearest Visitor Center: Van Damme State Park Visitor Center, (707) 937-5804. Open April through October daily 10 A.M.–4 P.M.; November through March weekends only.

Backpacking Information: Backcountry camping is allowed only at the 10 small but pleasant environmental campsites tucked along Little River 1.75 miles from the trailhead ($12 per site).

Nearest Campground: Van Damme State Park Campground (75 sites, $16). Reservations are imperative from April through October, when tourists and abalone divers routinely fill the campground.

COASTAL GREENBELT

Hike 37—Dune World

Location	MacKerricher Beach
Agency	MacKerricher State Park
Highlights	A vast dune field. MacKerricher from the north end.
Distance	1.0 mile round trip
Total Elevation Gain/Loss	50´/50´
Hiking Time	1–2 hours
Difficulty	★
Best Times	September through May
Optional Map	USGS 7.5-min *Inglenook*

Bordered north by the vibrant ecosystem of Ten Mile River, MacKerricher State Park stretches along the coast for over 4 miles. Usually approached from the crowded south entrance, this vast enclosure of shifting sands, endangered species, foaming ocean, and windswept beach is accessed here from the secluded north end.

The Hike is a stroll along Ten Mile Dunes to the ocean via Ten Mile River and can be extended to an up to 9-mile round trip along the beach. In order to protect several threatened species, Ten Mile Dunes themselves are off-limits; yet they can be admired from the trail and the beach. Summer months bring thick fog, obscuring views and chilling the air. A windbreaker and a warm sweater are always advisable. Crowds are refreshingly light from this unposted access point. No water is available at the trailhead.

To Reach the Trailhead, take Hwy. 1 to the Ten Mile River bridge, located 7 miles north of Cleone and 5 miles south of Westport. Park in the small turnout immediately south of the bridge on the west side of the road.

Description: From the trailhead, scramble briefly up the adjacent sandy slope to get a good vantage point of northern Ten Mile Dunes, and of the paved path leading down to the beach from beneath the bridge. The endangered Mendocino coast paintbrush grows in the area—be sensitive to the environment by henceforth following the paved path. Passing a sign reminding you of this, you soon reach the beach near the mouth of Ten Mile Creek.

Named for its distance north of the Noyo River mouth at Ft. Bragg, Ten Mile River protects 75 acres of salt marsh near its mouth, and provides habitat for spawning steelhead, salmon, and Pacific lamprey. In the dunes stretching south, the endangered Menzies wallflower and Thurber's reed grass grow. The threatened western snowy plover—a plump, 6"-tall bird with a white chest and sandy-brown markings on its head and back—nests in the sand. The view north is excellent, unimpaired beyond the Lost Coast to Punta Delgada and the town of Shelter Cove. It is possible to walk the length of Ten Mile Beach to the park's southern entrance—an adventure that can take all day, especially if you have to walk back!

Nearest Visitor Center: No park visitor center. For general information call (707) 964-9112 or 937-5804.

Nearest Campground: MacKerricher State Park Campground, located at the

main, south entrance (143 sites, $16).
Reservations are recommended in summer.

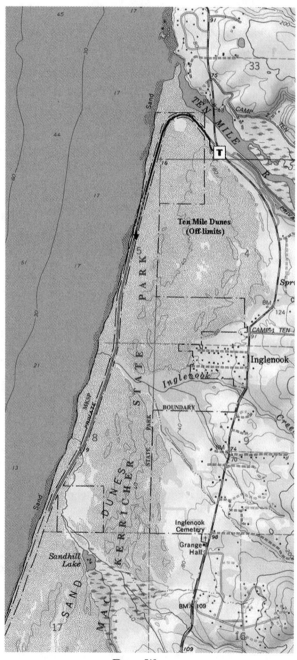

Dune World

Hike 38—Coast Range Delight

Location	Elder Creek
Agency	Northern California Coast Range Preserve
Highlights	Coast Range old-growth, mixed-evergreen forest.
Distance	3.5 miles round trip
Total Elevation Gain/Loss	300´/300´
Hiking Time	1–2 hours
Difficulty	★
Best Times	Year-round
Optional Map	USGS 7.5-min *Lincoln Ridge*

Euphonious streams of shimmering transparent clarity course beneath majestic trees here. In a land almost entirely felled by saw and ax, the little-known Coast Range Preserve protects a rare patch of pristine old-growth forest just inland from the coast.

The 7,500-acre Coast Range Preserve owes its existence to Heath and Marjorie Angelo, who acquired and lived in the heart of this deep wilderness tract during the mid-20th Century. Purchased by the Nature Conservancy in 1959, the preserve operates through a cooperative agreement with the BLM, protecting one of the best, old-growth mixed-evergreen forests left in California. The upper South Fork Eel River flows through the preserve and is joined by Elder Creek, a completely undisturbed drainage whose crystalline waters are used by the U.S. Geologic Survey as a benchmark for evaluating water quality around the state.

The Hike follows the narrow dirt road from the preserve entrance as it winds above the South Fork Eel River to reach the confluence with Elder Creek. The road continues for some distance past this point en route to a lodge at the road's end, but the views and experience do not change much. Ambitious hikers might consider the extra 4-mile round

trip to the summit of forested Black Oak Mountain (3708)—the posted trail junction is along the ridge where the road leaves the Elder Creek drainage. The hike can be done year-round, with cooler temperatures and rain common during the winter and fog always a possibility in the summer. The rivers swell after storms but quickly regain their remarkable clarity. While a University of California research station is located within the preserve and caretakers stay year-round, hikers are few and far between. The preserve is day-use only. No water is available at the trailhead.

To Reach the Trailhead, take Branscomb Rd. 9.2 miles east from Hwy. 1—the turnoff is 1.5 miles north of Westport by lower Westport-Union Beach. The recently paved road twists and turns steeply on its way to the easily missed turnoff for Wilderness Lodge Rd. (on the north side of the road). Approaching from the east, take Hwy. 101 to Laytonville and follow Branscomb Rd. 15 miles west to the turnoff. Follow Wilderness Lodge Rd. 3.3 miles to the small visitor center at the preserve entrance. Sign the register before proceeding another 0.1 mile to park in the posted day-use lot on the right.

Description: From the trailhead (0.0/1460), follow the narrow dirt road downhill a short distance and continue through the gate. The pristine nature of this preserve immediately becomes apparent as majestic redwood and Douglas-fir intermingle in a tall old-growth forest along the Eel River. Tan oak, madrone, big leaf maple, California bay, and canyon live oak fill in the middle story of the forest above an understory of huckleberry, sword fern, and moss. Wildlife here is plentiful, if reclusive. Mountain lion, black bear, river otter, bald eagle, osprey, gray fox, bobcat, mink, ring-tailed cat, Pacific giant salamander, black-tailed deer, and the rare fisher are all known to live within the preserve. Steelhead and silver salmon annually spawn here in the winter after migrating upriver more than a hundred miles from the sea.

Soon the remarkable waters of the South Fork Eel River are flowing below you. Containing 10% of the state's annual runoff, the Eel River is the third largest in California, and supports the second largest run of steelhead and silver salmon. Here in the preserve, less than 15 miles from the headwaters of the South Fork, the river is small and pristine. Unclouded by the muddy runoff associated with logging and agriculture, it flows an indescribable blend of greens and grays—a wonderful piece of an undisturbed California.

The road turns briefly away from the river before dropping to cross gurgling Elder Creek (1.7/1410). A plaque commemorating it as a registered natural-history landmark can be found on the opposite bank. Oregon and black oak grow on the surrounding slopes. Continue as far as you wish along the road before returning the way you came.

Nearest Visitor Center: The rustic visitor center is not staffed. For general information, call (707) 984-6653.

Nearest Campground: Westport-Union State Beach Campground, in several, separate units along the bluffs west of Hwy. 1, just north of Branscomb Rd. (100 sites, $10).

Additional Information:
www.nrs.ucop.edu/reserves/hmacrr.html

Coast Range Delight

Hike 39—Lost and Found

Location	The Lost Coast Trail (North to South)
Agency	Sinkyone Wilderness State Park
Highlights	Daunting coastal cliffs. Remote beaches.
Distance	16.7 miles one way
Total Elevation Gain/Loss	3800´/3800´
Hiking Time	16–24 hours (2–3 days)
Difficulty	★★★★★
Best Times	Spring and Fall
Optional Map	USGS 7.5-min *Hales Grove, Mistake Point, Bear Harbor; Trails of the Lost Coast* map, Wilderness Press, 2000

The Lost Coast can hardly be considered undiscovered. Ranching, logging, railroads, mills, and seaports have all left their mark on the land. But it is remote, too rugged for Highway 1, keeping all but the adventurous away.

The Lost Coast stretches from the Eel River delta near Ferndale south to Highway 1, a distance of more than 70 miles. Offshore is the Mendocino Triple Junction, the point where three tectonic plates meet. North of the junction, the Juan de Fuca Plate dives beneath the Pacific Northwest, triggering the volcanoes of the Cascade Range. South, the San Andreas Fault reaches its offshore terminus, knitting the landscape with a host of faults. All this tectonic mayhem combines to cause dramatic uplift, creating cliffs that tower more than 1,000 feet above the crashing sea. The dark cliffs weather to form unusual black-sand beaches, accessible only where small creeks have carved deep gullies between the bluffs. Sinkyone Wilderness State Park encompasses the southernmost section of the Lost Coast, an area of 7,367 acres that protects more than 22 miles of shoreline.

Wildlife thrives in the park today. A herd of Roosevelt elk, reintroduced from Prairie Creek Redwoods State Park,

wanders the coastal bluffs. Black bears and mountain lions prowl inland. Whales and seals can be spotted offshore. Raptors of all varieties soar above. And a few stands of old-growth redwood still remain.

The Hike follows The Lost Coast Trail between Orchard Camp and Usal Camp, a strenuous trek best done in three days. For being along the coast, there is virtually no level walking on this hike: the trail constantly encounters sheer creek canyons, descending quickly and ascending steeply hundreds of feet at a time. The two ends of The Lost Coast Trail are far apart by road (2–3 hours' driving time) and two vehicles are required for transportation to and from the trailheads. While the hike can be done in either direction, this description runs from north to south. Those wishing to dayhike from the north trailhead should turn around at Wheeler Camp, making a round trip of 9.4 miles with an elevation gain/loss of roughly 1,000 feet. Those interested in dayhiking from the south should see Hike 40.

Timing is key. Fog blankets the region from June through mid-September, obscuring views and chilling the air for days on end. Heavy storms usually strike by late October and can inundate the coast with torrential rainfall well into April. Your opportunity windows open in spring and fall. From late April through May, storms are less frequent, fog is only occasional, and the lush, green terrain explodes with wildflowers. In late September and October, fog tapers off and weather is most ideal. Avoid holidays and weekends and crowds will be light. Those planning a winter visit should call ahead to verify access: flooding and slides can close the roads for weeks at a time. Backcountry camping is allowed only at the three designated trail camps (see below). While no water is available at the trailhead, sources are plentiful along the trail.

To Reach the North Trailhead, take the Hwy. 101 exit for Redway and Shelter Cove. From Redway, take Briceland Thorn Rd. 16.5 miles west toward Shelter Cove to Chemise Mtn. Rd.—turn left (south). The road rapidly turns to dirt, reaching a four-way junction in 6.3 miles—turn right onto the least significant road. The descent from here is steep, narrow, and not passable for trailers or RVs. While 4WD vehicles will have an easier time, low-clearance cars can make a slow descent. The Needle Rock Visitor Center is 3.2 miles from the junction. Here, dayhikers pay a $2/vehicle day-use fee and backpackers pay their trail-camp fees. The trailhead at Orchard Camp is an additional 2.4 miles south at the road's end. After the first big rains of the season, the road is closed beyond the visitor center, making it necessary to walk this final stretch. For directions to the south trailhead, see Hike 40.

Description: Soon after leaving the trailhead at Orchard Camp (0.0/40), the trail is joined by a spur trail from Railroad Camp. Then, it winds down to Bear Harbor (0.4/00), a doghole port in the late 1800s with a spectacular coastal vista. Nothing remains of prior development but pleasant campsites tucked

away from the ocean. Next comes a general introduction to the Lost Coast Trail experience of repeated ascent and descent. Climbing a steep and narrow stream gully, the trail passes through luscious greenery. Large sword ferns splay everywhere, moss covers the thick trunks of alder and California bay, the large leaves of blue elderberry line the stream bank, and every possible nook and cranny bursts with life. You have time to enjoy all this because the trail is remarkably steep. After you attain the ridge, the trail traverses around Duffy's Gulch and through the first grove of old-growth redwoods before gently climbing along the blufftop. Views into the sheer gulch of Jackass Creek open up where the trail makes its steep descent to Wheeler Camp (4.7/10), passing through another old-growth redwood grove just before the first campsites.

Wheeler Camp was the location of a wood-processing facility from 1951 until 1960, run by the Wolf Creek Timber Company. The small company town with store, bunkhouse, and school was deliberately burned for liability reasons in 1969. Remnants of the mill include knee-high periscope-like tubes protruding from the ground, which were used to test the underground flow of toxic diesel fuel that leaked from the facility. While no fuel is known to have reached Jackass Creek, to be safe obtain your water upstream from the site. If it's raining or windy, the campsites nearest the redwood grove are nicest. If it's sunny and clear, continue along the trail to uphill sites south of the beach.

On your way to the beach, a trail diverges left as you enter the more open meadow—continue straight, winding along the edge of the beach before climbing steeply to almost 1,100 feet. Keep an eye out for the small trees lining the top of the cliff. Bonsai'd by exposure to the elements, these trees can be as old as those in the surrounding forest, with remarkably stout trunks hidden beneath their twisted foliage. Shelter Cove can be spotted north from near the cliff top, before the trail plummets down through dense tan oak forest to Little Jackass Creek Camp (9.2/20). Sites are fewer than at Wheeler Camp, and farther from the wonderfully secluded beach.

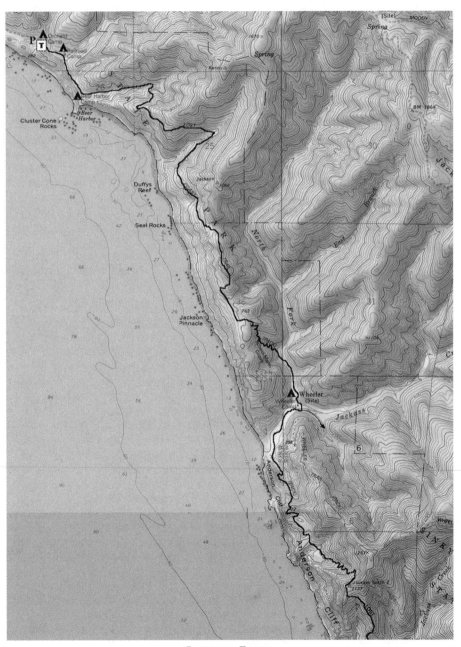

LOST AND FOUND
(end of route is shown on the next map)

The trail continues inland opposite the creek, quickly entering the Sally Bell Grove, an old-growth redwood stand named for a Sinkyone woman who fled here after a brutal attack on her village at Needle Rock (May 1864) by Lieutenant William Frazier and the Battalion of Mountaineers. Passing many substantial redwoods, the trail makes a very steep ascent to 800 feet before immediately dropping to Anderson Gulch Camp (11.7/250). Here, the campsites are small and hidden among the trees. You pass the best sites shortly after crossing the creek.

Another brief up-and-down brings you to Dark Gulch (12.3/350), where the final and most arduous section of the hike begins. A prolonged stretch of climbing brings you to—at over 1,100 feet—the highest point on this hike, almost directly above the ocean. The thick forest of tan oak, big leaf maple, and redwood opens into fields of low-lying coyote brush and blackberry tangles. South, the trail can be seen winding along the bare ridgetop. Ocean views are exceptional, Usal Beach is visible, and a keen eye can identify Highway 1, 7 miles south of here, twisting along the coast before turning inland. It's a gradual descent from here to Usal Beach, ending with several steep switchbacks that deposit you near some nice campsites.

Nearest Visitor Center: The Needle Rock Visitor Center is staffed year-round by volunteers and open approximately 20 hours per week. Park headquarters (open intermittently) is located on Briceland Rd. in Whitethorn, (707) 986-7711.

Backpacking Information: Backcountry camping is allowed only at the 3 designated trail camps—Wheeler, Little Jackass, and Anderson Gulch. There is a fee of $3 per person per night for the trail camps, payable outside the Needle Rock Visitor Center or at the Usal Camp fee station. There is no trail quota.

Nearest Campground: 18 walk-in campsites scattered around the Needle Rock area ($7/night October–April, $11/night May–September).

Hike 40—Found and Lost

Location	The Lost Coast Trail (South to North)
Agency	Sinkyone Wilderness State Park
Highlights	Daunting coastal cliffs. Remote beaches.
Distance	16.7 miles one way
Total Elevation Gain/Loss	3800´/3800´
Hiking Time	16–24 hours (2–3 days)
Difficulty	★★★★★
Best Times	Spring and Fall
Optional Map	USGS 7.5-min *Hales Grove, Mistake Point, Bear Harbor; Trails of the Lost Coast* map, Wilderness Press, 1996

This hike is for those opting to backpack The Lost Coast Trail from south to north, or for those wishing to hike an out-and-back section with easier access.

The Hike follows The Lost Coast Trail from Usal Camp to Orchard Camp, a strenuous multi-day trek (logistics are described in Hike 39). Those wishing to

FOUND AND LOST
(beginning of route is shown on the previous map)

dayhike from the south trailhead have a few options. Coastal access north of Usal Beach is non-existent until the beach at Little Jackass Creek Camp, 7.5 miles north of the trailhead. Motivated and fit hikers can complete this very strenuous 15-mile round trip in 10–14 hours. Those looking for a less-exhausting hike should climb to the top of the first bluff beyond Usal Beach, a steady ascent of over 1,000 feet, which offers superlative views of the ocean and coast. It is a 6-mile round trip that can be completed in 3–5 hours. While no water is available at the trailhead, sources are plentiful throughout the hike.

To Reach the South Trailhead, take Mendocino County (Usal) Rd. 431 north from Hwy. 1. Along Hwy. 1 the unmarked and easily missed turnoff is 13.9 miles west of its junc-

Roosevelt elk, The Lost Coast

tion with Hwy. 101, and approximately 3 miles north of Rockport at milepost 90.88. The one-lane dirt road is impassable for trailers and RVs but easily handled by all other vehicles. In 5.4 miles you reach the area's first campsites, located in a large grassy field. Trailhead parking is 0.3 mile farther on the left, immediately before a small bridge. From here, it's a short walk to the posted trailhead at the road's end. For directions to the north trailhead at Orchard Camp, see Hike 39.

Description: Read the Description for this route given in Hike 39, and follow it in reverse order.

Nearest Visitor Center: There is no visitor center at the southern end of the park. For information on the visitor centers at the northern end, see Hike 39.

Backpacking Information: Please see Hike 39.

Nearest Campground: 15 campsites are scattered around the Usal Beach area, and all are accessible by vehicle.

Hike 41—Humbling Humboldt

Location	Rockefeller Forest
Agency	Humboldt Redwoods State Park
Highlights	A vast forest of enormous redwoods.
Distance	11.0 miles
Total Elevation Gain/Loss	2800´/2800´
Hiking Time	5–7 hours
Difficulty	★★★★
Best Times	Year-round
Optional Map	USGS 7.5-min *Bull Creek, Weott*

The largest contiguous old-growth redwood forest on Earth is protected within Humboldt Redwoods State Park. Beyond amazement at individual trees, you experience an entire ecosystem that humbles all other redwood adventures in this book.

Named after the Prussian scientific explorer Alexander von Humboldt, the park began in 1921 with the purchase of 2,000 acres by the Save-the-Redwoods League on the South Fork Eel River. With completion of a railroad linking Humboldt County to the Bay Area in 1914 and construction of the Redwood Highway in 1922, increasing tourism and logging activity magnified pressures on the diminishing old-growth redwood forests. In 1927, California created a statewide system of parks, and passed a bond measure to provide matching funds for the acquisition of state park lands. The Save-the-Redwoods League immediately began soliciting private donations and, in 1930, J. D. Rockefeller contributed a remarkable gift of $2 million to purchase 10,000 acres along Bull Creek owned by the Pacific Lumber Company. His generosity and farsightedness now protects this unrivaled redwood forest.

Humboldt Redwoods State Park today is comprised of 51,000 acres, of which 17,000 nurture old-growth redwood forest. Most of The Avenue of the Giants winds through the eastern section of the park and the entire Bull Creek watershed is now protected in its western portion. Efforts to restore park watersheds damaged by past logging are ongoing.

The Hike follows a less-traveled route through a remote corner of Rockefeller Forest on Look Prairie, Peavine, and Thornton roads, before returning along the Bull Creek valley bottom. Because it climbs nearly 2,000 feet from Bull Creek to traverse along a ridgetop, this is not an easy hike. That old-growth forest does not occur during the first 1,000 feet of climbing also tends to limit traffic. The process of converting Thornton Rd. into a single-track trail will likely close this section through April '01, making the loop impossible until May. Construction may continue in following years—contact the state park ranger station at (707) 946-2409 for a current update. Otherwise, the hike can be done year-round: winters bring rain and guaranteed isolation; summers tourist crowds and fog; and spring and fall the best combination of crowds and weather. No water is available at the trailhead, and there are no reliable sources anywhere along the hike.

To Reach the Trailhead, take Hwy. 101 to the South Fork/Honeydew exit in northern Humboldt Redwoods State Park. Head 3.5 miles west on Mattole Rd. to a small dirt lot on the right marked with a gate and sign for Look Prairie Rd.

Description From the trailhead (0.0/220), go through the gate and begin climbing. The old-growth redwoods quickly disappear as the wide service road gradually ascends through open slopes of California bay, tan oak, and second-growth Douglas-fir. Obvious slumping and slides are indicative of the erosive effects that logging has had on slopes that would otherwise be held in place by redwood forest. Good views of the Bull Creek drainage open up as the trail relentlessly climbs.

Suddenly, old-growth redwood forest reappears (1.9/1400) and stays with you for almost the entire remainder of the hike. The redwoods are huge—up to 12 feet in diameter—and many of the more massive specimens exhibit a striking resemblance to their giant sequoia cousins. Some of the largest Douglas-firs you will ever see mingle with the redwoods, and gigantic madrones twist high through the understory. The Rockefeller Forest is thick, containing the greatest density of biomass (amount of total organic material) ever measured. Estimates made at other locations in the park place the total biomass per acre at approximately 1,800 tons, seven times the density of an acre of the Amazon rainforest! Near the ridgetop, you encounter the junction with Peavine Rd. (3.5/2230)—go left.

After a brief, continued climb to the hike's greatest elevation (2500), Peavine Rd. traverses west along the park's northern boundary. Lands north have been completely logged, harvested to the exact limit of the park's protected lands. Thankfully, these discouraging views are few and the road generally remains in

Humbling Humboldt

undisturbed forest. After a long, gentle ramble along Peavine Rd., you reach the posted junction with Thornton Rd. (7.0/2300)—turn left. Steadily descending the ridge that divides Mill and Albee creeks, you soon pass a patch of incredibly thick madrones before continuing on the long descent to Albee Creek Campground (9.6/400). From the campground, two trail options will return you to the trailhead about a mile east. The first passes through redwoods immediately north of Mattole Rd.; it begins from the campground access road. The second closely parallels Mattole Rd. on its south side; it begins opposite the campground turnoff. Growing in near-optimal conditions by a perennial water source, the redwoods along Bull Creek Flats are the most massive specimens of the entire hike.

Nearest Visitor Center: Humboldt Redwoods Visitor Center, (707) 946-2263, located 1 mile south of Weott on The Avenue of the Giants. Open in summer daily 9 A.M.–5 P.M.; in winter daily 10 A.M.–4 P.M.

Nearest Campground: Albee Creek Campground is only open from mid-May through September (40 sites, $12–16). Burlington Campground, located near the visitor center on The Avenue of the Giants, is open year-round (57 sites). Reservations are recommended during the summer.

Additional Information: *www.humboldtredwoods.org*

Hike 42—Get Lost

Location	Punta Gorda Lighthouse
Agency	King Range Conservation Area
Highlights	A remote abandoned lighthouse. A remote abandoned coastline.
Distance	6.4 miles round trip
Total Elevation Gain/Loss	100´ / 100´
Hiking Time	3–4 hours
Difficulty	★★
Best Times	Spring and Fall
Optional Map	USGS 7.5-min *Petrolia; Trails of the Lost Coast* map, Wilderness Press, 2000

Where California bulges farthest west at Cape Mendocino, powerful tectonic forces have crushed the coastal King Range skyward. Touched by man and then forgotten, the mountains compose a remote topography jammed against the Pacific edge.

Eleven miles north of the Mattole River mouth, Cape Mendocino marks the westernmost point in the lower 48 states. Due west from the cape, less than 10 miles from shore, three tectonic plates meet at the Mendocino Triple Junction. Land north lies along an active subduction zone where the tiny Juan de Fuca Plate dives beneath the North American continent in an underwater trench almost 2 miles deep. South, the San Andreas Fault careens offshore, slicing the land in a myriad of related faults. As the triple junction slowly migrates north, combined tectonic forces produce the most seismically active spot in the entire earthquake-prone state. The mountains are pushed upward at an astounding rate and major earthquakes are a frequent occurrence—a 1992 earthquake lifted the entire King Range up 3–5 feet! Kings Peak (4087), the highest summit in the range, is barely 3 miles from the sea.

Twenty-one miles south of Cape Mendocino is Punta Gorda, another bulge in the coastline sheltering remote Punta Gorda Lighthouse. Staffed for only 40 years, the lighthouse was shut down in 1951. The whole region bears traces of a 19th Century boom that busted, leaving the landscape empty and forgotten by today's world. The first oil well in California was drilled near Petrolia in 1865, and ranching and logging quickly pruned the sweeping hills and ridges. Today, the mouth of the Mattole River marks the northern limit of the King Range National Conservation Area, 60,000 acres of land protected south along the coast and inland through the heart of the King Range. Its seaside mountain topography catches a lot of rain, making this area the wettest in the entire state. While the mouth of the Mattole River receives an average of 50 inches per year, the surrounding ridges have recorded in excess of 200 inches—nearly 17 feet—during wet years.

The Hike follows the coastline south from Mattole River to Punta Gorda, a sandy walk that ends at the lighthouse turret. Just south of sheltering Cape Mendocino, the coastline here is reputed to have regular fog-free days during the summer months, a rarity on the North Coast. Spring and fall are the best times to come; avoid winter when storms swelling Fourmile Creek are likely to obstruct the hike. The region around Punta Gorda can be treacherous at high tides—tide tables are usually posted at the trailhead and your hike should coincide with low tide. People are few out here, and supplies are limited and very expensive. Water is available at the trailhead.

To Reach the Trailhead, you have to drive a lot of twisting roads. The easiest approach is via Ferndale, located 5 miles west of Hwy. 101 on Hwy. 211—the turnoff from 101 is at Fernbridge. In Ferndale, turn right off Main St. onto Ocean Rd., and then turn immediately left at Fifth St. to head south toward Petrolia, 27 miles away. One mile south of Petrolia, turn right on Lighthouse Rd. and follow it 4.6 miles to the campground and day-use parking lot at the road's end. It is also possible to get here by taking sinuous Mattole Rd. west from Humboldt Redwoods State Park to the town of Honeydew, located 23 miles (60–90 minutes) from Hwy. 101. Cross the Mattole River and continue west (downstream) on Mattole Rd. for 13.4 miles to reach Lighthouse Rd. There is a $2 day-use fee for those not staying overnight at the campground.

Description: From the trailhead, go through the gate by the information sign and head south through the dunes to quickly reach a fenced-off shell midden used by the Mattole Indians. Interpretive signs explain its potential archaeological significance and provide an excellent diagram of the tectonic forces at work in the region. Looking north, the striking point of Cape Mendocino can be seen jutting into the ocean beyond the nearby Mattole River drainage.

As you head south, follow either a trail often found running below the base of the steep bluffs or the sandy beach.

Note the slopes covered with coyote brush, cow parsnip, lupine, yarrow, and mint, but beware the extensive poison oak. Wildlife is rich in the offshore waters and you may see harbor seals eyeing you from inside the breakers. As you slowly round Punta Gorda to reach Fourmile Creek, the lighthouse appears

Get Lost

down the coast, dwarfed in scale by the landscape.

A private dwelling is located near the mouth of Fourmile Creek (2.5/00)—please respect the property rights and the privacy of the owners here. Crossing the creek and continuing south, you soon reach the lighthouse, where informative placards detail the site's history. The tower itself is open and accessible from the inside via a very tight stairway ladder; it makes a great spot for lunching and relaxing. While the Lost Coast Trail continues 21 miles south along the beaches to Shelter Cove, you avoid that long sandy walk by returning the way you came.

Nearest Visitor Center: Nothing remotely close. The BLM has an office in Arcata, (707) 825-2300, located at the north end of town. Open Monday through Friday 7:45 A.M.–4:30 P.M. There

is also a visitor center at Thorn Junction, (707) 986-5400, located 14 miles (30–45 minutes) west of Hwy. 101 on Briceland Rd., going toward Shelter Cove. Office hours vary but they're generally open in summer Tuesday through Saturday 10 A.M.–5 P.M.; in winter they're open Monday through Friday roughly 8 A.M.–5 P.M.

Backpacking Information: Beach camping is permitted along this hike and at points farther south along the coast. Proper human waste disposal is critical along the beaches—bury it at least 6 inches deep in the sand of the intertidal zone. Campfires are allowed on the beach but a valid campfire permit is required (a CDF permit is valid).

Nearest Campground: Mattole Campground, located at the trailhead (9 sites, $5).

Punta Gorda Lighthouse

Hike 43—Hike a Head

Location	Trinidad Head
Agency	City of Trinidad
Highlights	The North Coast. Ocean views.
Distance	2.0 miles
Total Elevation Gain/Loss	400´/400´
Hiking Time	1–2 hours
Difficulty	★
Best Times	Spring and Fall
Optional Map	USGS 7.5-min *Trinidad*

Beaches are few on the North Coast and the ocean cannot be seen for long stretches along Hwy. 101. Trinidad Head shelters a sandy stretch of protected coastline and offers sweeping coastal vistas from its slopes. Perfect.

The Hike follows Trinidad State Beach south the short distance to Trinidad Head (362) and makes a circuit below the summit before returning back along the beach. This is not a hike offering an isolated, wilderness experience—the small town and harbor of Trinidad are nearby—but it is an easy taste of the North Coast. Fog can be thick during the summer months, chilling the air, obscuring views, and making this a much less enjoyable hike. Be prepared for wind on Trinidad Head, and watch out for the poison oak that thrives in brush along this hike. Water is available at the trailhead.

To Reach the Trailhead, take Hwy. 101 to the Trinidad exit and go west toward town. After crossing Patricks Point Drive, make a right at the T-junction to reach the Trinidad State Beach entrance. Park by the picnic area.

Description: From the west end of the parking lot, the trail briefly passes through Sitka spruce and shore pine before descending via several switchbacks to the beach. A short spur trail near the bottom accesses the lush gully of Mill Creek. Around the immediate point north is College Cove, another sandy beach always accessible from the parking lot, and from the main beach at low tide.

Turning south, you walk along the beach toward Trinidad Head. Keep an eye out offshore for sea lions and harbor seals. Approaching the base of Trinidad Head, you can find the start of the trail in the large parking lot surrounded by mountains of old tires. After you quickly climb 60 feet up some sandy stairs, the trail follows a paved road—bear right and walk up the road for a short distance. By several benches with good views north, the narrower, unpaved trail soon splits right from the road and begins winding through a dense corridor of coastal shrubbery. Thimbleberry, fern, sticky monkey flower, poison oak, and impenetrable brush obscure the view but provide a good windbreak; the trail slowly traverses west around the head. Making a few switchbacks, you soon arrive at the first unobstructed views north of the jagged coastline.

The bulk of the coastline here is easily eroded sandstone and mudstone with large chunks of more resistant rocks randomly interspersed. The waves' erosive power readily strips away most material, leaving the more resistant blocks as jagged offshore rocks. The area around Trinidad is a prime example of what is known as an *emergent coastline*.

The trail continues its circuit, passing below a rocky rise easily accessible by an obvious spur trail. The view from on top of this small ridgelet is the best of the hike; the coastline can now be seen stretching south into the distance. Large Pilot Rock sits more than a half mile offshore south of Trinidad Head, and the city of Eureka is visible far beyond it on the distant coastline.

Resuming the circuit, you soon reach a large granite cross commemorating June 9, 1775, when the Spanish explorers Heceta and Bodega raised a cross here

on Trinity Sunday, giving the location its name. From here, a complex of small buildings and access roads somewhat spoil the natural feel. Follow the gravel road down the east side of the head to rejoin the paved road and return to the beach.

Nearest Visitor Center: No visitor center. Contact the North Coast Redwoods District of the California Department of Parks and Recreation at (707) 445-6547 for general information.

Nearest Campground: Patricks Point State Park Campground, located 5 miles north of Trinidad just west of Hwy. 101. Arrive early or reserve in advance if you plan on staying at this popular state park (124 sites, $14–16).

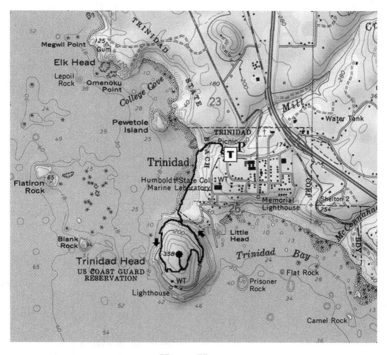

HIKE A HEAD

Hike 44—The Spit

Location	Klamath River Mouth
Agency	Redwood National Park
Highlights	Gigantic driftwood in a dangerous place.
Distance	1–2 miles round trip
Total Elevation Gain/Loss	150′/150′
Hiking Time	1–2 hours
Difficulty	★
Best Times	April through October
Optional Map	USGS 7.5-min *Requa*

It is a world like no other, an enormous sandy spit regularly swept clean by the fury of the ocean. Driftwood litters it, enormous stumps are buried within it, a mighty river flows behind it, and the Pacific breaks upon it.

The Hike explores the length of the broad sandbar formed at the Klamath River mouth, an easy hike that places you deep within Nature's domain. **WARNING:** This can be a very dangerous place—especially near the mouth

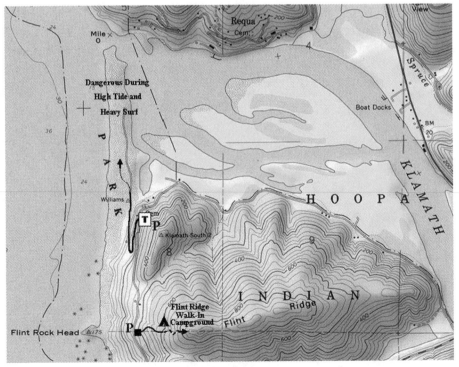

THE SPIT

itself—where strong surf and high tides can completely wash across the spit and sweep the unsuspecting into the Klamath River and out to sea. **Do not venture onto the sandbar if you see water washing across it.** While the hike can be done year-round, torrential winter rains are worth avoiding. The mouth of the Klamath is included within Redwood National Park but this is not an official or posted trail. Crowds will be minimal. No water is available at the trailhead.

To Reach the Trailhead, take Hwy. 101 a half mile south of its Klamath River crossing, turn west onto Hwy. D8, and proceed 3.3 miles to a Y-junction near the river level. Bear left and go 0.2 mile to the end of the pavement. Park in the small dirt lot across from the gated paved road.

Description: Be respectful of the adjacent private residence as you go through the gate and begin descending toward the beach. A few salt-pruned Sitka spruce line the upper sections but the vegetation rapidly turns to thick brambles. Once you step onto the sandbar the world of plants has been left behind. The spit is roughly a half mile long and the washed up remains of many a gigantic redwood tree can be found along its length. Flint Rock Head (175) can be seen protruding from the jagged coast a mile south.

Surpassed in size only by the Sacramento, the Klamath River is the second largest river in California, draining 15,500 square miles as it winds 263 miles from its headwaters in the Cascades of southern Oregon. Supporting the state's largest run of salmon and steelhead, it also provides habitat for a great diversity of life in the estuary tucked behind its mouth. Starry flounder, Pacific lamprey, American shad, and striped bass are but a few of the species that swim in the nearby waters. The wetlands just inland also attract numerous shorebirds, including godwits, willets, pintails, buffleheads, and green-winged teals. Harbor seals and sea lions can often be seen on the offshore rocks north of the river. Osprey and spotted owls nest in the surrounding forest and bald eagles are occasionally sighted here as well.

Nearest Visitor Center: Please see Hike 45.

Nearest Campground: Flint Ridge Walk-in Campground, located a half mile south of the trailhead on unpaved Coastal Drive (10 sites, free, no water).

Hike 45—Damnation

Location	Damnation Creek
Agency	Del Norte Coast Redwoods State Park
Highlights	Extraordinary old-growth forest. Remote coastal access.
Distance	4.2 miles round trip
Total Elevation Gain/Loss	1200´/1200´
Hiking Time	3–4 hours
Difficulty	★★
Best Times	April through October
Optional Map	USGS 7.5-min *Sister Rocks, Childs Hill*

Damnation Creek flows a scant two miles to the sea, yet slices a gorge more than 1,000 feet deep and preserves an isolated, undisturbed old-growth forest within its sheltered walls. Its mouth provides the only coastal access point for three miles in either direction, a remote and rugged slice of the North Coast.

Damnation Creek lies within Del Norte Redwoods State Park, one of three state parks founded during the 1920s and included today within the Redwood National and State Parks system. There are currently 856 known plant species within the parks and 202 native wildlife residents, including the threatened marbled murrelet and northern spotted owl. The parks are collectively designated a World Heritage Site and International Biosphere Preserve, testament to their unique and irreplaceable qualities. Damnation Creek is a choice example.

The Hike is a quick descent into the Damnation Creek drainage on more than 20 gentle switchbacks, passing through an awe-inspiring forest to reach a rocky and isolated beach. While fog can obscure the far-reaching coastal views, it enhances the primeval tranquility of the forest and should not dissuade you from this hike. Fog is heaviest during the summer months, with spring and fall providing the most consistent sunshine. The

trail is open year-round but torrential winter rains are best not trifled with. Expect cool conditions at all times and bring a warm sweater. Crowds are relatively light but you are seldom entirely alone. No water is available at the trailhead.

To Reach the Trailhead, take Hwy. 101 north of the Klamath River bridge for 11 miles to milepost 16.0, and park in the dirt lot on the west side of the highway. The turnout is easily missed so keep your eyes open. Approaching from the north, the trailhead is 3 miles south of the Mill Creek Campground turnoff.

Description: From the trailhead, the wide root-studded path rises briefly to its highest point (1100); it passes through a thick ground cover of redwood sorrel and wild ginger while—overhead— enormous redwoods tower above spindly rhododendron trees. After cresting the divide the trail gradually descends, soon reaching the wide dirt road of the Coastal Trail, a former Hwy. 101 roadbed. Cross the road and continue down the posted STEEP, STRENUOUS TRAIL. As you begin the long switchbacking descent, Douglas-fir become increasingly common; they are easily identified by their rough, unfurrowed bark, so distinct from that of redwood. Fire scars are abundant in the trees along the trail, and several exciting caverns can be found within their ponderous trunks.

Sitka spruce are a special highlight of this hike and begin to appear about halfway down the gorge. You can identify them by the flaky scales on their trunks and their small feathery cones. Growing in a narrow 1,800-mile-long coastal belt extending from Northern California to Alaska, these majestic trees can achieve heights in excess of 300 feet, and have long been prized for their golden wood. Pound for pound stronger than steel, this spruce has been utilized to build boats, airplanes, and the soundboards of concert harps, grand pianos, and violins. Victim to heavy logging, few old-growth stands remain—the trees around you are some of the largest left in California.

Thimbleberry and salmonberry twine thickly among the brush as the trail approaches the bottom. The thin trickle of Damnation Creek is heard for the first time where the trees suddenly thin, unable to withstand the salt-laden sea air. You encounter the ocean at a small promontory, and the adventurous can explore along the coast for some distance both north and south. Then, back up you go.

Nearest Visitor Center: Redwood National Park Headquarters and Visitor Center, (707) 464-6101, located in Crescent City at 2nd and K streets. Open daily 9 A.M.–5 P.M. Also try Redwood Information Center, (707) 464-6101 ext. 5265, located to the south in Orick. Open daily 9 A.M.–5 P.M.

Nearest Campground: Mill Creek Campground, located 3 miles north of the trailhead (145 sites, $16). Open summer only. Year-round campgrounds can be found in Prairie Creek and Jedediah Smith Redwoods state parks.

Additional Information: *www.nps.gov/redw*

DAMNATION

Hike 46—Rain Forest

Location	Stout Grove
Agency	Jedediah Smith Redwoods State Park
Highlights	The lush diversity of a unique temperate rain forest.
Distance	1.0 mile round trip
Total Elevation Gain/Loss	50´/50´
Hiking Time	1 hour
Difficulty	★
Best Times	April through October
Optional Map	USGS 7.5-min *Hiouchi*

North America's temperate rain forest extends from northwest California to Alaska in a narrow coastal strip where rainfall is significant year-round and snow is infrequent. The coast redwood forest range extends north from Big Sur to a few miles past the Oregon border and exists in an equally narrow coastal belt. Jedediah Smith Redwoods State Park is one of the few places where you can experience the rare juxtaposition of these two impressive worlds.

Three members of the forest readily seen in the park are western hemlock, western red cedar, and Port Orford cedar. Common throughout the temperate rain forest, western hemlock has needles that closely resemble those of mountain hemlock—very short and continuously wrapping the ends of its drooping branches. Because germinating in the mossy green carpet on the forest floor is difficult, western hemlock utilize fallen trees as nurse logs. Elevated above the understory below, the trees gradually grow roots through the log and into the ground. As the log rots away, the trees are left standing in a line with their roots exposed above the surface.

Western red cedar is readily identified by the flattened sprays of delicate foliage that extend from the length of its thin branches. Cones are less than a half

inch in diameter and have from four to six pairs of opposite scales. The needles are pleasantly fragrant when crushed. Also common throughout the temperate rain-forest belt, it is widely used as lumber for housing construction.

Occurring only in the Klamath Mountain region, Port Orford Cedar is a valuable lumber tree that can fetch up to $50,000 for a mature specimen. A waterborne fungus is currently decimating these trees throughout the Smith River drainage, and many unpaved Forest Service roads are closed during the rainy season to prevent further spread of the disease. They can be identified by the resemblance of their foliage to incense cedar, equally small cones (less than a half inch) with from six to ten shieldlike scales, and the deeply grooved brownish-gray bark on taller specimens. Other large trees that occur in the park are Sitka spruce (better seen on Hike 45), Douglas-fir, and grand fir.

Flowing through the park is the Smith River, the only major undammed river system left in California. Roughly 300 miles of it are designated as part of the National Wild and Scenic River System—more than on any other river in the country—and its mesmerizing waters support healthy runs of salmon and steelhead throughout the winter months.

In 1990 Congress created the Smith River National Recreation Area to preserve a huge portion of land in the Smith River watershed, assuring the long-term health of this remarkably pristine corner of California.

The state park is named for Jedediah Smith, who between 1822 and 1830 became the first Anglo-American to reach California from the east, the first to cross the Sierra Nevada, the first to travel the length of the state and, in 1828 the first to reach the Pacific Ocean overland through northwest California, camping near the future state park. During his travels he was mauled by a grizzly bear and almost lost an ear, nearly died in the Colorado River when 10 of his 19 men perished, and survived an Indian attack farther up the coast in 1828 that killed 16 of his 20-man party.

The Hike is a meandering stroll through the Stout Grove forest and the park campground on an easy, level trail. Stout Grove is across the Smith River from the campground and in summer a temporary bridge links the two. In the off-season it is necessary to drive 4 miles from the campground to the Stout Grove trailhead. Tourist crowds are heavy during summer months, making spring and fall—with regularly occurring warm weather—the best times to visit. Winter rains can be torrential and make tent camping a dubious proposition. Expect cool, damp conditions year-round. Water is available at the trailhead.

To Reach the Trailhead, take Hwy. 199 east from Hwy. 101 (above Crescent City) for 4.5 miles to the park entrance. There is a day-use fee of $5. To reach the Stout Grove trailhead from the north side, continue 2.2 miles west on Hwy. 199 past the park entrance, turn right on South Fork Rd., and then quickly right again on unpaved Howland Hill Rd./ Douglas Park Dr. After crossing the two forks of the Smith, the trailhead is on your right in 2.5 miles. Trailers and RVs are not permitted on Howland Hill Rd.

Description Wander the campground first and look for all the trees mentioned above before heading to the river crossing near campsite 83. Then stroll through the Stout Grove, named not for the gigantic redwoods but for the Stout family who donated the 200-acre grove. An easy loop trail winds through it. As you mosey, look in the understory for salal, oxalis, western azalea, rhododendron, trillium, huckleberry, salmonberry, numerous spring wildflowers, and the nine species of ferns found within the park. Longer hikes are available for those intrigued by this short ramble—try Mill Creek Trail.

Nearest Visitor Center: Hiouchi Information Center, located 0.2 mile west of the park entrance on Hwy. 199. Open May through September daily 9 A.M.– 5 P.M., closed in the off-season. Also Redwood National Park Headquarters and Visitor Center, (707) 464-6101, located in Crescent City at 2nd and K streets. Open daily 9 A.M.–5 P.M.

Nearest Campground: State park campground (106 sites, $12–16 depending on season). Reservations are recommended in summer. Otherwise, try the National Forest campgrounds east of Gasquet on Hwy. 199.

Additional Information:
www.nps.gov/redw

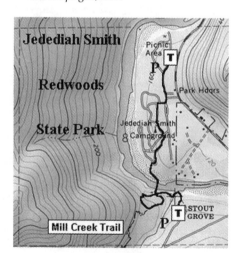

RAIN FOREST

Hike 47—Go Hobo

Location	North Fork Trinity River
Agency	Trinity Alps Wilderness
Highlights	Klamath Mountain wilderness.
Distance	3.0 miles
Total Elevation Gain/Loss	650′/650′
Hiking Time	1–2 hours
Difficulty	★★
Best Times	June through October
Optional Map	USGS 7.5-min *Thurston Peaks*

Deep in the wilderness, a quick jaunt along a pristine river rewards you with a taste of the Klamath Mountains.

The Klamath Mountains are a complex mountain range sliced by deep river canyons that support a rich diversity of life. At relatively lower elevations, the Klamath escaped the thick ice sheets that have intermittently covered the Sierra Nevada over the past few million years. They occupy the geographic crossroads of three other major ranges—the Sierra Nevada, Cascade Range, and Coast Ranges. As a result of all this, the flora and fauna of the region are lush, diverse, and include many rare and unusual species found nowhere else.

The Hike is an easy adventure at the end of a long access road into the central Trinity Alps Wilderness. The Hobo Gulch trailhead is primarily an access point for extended trips into the wilderness, but a short loop around the North Fork Trinity River offers a quick introduction to the Klamath region. Being at a low elevation, any winter snow melts quickly; the trailhead should be open in May. Double-check the access road conditions if you are planning an early visit, and don't expect to be able to cross the swollen Trinity River before July at the very earliest. Fall colors are excellent. Crowds will be light relative to the more popular Trinity Alps trailheads. Fishing is prohibited in the North Fork Trinity River and its tributaries. No water is available at the trailhead but the river is soon accessible.

To Reach the Trailhead, take Hwy. 299 west from Junction City 6.2 miles to East Fork Rd. (posted for nearby Helena) and turn north. Approaching along Hwy. 299 from the west, the turnoff is 0.4 mile past Pigeon Point Campground. The narrow paved road reaches unpaved Forest Service Rd. 34N07Y in 3.6 miles at an easily missed fork. Bear left on FS Rd. 34N07Y and continue 11.4 exciting miles to a final fork in the road. Bear right for the nearby trailhead or left for the adjacent campground.

Description From the trailhead (0.0/3070), your route immediately crosses into the wilderness at a sign surrounded by vine maple. It is soon joined from the left by a short spur trail originating from the campground. Big leaf maple, dogwood, black oak, canyon live oak, and large Douglas-fir up to 5 feet in diameter make up this forest around you. The trail briefly rises before dropping to cross Backbone Creek (0.7/2950), a crystalline stream supporting lush plant life. On the opposite creek bank is a four-way junction—continue straight on the High Water Trail. River-crossing conditions permitting, you'll return on the Low Water Trail (branching left here). The trail to the right follows Backbone Creek more than 3 miles before dead-ending at an old cabin site.

After climbing briefly up the ridge, you begin a level traverse through thick forest on a narrow path cut into the steep slopes. Where the trail slowly descends, views of the sheer Whites Creek drainage open up across the canyon. The creek plummets more than 4,000 feet from bare Limestone Ridge. Once on the bottom of an ancient sea, the limestone has since been exposed on this ridgetop by powerful tectonic forces. When you reach the junction with the Low Water Trail (1.7/3070) near the riverbed, cut back left and descend to the river.

The broad riverbed speaks of the flood potential present here. The exposed channel is very wide, filled with huge rocks, and scattered with enormous logs, testament to the power that can rage through these canyons during times of heavy rain. The river channel provides the only opening through the dense forest and can be a good place to see wildlife, especially in the early morning or evening. Black bears are common, and sightings of rare bald eagles and osprey have been increasing in the region.

Conditions permitting, ford the river near the confluence of Whites Creek and head south along the sometimes faint Low Water Trail. It passes through a long, level section of Douglas-fir, incense cedar, ponderosa pine, and the less-common knobcone pine. Where the trail rejoins the riverbed, your return crossing (2.4/2940) should be clear, just upriver from the confluence with Backbone Creek. Upon reaching the previous four-way junction, return the way you came.

Nearest Visitor Center: Weaverville District Ranger Office, (530) 623-2121, located on Hwy. 299 on the west side of Weaverville. Open Monday through Friday 8 A.M.–4:30 P.M., during summer also Saturday 8 A.M.–5 P.M.

Backpacking Information: A wilderness permit is required, obtainable free either outside the Weaverville District Ranger Office or at the Junction City ranger station (0.1 mile east of Canyon Creek Rd. in Junction City). Campsites are plentiful along the river.

Nearest Campground: Hobo Gulch Campground, located near the trailhead, has several primitive sites that can get overrun during peak periods (free, river water only). Also try the campgrounds along Hwy. 299—Pigeon Point Campground is 0.4 mile west of East Fork Rd.

Additional Information: *www.r5.fs.fed.us/shastatrinity/trinity_al ps.htm*

Go Hobo

Hike 48—The Trinity Alps

Location	Canyon Creek Lakes
Agency	Trinity Alps Wilderness
Highlights	A serrated granite divide above lush wilderness.
Distance	15.0 miles round trip
Total Elevation Gain/Loss	3000´/3000´
Hiking Time	12–14 hours
Difficulty	★★★★
Best Times	Late June through October
Optional Map	USGS 7.5-min *Mount Hilton*

A land of deep canyons and jagged granite ridges, the Trinity Alps are the greatest alpine highlight of the Klamath Mountains. Impossibly alluring, they crown the thick forest of the region, a vibrant playground of lakes, rivers, and wildlife.

The Hike follows Canyon Creek Trail to Lower Canyon Creek Lake in the heart of the Trinity Alps, a very long dayhike that can easily be turned into a two- or three-day adventure. The Klamath Mountains receive heavy precipitation and, despite the relatively low elevation of this hike, snow can linger on the trail into June. Crowds funnel into this small area in unfortunate numbers during July and August, making September and even early October the best times to visit. Fishing is possible in the lakes but Canyon Creek is too small for angling. While no water is available at the trailhead, sources are plentiful along the way.

To Reach the Trailhead, take Hwy. 299 to Junction City, located 7.7 miles west of the Hwy. 3/299 intersection in Weaverville and 6 miles east of East Fork Rd. and the turnoff for Helena. Turn north on Canyon Creek Rd. (Hwy. 401)—the turnoff is directly opposite the Junction City Store—and follow the increasingly narrow paved road 12.4 miles to the large parking lot at the road's end.

Description From the trailhead (0.0/3150), both paths leaving the parking lot quickly join to reach a posted junction for Bear Creek Trail—head left on Canyon Creek Trail. Entering the wilderness, the trail passes beneath ponderosa pine, Douglas-fir, incense cedar, madrone, black oak, big leaf maple, dogwood, and alder. Thimbleberry and vine maple thrive in the lush understory. Initially traversing above rushing Bear Creek, you soon descend to cross the transparent stream. A few canyon live oak can be seen as you climb out of the gully to begin paralleling above Canyon Creek.

While Canyon Creek is often visible below through the trees, access is generally not possible. The pale granite boulders that fill the creekbed are in stark contrast to the dark metamorphic rocks of the opposite peaks, and are representative of the overall regional geology. Occupying all of northwest California, the Klamath Mountains are a complex geologic mosaic formed from a wide variety of metamorphic rocks, which accreted to the continent over the past few hundred million years. Once connected with the northern Sierra Nevada, the mountain range was intruded by magma rising through the crust in enormous subterranean bubbles between 150 and 120 million years ago. Solidifying as granite before reaching the surface, these bubbles became exposed as erosion stripped away the overlying rock. Unlike the heavily intruded central and southern Sierra, the Klamath Mountains contain only isolated pockets of granite—the Trinity Alps is the most spectacular example. The rocks of Canyon Creek have been washed down from the granitic heart of the mountains, but here the trail still winds above a complex metamorphic assemblage. However, you soon cross the geologic divide where soaring peaks of granite become visible up-canyon.

The trail steadily climbs above Canyon Creek, becoming increasingly rocky as it navigates a few intermittent switchbacks before reaching beautiful Canyon Creek Falls (3.8/4450) and the first easy river access. The falls mark the halfway point for the hike, and the end of the deep V-shaped river gorge of lower Canyon Creek. Above the falls, relatively recent glaciation has carved the valley into a broad U, with a delightfully flat canyon bottom. Vegetation is lush and California redbud, huckleberry oak, and seasonal wildflowers line the trail. Leaving the vicinity of the creek, the trail switchbacks 200 feet to reach the junction with Boulder Creek Trail (6.0/5000).

Continuing up-canyon on Canyon Creek Trail, notice the appearance of mountain hemlock and western white pine in the forest mix. As the trail begins to climb again, notice

the glacial polish in evidence on nearby rocks. Red fir and aspens appear next. Soon the final push to Lower Canyon Creek Lake begins near another beautiful waterfall, this one only visible through the trees. Becoming rocky and narrow, the trail is marked by numerous small cairns as it climbs 200 feet to a rockhop across Canyon Creek. The lake is just ahead (7.5/5606).

With a backdrop of Wedding Cake (8569) and more distant Thompson Peak (9002) at the head of the canyon, the lake is scenic. It also harbors numerous specimens of Brewer spruce around the shore. The rarest spruce in the world, Brewer spruce exists only in scattered locations throughout the Klamath Mountains and

Canyon Creek Falls

is easily identified by its distinctive dangling branches. Useless for lumber, and growing in generally remote locations, the tree has been little studied and its origins remain a mystery.

Several adventurous side trips are possible from the lake. Past the lake's northwest corner, more rugged Upper Canyon Creek Lake is accessible via a short brushy scramble. Tiny El Lake perches northeast nearly 800 feet above the upper lake and is reputed excellent for fishing. Thompson Peak, the highest summit in the Trinity Alps, cannot be bagged from this approach without technical equipment. Revel in the majesty of these mountains before returning the way you came.

Nearest Visitor Center: Weaverville District Ranger Office, (530) 623-2121, located on Hwy. 299 on Weaverville's west side. Open Monday through Friday 8 A.M.–4:30 P.M., during summer also Saturday 8 A.M.–5 P.M.

Backpacking Information: A wilderness permit is required, obtainable free either outside the Weaverville District Ranger Office or at the Junction City ranger station (0.1 mile east of Canyon Creek Rd.). Campsites are abundant in the valley above Canyon Creek Falls but only a few good sites exist around Lower Canyon Creek Lake; there are none at the upper lake. Black bears are common in the area—hang your food or bring a canister. No quota is currently in effect for this very popular trailhead.

Nearest Campground: Ripstein Campground, located on Canyon Creek Rd. 0.7 mile before the trailhead, has excellent walk-in sites (free, no water).

Additional Information:
www.r5.fs.fed.us/shastatrinity/trinity_alps.htm

THE TRINITY ALPS

Hike 49—The Marbles

Location	Marble Rim
Agency	Marble Mountain Wilderness
Highlights	Sky High Basin. The Marble Mountains.
Distance	17.0 miles
Total Elevation Gain/Loss	2800´/2800´
Hiking Time	10–14 hours
Difficulty	★★★★
Best Times	mid-June through October
Optional Map	USGS 7.5-min *Marble Mountain*

Designated a primitive area in 1931 and established as one of California's first wilderness areas in 1953, Marble Mountain Wilderness protects nearly a quarter million acres of pristine California. You might think that the deep lakes, striking mountains, lush forest, abundant wildlife, and isolation would attract droves of hikers. But they don't.

The Hike ascends to the impressive cliffs of the Marble Mountains via serene Sky High Lakes Basin, a long dayhike best done as an easy overnight trip. Despite the low elevation, snow lingers on the trail well into June and usually returns by the end of October. This is (deservedly) the most popular hike in the wilderness, but crowds will be light relative to other alpine regions of the state. Fishing is possible in the Sky High lakes. Water is available at the trailhead until late September and sources are plentiful along the hike.

To Reach the Trailhead, take Scott River Rd. 13.4 miles west from Fort Jones on Hwy. 3 to Indian Scotty Campground and turn left (south) onto Forest Service Rd. 44N45, posted for Lovers Camp. Bear left at the immediate fork and continue on the sinuous, one-lane paved road as it climbs 6.8 miles to a large parking lot at the road's end.

Description: From the trailhead (0.0/4150), start out on Canyon Creek Trail, passing two established campsites and entering the lush forest. Douglas-fir, tan oak, and big leaf maple are common sights overhead; and trail markers, wild ginger, and ferns line the path. In 0.1 mile, the trail reaches a confusing intersection of unpaved roads—continue on the trail found diagonally across the road. Passing a wilderness-boundary sign hammered to a Douglas-fir, you soon reach a posted fork (0.7/4250) in the level trail. The trail to Red Rock Valley heads left, but you continue right on Canyon Creek Trail toward Marble Valley.

While the hike parallels rushing Canyon Creek for several miles, it remains unseen below you for the duration. Crossing flowing Death Valley Creek, the trail then climbs briefly before dropping to cross Big Rock Fork. The logs that litter the bouldery watercourse provide evidence of the ferocity that winter rains and flood bring to the region's otherwise small streams. Shortly thereafter, the trail abruptly turns upslope and begins climbing steeply uphill. Intermittent switchbacks eventually bring you to the junction for Marble Valley (4.1/5320). Marble Valley provides faster and more direct access to the Marble Mountains but entirely misses Sky

Marble Rim

Northwest, sub-alpine fir's range extends north to the subarctic. But in Northern California it only occurs here and in scattered locations within nearby Russian Wilderness, and both populations are more than 50 miles distant from the next closest stand in southern Oregon (Lanner 1999). Despite existing at the extreme southern limit of their range, the trees seem to be thriving. Identify them by their narrow spire shape, strongly aromatic crushed needles, and close resemblance to red fir. Within the lakes amphibians thrive: frogs, tadpoles, and the ubiquitous, orange-bellied rough-skinned newt all entertain along the shorelines. In early October, cattle graze here as well.

Continuing west toward the Marble Mountains, the trail climbs steeply up the slopes and offers superlative views of the entire basin before attaining the divide and reaching a junction with the PCT (7.1/6400). From the ridge, the entire drainage of Wooley Creek reveals itself within a horseshoe of peaks dominated west-southwest by granite Medicine Mountain (6837). From its headwaters here, Wooley Creek plummets more than 5,000 feet through dense, undisturbed forest to join the Salmon River 20 miles away. Its entire pristine watershed is protected within the wilderness.

Once on the ridge, turn right and follow the PCT descending gently northwest to a four-way junction (8.6/6230), where you continue straight toward Marble Rim. Right leads down into Marble Valley, the possible shortcut or

High Lakes Basin. If you are short of time, bear right and continue uphill to the Marble Valley Cabin (closed to the public) and the Pacific Crest Trail junction. Head south on the PCT until you reach the Marble Rim Trail. This marble-strewn route also makes an excellent return trail at the end of the day.

Bearing left toward Sky High Lakes, you climb more gradually and soon pass another junction for Marble Valley (4.4/5500) on the right. Curving east, the trail offers the first views of the Marble Mountains to the west before making a final ascent into Sky High Lakes Basin. After you crest a final rise, diminutive and willow-choked Gate Lake welcomes you to the gently rolling basin.

Carved out by recent glaciation within the past two million years, the basin holds several lakes. While use paths crisscross the area, the actual trail leads first to larger Lower Sky High Lake (6.0/5775) in the basin's southeast corner, before turning west toward tiny Frying Pan Lake, and then climbing out of the basin. The trees are diverse—white fir, red fir, mountain hemlock, western white pine, and large groves of aspen can all be found. In addition, a rare stand of subalpine fir grows here as well. A common tree throughout the Pacific return route mentioned above. Left drops down in just over a mile to Big Elk Lake, visible southwest in an open grassy area. Now climbing again toward the marble slopes, the trail remains below the divide until it reaches the low, treeless notch along Marble Rim (8.7/6480).

Part of the complex geologic mix of the Klamath Mountains, the Marble Mountains most likely originated more than 200 million years ago from coral reefs surrounding an ancient, offshore island or landmass. Over the millenia, the reefs' skeletal remains collected in thick layers that eventually solidified into the sedimentary rock, limestone. Smashed into North America, the limestone was transformed to marble and exposed by erosion to form the spectacular cliffs before you. North, Rainy Valley trails away more than a thousand feet

below. Southeast are the jagged peaks of the highest mountains in the wilderness, and the Trinity Alps (Hike 48) can often be seen on the distant southern skyline. Return as you came via Sky High Lakes Basin or take the Marble Valley shortcut.

Nearest Visitor Center: Scott River Ranger Station, (530) 468-5351, located in Fort Jones by the intersection with Scott River Rd. Open Monday through Friday 8 A.M.–4:30 P.M.

Backpacking Information: No wilderness permit is necessary, but a valid campfire permit is required. Sites are abundant in the Sky High Lakes Basin.

Nearest Campground: Free overnight camping is permitted in sites around the trailhead. Otherwise, try Indian Scotty Campground at the Lovers Camp turnoff from Scott River Rd. (28, sites, $10).

THE MARBLES

Hike 50—Russian Flavor

Location	Taylor Lakes
Agency	Russian Wilderness
Highlights	A mini-wilderness of lakes and astounding ecological diversity.
Distance	1.0 mile round trip
Total Elevation Gain/Loss	100´/100´
Hiking Time	1 hour
Difficulty	★
Best Times	mid-June through October
Optional Map	Forest Service *Marble Mountain Wilderness and Russian Wilderness* topographic map

A world of metamorphic ridges and peaks sliced by canyons thousands of feet deep, the Salmon Mountains harbor a small island of granite within tiny Russian Wilderness, where lakes rare to the region nestle in forests boasting the greatest diversity of conifers found anywhere on Earth.

The Salmon Mountains are one of the many small ranges included within the greater Klamath Mountain geographic province, an area stretching from near the Pacific Coast to just west of Mt. Shasta, which includes most of northwest California. The region preserves an ecological story begun millions of years ago when California was composed of low-lying hills and had little topography. A more tropical climate produced abundant rainfall, providing habitat for a lush forest. As the towering mountain ranges started to rise 15 million years ago, the climate began to change. Rainfall diminished, temperatures cooled, deserts formed, and higher-elevation regions became intermittently smothered by glaciers. All but eliminated in the Sierra Nevada, the ancient forest was largely preserved in the Klamath Mountains.

The Klamath Mountains' northerly location and proximity to the sea has kept rainfall abundant. Their lower elevation prevented extensive ice sheets from forming during past ice ages. Their situation at the crossroads of the Cascade Range, Sierra Nevada, and Coast Ranges allows an unusual intermingling of species. As a result, a startling ecological diversity is preserved within the Klamath Mountains—and Russian Wilderness has the greatest diversity of all!

More than 450 plant species exist within the wilderness and 17 different species of conifers have been identified within a one-square-mile plot around the Russian Peak-Little Duck Lake area. They are: Jeffrey, ponderosa, lodgepole, foxtail, western white, sugar, and whitebark pine; white, Shasta red, and subalpine fir; Douglas-fir; Engelmann and Brewer spruce; incense cedar; mountain hemlock; western yew; and prostrate juniper (Wallace 1983). Many of them can be observed on the short hike to Taylor Lake.

The Hike is an easy introduction to Russian Wilderness, following a trail so gentle that those in wheelchairs can make it, designed to whet your appetite for deeper adventuring on your own. Taylor Lake's easy accessibility makes this a popular destination, so don't expect to be alone. The lake is regularly stocked with brook trout and fishing is possible from around the shore. No water is available at the trailhead.

To Reach the Trailhead, take Hwy. 3 to the town of Etna and turn west down Main St., passing through two miles of residential area before the narrow street becomes a small two-lane road (Hwy. 1C01). The road crests a spectacular divide (crossed by the PCT) 10 miles from Etna into the North Fork Salmon River drainage. Descend 0.3 mile beyond this divide and turn left on unpaved Forest Service Rd. 41N18, posted for Taylor Lake. In 1.8 miles, another road cuts steeply left but you continue straight, reaching the trailhead at the road's end in another 0.4 mile.

Description: From the trailhead (0.0/6450), the recently refurbished trail passes among white and red fir, incense cedar, mountain hemlock, and lodgepole and western white pine. At the trailhead,

Taylor Creek is more than 400 feet below the trail but soon the two meet by an old granite wall at the edge of Taylor Lake (0.5/6400). A trail crosses the creek and continues on for 3 miles to Hogan Lake, but you continue on the trail along the eastern shore, soon passing several good campsites. It is possible to circumnavigate the lake. Return the way you came.

Nearest Visitor Center: Salmon River Ranger District Office, (530) 468-5351, located in Ft. Jones. Open Monday through Friday 8 A.M.–4:30 P.M.

Backpacking Information: The wilderness is small at only 12,000 acres, but there are 22 lakes to explore. No wilderness permit is needed but a valid campfire permit is required. There are several sites around Taylor Lake.

Nearest Campground: Idlewild Campground, located 8 curvaceous miles west of the divide on Hwy. 1C01 at the confluence of North Fork Salmon and North Russian rivers (12 sites).

RUSSIAN FLAVOR

Hike 51—The Granite Castle

Location	Castle Dome
Agency	Castle Crags State Park
Highlights	Jagged thrusting pillars of granite.
Distance	5.4 miles round trip
Total Elevation Gain/Loss	2300′/2300′
Hiking Time	3–5 hours
Difficulty	★★★★
Best Times	April through October
Optional Map	USGS 7.5-min *Dunsmuir*

Raking the sky, a jagged protrusion of granite bursts from the slopes above Interstate 5. Needle-sharp spires, bulbous domes, a mania of fantastical granite blades, Castle Crags is unlike anywhere else in California. Add to this views of Mt. Shasta and you have a hike that must be done.

The Hike follows the steep trail to Castle Dome (4966), a tall rounded peak in the middle of Castle Crags. Unlike trails in nearby high-elevation areas, the hike here usually becomes free of snow by April and does not receive snowfall again until November. While summer months are crowded, spring and fall offer increased solitude and views of a snow-mantled Mt. Shasta. While no water is available at the trailhead, sources can be found by the visitor center, in the campground, and halfway at Indian Springs.

To Reach the Trailhead, take the Castella off-ramp from I-5 and head west, immediately turning right into Castle Crags State Park. Turn right past the entrance station toward Crags Trail and Vista Point and proceed 1.8 miles, passing the campground before reaching the parking lot at the road's end—RVs and trailers are not allowed on this steep and narrow road. There is a day-use fee of $5.

Description: From the trailhead at the west end of the lot (0.0/2580), the level double-track trail begins climbing among second-growth Douglas-fir, incense cedar, big leaf maple, alder, ponderosa pine, black oak, and poison oak to quickly reach a junction with Root Creek Trail—bear left and continue on Castle Crags Trail. After a few switchbacks, the trail crosses the Pacific Crest Trail beneath some power lines (0.4/2680) and continues climbing. Canyon live oak begins to appear and the small Indian Creek drainage is visible below you to the west, before a gradually rising traverse brings you to the junction with Bob's Hat Trail (0.6/2910)—continue upward on Castle Crags Trail. Crossing into Castle Crags Wilderness, the rising trail briefly levels out on the eastern slope of Indian Creek, and offers the first tantalizing glimpses of granite crags and the deep east-west drainage of Castle Creek. Formed between 170 and 225 million years ago when the Klamath Mountains and Sierra Nevada were joined as one continuous mountain range, the granite of Castle Crags closely resembles the rock of the eastern Sierra Nevada in both age and composition.

At the posted junction for Indian Springs (1.5/3560), a brief and highly recommended side trip leads to a series of lush springs emerging from the hillside and dribbling out of cracks in a mossy 25-foot-high block of granite. Back on the main trail, the route gets rocky and steep, switchbacking rapidly as sugar pine and increasing manzanita line the path. Mt. Shasta soon appears for the first time beyond the sheer east face of Castle Dome. The fire lookout on top of Mt. Bradley (5556) is visible between the two.

Weaving through jagged pillars of granite surmountable only by climbing spidermen, the trail, occasionally hewn into solid rock, begins to diverge into a maze of use paths near the top. The wider main trail is generally easy to follow; it terminates at a fenced overlook with a view into the deep crevice between Castle Dome and the neighboring crags. The thick ground cover of the upper crags is primarily manzanita and huckleberry oak; the trees are sugar and ponderosa pine. The summit of Castle Dome (2.7/4966) can be bagged from the south with some precarious scrambling—follow the easiest route up the south face and wrap around to the east. Return the way you came.

Nearest Visitor Center: Castle Crags State Park Visitor Center, (530) 235-2684, located at the park entrance. Open May through September daily 8 A.M.–6 P.M.; October through April open sporadically.

Backpacking Information: While not allowed within the state park, backcountry camping is allowed within Castle Crags Wilderness—no wilderness permit is needed. A few possible sites exist around Castle Dome but there is no water above Indian Springs.

Nearest Campground: Castle Crags State Park Campground (76 sites, $12). Reservations are recommended in the summer.

THE GRANITE CASTLE

Hike 52—Lighthearted

Location	Heart Lake
Agency	Shasta-Trinity National Forest
Highlights	The quick and easy Shasta-Trinity experience.
Distance	1.8 miles round trip
Total Elevation Gain/Loss	700´/700´
Hiking Time	1–2 hours
Difficulty	★★
Best Times	June through October
Optional Map	USGS 7.5-min *Seven Lakes Basin*

Just north of Castle Crags Wilderness, tiny Heart Lake perches among boulders and trees high above Castle Lake. The massif of Mt. Shasta looms beyond, a great geographic transition easily observed without the physical punishment of other nearby hikes.

The Hike climbs past Castle Lake to reach Heart Lake, an easy hike with easy access that provides a quick sample of the region's geography. Fishing is popular in deep Castle Lake for brook and rainbow trout. Water is available at the trailhead.

To Reach the Trailhead, take the Mt. Shasta exit from I-5 and head west, immediately turning left (south) at the stop sign by the fish hatchery. Continue straight on W.A. Barr Rd. for 2.4 miles, bearing left on Castle Lake Rd. at the **Y-**

Castle Lake and Mt. Shasta

junction immediately after crossing the outflow from Siskiyou Lake. Castle Lake Rd. twists uphill for 6.9 miles to a large circular paved lot at the road's end.

Description: From the trailhead, drop down to Castle Lake (5436). Known to the local Shasta-Wintun Indians as "Castle of the Devil," home of the evil spirit Ku-Ku-Pa-Rick, Castle Lake is one of the most extensively studied mountain lakes in all of California and numerous informative placards highlight the work done here over the past 60 years. The wide trail strikes south along the lake's east shore among white fir and lodgepole pine, passing several heavily used primitive campsites before reaching a posted sign for Little Castle and Heart lakes.

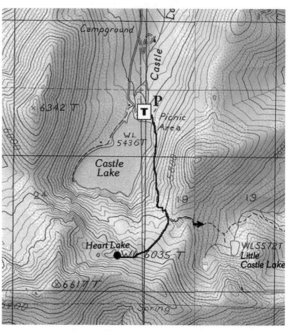

LIGHTHEARTED

The narrower trail begins to climb, traversing above Castle Lake and becoming increasingly rocky and rooty. Red fir begins to appear trailside, tantalizing views begin to appear between the peaks, and you soon crest the low divide above Castle Lake. The junction for Heart Lake is precisely at this divide. Continuing straight on the obvious trail leads to Little Castle Lake in a quick half mile, but the unposted spur to Heart Lake strikes a hard right from the main trail and soon reaches its destination. Western white pine appear here, Mt. Eddy (Hike 53) is visible northwest through a notch in the ridge, and Mt. Shasta is apparent in its entirety.

Castle Lake is located at the eastern edge of the Klamath Mountains, a geologically complex range whose ancient rocks vary in age from approximately 80 to over 300 million years old. You are so close to the edge of this geologic province that you can see beyond it to the young rocks mantling Mt. Shasta, rocks formed less than 10,000 years ago. Here in the eastern Klamath Mountains, however, the peaks are composed primarily of the Trinity Complex—the largest exposure of ancient sea floor in all of North America. Yet the rocks around you are granite, the exposed surface of a small bubble of magma that rose through the older rock between 170 and 225 million years ago and solidified before reaching the surface. Castle Crags (Hike 51), a mere 6 miles south of here, represents the southern edge of this granite outcropping. The darker rocks of the Trinity Complex can be found mixed in with the lighter granite on your return trip. So back you go!

Nearest Visitor Center: Mt. Shasta Ranger District Office (see Hike 54).

Nearest Campground: Castle Lake Campground, located a half mile north of the lake on Castle Lake Dr. (6 sites, free, no water). Always full.

Additional Information:
www.r5.fs.fed.us/shastatrinity

Hike 53—Eddy

Location	Mt. Eddy
Agency	Shasta-Trinity National Forest
Highlights	Killer views of Mt. Shasta and the Klamath Mountains.
Distance	10.0 miles round trip
Total Elevation Gain/Loss	2100´/2100´
Hiking Time	5–7 hours
Difficulty	★★★★
Best Times	mid-June through September
Optional Map	USGS 7.5-min *South China Mountain, Mount Eddy*

Dwarfed by its towering neighbor, the rocky rise of Mt. Eddy may not immediately catch your attention but, if you want a secluded valley and a summit with sweeping 360° views, it should.

The Hike ascends Mt. Eddy (9025) from the west, passing through a broad valley with easy access to Upper Deadfall Lake before steeply climbing to attain the summit. The high elevation of Mt. Eddy means that snow can linger well into June and return anytime in October. Crowds are unfortunately thick during the summer months, when as many as 60 cars can be found parked at the trailhead. Fishing is good in Upper Deadfall Lake and wildflowers are abundant in June and July. No water is available at the trailhead but it can always be obtained from Deadfall Creek 2.5 miles from the trailhead.

To Reach the Trailhead, take the Edgewood exit from I-5—located 2 miles north of Weed—and go west. Just past the freeway, turn right and then quickly left in 0.2 mile to stay on Stewart Springs Rd. for 3.8 miles. At the wooden gate marking the entrance to Stewart Springs, turn right onto Forest Service Road 17. Proceed 8.6 miles on the paved road to the posted Parks Creek trailhead on the left, just past the divide. An alternate trailhead can be found 1.2 miles farther

down the road, from a gravel lot at a sharp U-turn in the road. The trail leading from here follows Deadfall Creek along the valley bottom, joining the trail described below in 1.5 miles, and adding an extra 750 feet of elevation gain to the hike.

Description: From the trailhead (0.0/6850), the hike begins on the PCT and briefly parallels the road as it passes among Jeffrey pine, white fir, and western white pine. It then curves east to begin a long, gradually rising traverse above the valley. As views open up, the glacial origin of the valley is readily apparent in its broad U-shape.

In season, wildflowers abound along the trail—please do not pick them. The reddish-brown rocks here are part of the Trinity Complex, the largest exposure of ancient sea floor found in North America. Accreted to the continent roughly 250 million years ago, these rocks weather to form a nutrient-deficient soil that provides habitat for many rare and unusual plants found only where such rocks are exposed. Let them live.

Reaching the valley floor, you come to a four-way junction (2.6/7230). The PCT continues straight and the trail from the alternate trailhead joins from the right but you turn left toward Mt. Eddy, visible due east from here. Lodgepole pines now predominate. In 0.1 mile you reach an unmarked spur trail that splits right to Upper Deadfall Lake—fishing and swimming opportunities abound around the lakeshore.

Back on the main trail, your route quickly steepens where the trail switchbacks to reach several ponds in a small basin, the last source of water for this hike. As the trail continues to climb, an unusual stand of foxtail pine appears among mountain hemlock and western white pine.

Foxtail pine exists in two distinct populations separated by a gap of nearly 300 miles: one in the Klamath Mountains, of which the trees around you are the easternmost representatives; and one in the southern Sierra Nevada, found primarily in Sequoia and Kings Canyon national parks. How such a wide gap developed remains unresolved, but it seems likely that the two populations are remnants of a once extensive forest across California. Closely related to the ancient bristlecone pine (Hike 91), foxtail pines are able to survive in soils inhospitable to most

other conifers. They are easily identified by the namesake needle clusters that extend densely along the branches.

Reaching a divide (4.0/8000), you come to another junction—turn left and begin the grueling push to the top. The rocky path switchbacks more than a dozen times as it climbs the south ridge and provides increasingly airy views. Approximately halfway to the top, scrubby whitebark pines, the only conifer capable of surviving at such high elevations, have been twisted into krummholz form by the harsh elements. Ever-tightening switchbacks finally deposit you on the summit (5.0/9025).

An old abandoned fire lookout blown over during the winter of 1998–99 crowns the summit, providing some shelter from windy conditions. The view is unbelievable. Mt. Shasta dominates the landscape east above the thin ribbon of I-5 and the perfect cone of Black Butte (6325). To the west, a large stretch of the Trinity River drainage can be identified, and the distant peaks of the Trinity Alps (Hike 48) rake the skyline southwest.

EDDY

Due west are the mountains of Russian Wilderness (Hike 50), and Marble Mountain Wilderness (Hike 49) forms the skyline west-northwest. Return the way you came.

Nearest Visitor Center: Mt. Shasta Ranger District Office (see Hike 54).

Backpacking Information: A campfire permit is required. Besides a large campsite by Upper Deadfall Lake, the adventurous can sleep on the often-windy summit of Mt. Eddy.

Nearest Campground: There are several campgrounds along Hwy. 3 including: Scott Mountain Campground, located 5 miles north of the Hwy. 3/FS Rd. 17 junction; and Eagle Creek Campground, 6 miles south of the junction. Hwy. 3 can be accessed from the trailhead by driving west on FS Rd. 17 for 13 twisty miles.

Additional Information: *www.r5.fs.fed.us/shastatrinity*

Hike 54—Hidden Valley

Location	Mt. Shasta Wilderness
Agency	Shasta-Trinity National Forest
Highlights	The mountain. The views.
Distance	6.0 miles round trip
Total Elevation Gain/Loss	2300´/2300´
Hiking Time	4–6 hours
Difficulty	★★★★
Best Times	July through October
Optional Map	USGS 7.5-min *McCloud, Mount Shasta*

An active volcano, Mt. Shasta towers over the landscape of Northern California and hides a secluded world of rock and snow on its southwest flank. Hidden Valley awaits.

Mt. Shasta (14142) is part of the Cascade Range of volcanoes that extends from Northern California to northern Washington State, and includes such notable peaks as Mt. St. Helens and Mt. Rainier. With a volume of roughly 80 cubic miles, Mt. Shasta is substantial—the largest of the Cascade Range—and while its vents have been active for at least 100,000 years, the bulk of the current mountain has been constructed over only the past 10,000 years in a series of at least 13 separate eruptions. Hotlum

Sierra Club hut

Cone at the summit has erupted eight times during this period, covering the mountain and surrounding landscape with lava and debris flows. Its most recent eruption occurred in 1786 and there is no doubt that the mountain will flare again—current studies indicate that on average eruptions take place once every 250–300 years.

The Hike follows the popular trail to Horse Camp from Bunny Flat before continuing on an open cross-country traverse over loose and rocky slopes to Hidden Valley, a secluded depression offering outstanding views of the mountain. Because Mt. Shasta is primarily a mountaineer's playground and Bunny Flat the principal trailhead for the summit, crowds will be thick during mountain-climbing season (roughly April through July). The period following climbing season is best for hikers as crowds reduce drastically and the snow preferred by aspiring climbers melts off the trail. No water is available at the trailhead. Horse Camp has a freshwater spring and provides the hike's only water source.

To Reach the Trailhead, take I-5 to the town of Mt. Shasta and proceed east on Lake St. to join Everitt Memorial Highway and continue toward the mountain—Bunny Flat trailhead is 10 miles from town on the north side of the road.

Description: At the trailhead (0.0/ 6900), be sure to complete a self-issued day-use permit before striking out on the wide trail. Shasta red fir, manzanita, and lupine surround you as the trail climbs above a broad, dry meadow swept clean by the occasional heavy winter avalanche. Use trails crisscross the area—stay on the main trail and bear left at the next obvious junction.

Winding through open forest, the path curves west toward the edge of Avalanche Gulch, climbing more steeply now along the edge of a lateral moraine carved by recent glaciation. A trail from

Sand Flat trailhead joins from the left (1.0/7330) and you soon cross the wilderness boundary. The steady ascent leaves the shaded forest just before reaching the open vistas of Horse Camp (1.7/7880). The Sierra Club hut located here is an historic shelter open to everyone for browsing, relaxing, and reflecting. The hut is manned by a seasonal caretaker until early October, and supplies are available here in the event of an emergency. The standard climbing route is visible northwest, winding east around the distinctive Red Banks near the top before reaching unseen Misery Hill and the final push to the summit. Campsites and well-marked trails crisscross the area around Horse Camp, and an excellent outhouse is nearby.

From Horse Camp, the route to Hidden Valley follows a generally distinct trail that has been marked in recent years by wands to minimize hiker impact. Please stay on the marked route—the loose slopes are easily scarred. The rocky route begins beyond the northern campsites and is clearly discernible as it immediately begins climbing north out of Avalanche Gulch. Lassen Peak (10457), the southernmost volcano of the Cascade Range, soon appears southeast beyond the eastern ridge of Avalanche Gulch. Cresting a rise, the trail levels out briefly in a flat bowl (2.0/8100) where spectacular views west open up. The Eddys rise across the valley, with the high point of Mt. Eddy (9025, Hike 53) visible just south of the perfect cone of Black Butte (6325). Beyond Mt. Eddy, the distant skyline peaks of the Trinity Alps (Hike 48) can be picked out southwest on a clear day.

As the route begins climbing steeply out of the bowl, shrubby and twisted whitebark pines appear among the rocks, shrunken to krummholz form by the powerful elements so high on the mountain. The final trail section is less discernible, where the route scrambles above sheer Cascade Gulch to crest into barren Hidden Valley (3.0/ 9220). Shastina (12330) dominates to the north, a subsidiary cone formed between 9,300 and 9,700 years ago. The southern edge of Hidden Valley is part of Casaval Ridge, the sharp spine winding northwest toward the main summit, which offers some of the mountain's more technical routes when snow and ice are present. Return the way you came.

Nearest Visitor Center: Mt. Shasta Ranger District Office, (530) 926-4511, located in the town of Mt. Shasta on West Alma St. (parallel to Lake St.). Open Memorial Day through Labor Day daily 8 A.M.–4:30 P.M.; open Monday through Friday only the rest of the year.

Backpacking Information: Wilderness permit required, available for free anytime outside the Mt. Shasta Ranger District Office. A donation is requested for camping in the sites around Horse Camp ($5 per tent, $3 per person without tent). The only other option are the small sites in Hidden Valley (no water). Be sure to follow the guidelines for the human waste pack-out program, if you are camping beyond an outhouse—supplies are available at the trailhead. While you will often find a community fire by the Sierra Club hut, no campfires are allowed elsewhere on the mountain.

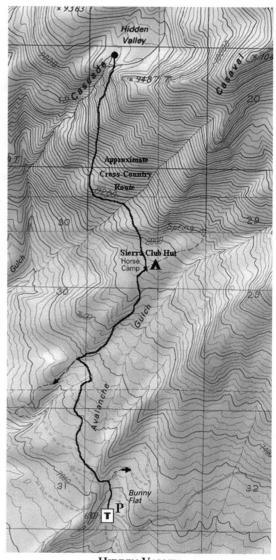

HIDDEN VALLEY

Nearest Campground: Panther Flat Walk-in Campground, located 2 miles east of Bunny Flat trailhead on Everitt Memorial Highway (10 sites, free, no water). Also try McBride Springs Campground on Everitt Memorial Highway (10 sites, $10). Both are always full during the summer.

Additional Information: *www.r5.fs.fed.us/shastatrinity*

Hike 55—North Gate

Location	Mt. Shasta Wilderness
Agency	Shasta-Trinity National Forest
Highlights	The more removed north side of Shasta.
Distance	4.0 miles round trip
Total Elevation Gain/Loss	1600´/1600´
Hiking Time	3–5 hours
Difficulty	★★★
Best Times	July through October
Optional Map	USGS 7.5-min *Mount Shasta*

California's largest glaciers spill north from the summit of Mt. Shasta, permanent icy expanses extending thousands of feet down the mountainside. The portal to the region is North Gate, removed from the bustle by a maze of dirt roads, access point for up-close views of glaciers and summit.

   The Hike follows an obvious trail through an unusual whitebark pine forest to reach exceptional views of Shasta's upper north flank. The adventurous can continue for some distance up the mountain but the slopes require increasing technical skills and equipment above 10,000 feet. Because the area offers challenging mountaineering problems, climbers are plentiful here in late spring and early summer. As the snow melts away in July, climbing routes become hazardous; the region remains little visited until the following spring. No water is available at the trailhead or anywhere along this hike, once the snow has melted.

   To Reach the Trailhead, take Hwy. 97 north from Weed for 13.9 miles to Military Pass Rd. (Forest Service Road 43N19) and turn right. The route from here is rough, unpaved, and passes along a maze of logging roads—zero your odometer at the turnoff from Hwy. 97. Follow FS Rd. 43N19 to mile 4.5 and

go left at the posted **Y**-junction for North Gate. At mile 5.1, bear left at the unsigned fork. At mile 7.7, go right at the posted fork on FS Rd. 42N97. At mile 7.8, go left at the junction and follow the road to the parking lot at mile 8.3. There is a $5 parking fee.

   Description For general information on the geology of Mt. Shasta, please see Hike 54. At the trailhead (0.0/7000), be sure to complete a self-issued day-use permit before beginning on the dusty single-track trail. Mt. Shasta's summit looms over the trees from the parking lot but soon disappears as you pass beneath the branches of Shasta red fir and whitebark pine.

   The trail ascends gently at first, but soon steepens noticeably as it climbs through a thick forest increasingly dominated by whitebark pine. Rarely attaining the size of the trees found here and seldom forming its own forest, whitebark pine is usually limited to shrubby growth just below tree line. It owes its existence to a unique symbiotic relationship with the Clark's nutcracker, a bird that harvests the pine seeds and caches them by the thousands in the ground for later consumption. Those left uneaten sprout, often forming thick clumps of trees from the bird's forgotten meal. The stubby, purple cones of whitebark pine usually glisten with sap, and their visibility at the end of sweeping upturned branches helps attract the nutcracker. Interestingly, the seeds will not drop of their own accord and must be harvested by these birds to plant future generations. Built like a small crow, a Clark's nutcracker can be identified by its light gray body and the white patches on its black wings and tail. Its call is a flat "khaa" or "khraa."

Where views begin to first open up (1.3/8000) the trail levels out somewhat, and the broad rounded summit of The Whaleback (8528) becomes visible nearby to the northeast. The path becomes faint as you proceed through a sandy valley littered with avalanche-swept trees—wands are usually placed to mark the route. Please follow the designated route as the fragile ecosystem here is easily scarred.

This hike ends where the broad valley curves west, providing an awesome view of Mt. Shasta (2.0/8550). Looking south toward the summit, the broad expanses of Bolam Glacier (west) and Hotlum Glacier (east) merge into a large snow and ice field covering all angles of the upper mountain. Both are technical climbs with dangerous crevasses, requiring roped glacier travel for an ascent. Those feeling adventurous can continue south up the rocky slopes to 10,000 feet, but be aware that distances are deceiving—the top of the nearby slope here is 1,500 feet farther up the mountain—and a summit pass is required to continue above 10,000 feet. Return the way you came.

Nearest Visitor Center: Mt. Shasta Ranger District Office (see Hike 54).

Backpacking Information: Wilderness permit required, available for free anytime outside the Mt. Shasta Ranger District Office. Campsites are plentiful in the upper valley. No water is available once the snow has melted. No campfires allowed.

Nearest Campground: Nothing very close. Try the campgrounds on Everitt Memorial Hwy. (see Hike 54) or at Castle Lake (see Hike 52).

Additional Information:
www.r5.fs.fed.us/shastatrinity

North Gate

Hike 56—Tule or not Tule

Location	Sheepy Ridge
Agency	Tule Lake National Wildlife Refuge
Highlights	The land of a million birds.
Distance	0.6 mile round trip
Total Elevation Gain/Loss	180′/180′
Hiking Time	1 hour
Difficulty	★
Best Times	Year-round
Optional Map	USGS 7.5-min *Hatfield*

Tule (TOO-lee) Lake sits in the Klamath Basin, a region of vast wetlands providing habitat for 263 species of birds. Many are migratory, stopping over to rest and refuel before continuing on their journeys. Geese, swans, and ducks of all types pass through, peaking in numbers during March and early November and swelling the number of birds in the Klamath Basin to over one million. Winter is a magical time—Tule Lake freezes over and raptors of all kinds congregate here. From December through February, the Klamath Basin hosts the largest concentration of bald eagles in the contiguous United States—over 1,000 can be present in the Basin—and Tule Lake is one of the best spots to observe them. During the summer resident ducks and other waterbirds raise their young, livening the area with their darling broods. Options for bird watching include an auto tour, self-guided canoe trails, and reservable photo blinds. The visitor center (see below) has all the details.

The Hike climbs Sheepy Ridge behind the Klamath Basin Wildlife Refuges Visitor Center, an easy hike that is primarily an introduction to adventuring around Tule Lake. It offers broad views of the landscape from an unusual stone hut perched above the sheer cliffs. The exposed trail is scorching during summer months, so sun protection is essential. While snow can cover the trail in the winter, the Tule Lake region is worth visiting year-round for its ever-changing seasonal birdlife. Water is available at the trailhead.

To Reach the Trailhead, take East-West Rd. west from the town of Tulelake on Hwy. 139. In 4.4 miles, turn left on Hill Rd. to reach the visitor center in 0.5 mile. The trail starts in the upper parking lot. Approaching from Lava Beds National Monument, take Hill Rd. 8.5 miles north from the park road—the junction is located immediately west of the Lava Beds north entrance station.

Description: Pick up an interpretive brochure at the trailhead before you begin. Climb through rabbit brush and sage, making three switchbacks before traversing over to the stone lookout at the trail's end. Constructed by the CCC in 1938, the enclosed hut offers respite from the sun's blistering rays.

Sheepy Ridge was formed as the adjacent land to the east slipped downward along a long, linear fault, forming a north-south ridge that extends more than 10 miles south into Lava Beds National Monument. Looking south down the ridge, notice the several cinder cones east of its terminus. The farthest east is Schonchin Butte (Hike 57). The

Tule or not Tule?

collapsed form of Medicine Lake Volcano (Hike 59) occupies the distant
southern skyline. As you face east, the
perfect squares of reclaimed wetland
surround Sump 1-A and the northern
section of Tule Lake. The hills of Oregon
recede into the northern distance.

Nearest Visitor Center: Klamath
Basin Wildlife Refuges Headquarters
and Visitor Center, (530) 667-2231. Open
Monday through Friday 8 A.M.–4:30 P.M.,
weekends and holidays 10 A.M.–4 P.M.

Nearest Campground: Lava Beds
National Monument (see Hike 57).

Additional Information:
www.klamathnwr.org

Tule or not Tule

Hike 57—Scorchin' Schonchin

Location	Schonchin Butte
Agency	Lava Beds National Monument
Highlights	A sweeping vista of volcanic wasteland.
Distance	1.4 miles round trip
Total Elevation Gain/Loss	500´/500´
Hiking Time	1–2 hours
Difficulty	★
Best Times	Year-round
Optional Map	USGS 7.5-min *Schonchin Butte*

Lava Beds National Monument is a land smothered by recent lava flows, pocked with cinder cones, devoid of all surface water. A world both hostile and fascinating, it's almost entirely visible from the fire lookout atop Schonchin Butte (5253).

This is an active volcanic area. The entire landscape was formed less than one million years ago when lava spilled across the surface and smothered it beneath thick flows of black basalt. Much of the lava originated in Medicine Lake Volcano to the west, but several vents within the monument have been active during the past 10,000 years. The Modoc Plateau is a part of the Earth's crust that is undergoing extension, thinning and cracking in places as it is pulled

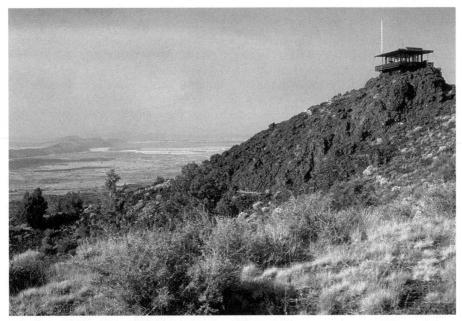

Fire Lookout atop Schonchin Butte

Scorchin' Schonchin

apart. These cracks allow liquid basalt from the Earth's interior to well up onto the surface, creating the lava flows and cinder cones seen in the monument today.

Schonchin Butte is a cinder cone that was produced by an active vent sometime during the past 10,000 years. As a new fissure allows magma to rise toward the surface, ground water is overheated, blowing large chunks of rock into a distinct cone shape around the surface opening. Once the actual magma reaches the surface it typically pours out at the base of the cone, flowing with gravity over the land. Schonchin Butte and the Schonchin Lava Flow, which flowed north over the heart of the monument, are textbook examples. This type of eruption is generally small and short-lived, producing a volcano in miniature that rarely erupts again.

The Hike climbs Schonchin Butte via a well-maintained trail to the summit fire lookout, an easy hike with several,

strategically located rest benches. While the hike is partly shaded, the sun is intense during summer months on the exposed portions of trail. The monument is open year-round and receives light snowfall from November through April. Despite the intense sun, Lava Beds receives most visitors during summer months, making the rest of the year preferable for a hike. No water is available at the trailhead or anywhere along the way.

To Reach the Trailhead, take Hwy. 139 northwest from Hwy. 299—the turnoff is just west of Canby. In 26 miles, turn west onto Hwy. 97. When you reach a fork in 2.5 miles, bear right onto Hwy. 10. Drive 9.4 miles to the monument border. From here, the visitor center is 3.6 miles and the turnoff for Schonchin Butte 5.7 miles. (Approaching from the north, the turnoff is 6.7 miles south of the north entrance station.) The unpaved road to the trailhead is easily passable for all vehicles, and reaches the parking area in 0.9 mile. There is a $4 entrance fee, valid for seven days.

Description: From the trailhead (0.0/4800), the wide path traverses up the north flank of the cone. Juniper, sage, rabbit brush, and mountain mahogany cover the slopes, and the fire lookout is visible above you. After two switchbacks, the trail forks. While both paths lead to the summit, the left is more direct, but the right traverses around the old cinder crater providing good views of the lookout's precarious roost. Go for the loop!

A wooden railing rings the lookout and you may have the opportunity to converse with the seasonal worker that staffs this active facility. Placards identify the surrounding landmarks, including Glass Mountain (Hike 59) and Mt. Shasta (Hikes 54–55). The fresh-looking, razor-sharp rocks of the Schonchin Lava Flow cover the ground below you to the north, barely colonized by plant life after thousands of years of erosion. Hidden among the cracks at the flow's northern end is Captain Jack's Stronghold, where a small band of Modoc Indians successfully resisted army attack for over six months by utilizing the maze of caves and passageways in the lava flow. Lasting from November 1872 until June 1873, the Modoc War was the last Indian war fought in the United States.

Nearest Visitor Center: Lava Beds National Monument Visitor Center, (530) 667-2282. Open year-round daily 8 A.M.– 5 P.M.

Nearest Campground: Indian Well Campground, located 0.5 mile from the visitor center (water, 43 sites, $10).

Additional Information: *www.nps.gov/labe*

Hike 58—The Underground

Location	Valentine Cave
Agency	Lava Beds National Monument
Highlights	Spelunking in a lava tube.
Distance	0.5 mile round trip
Total Elevation Gain/Loss	10´/10´
Hiking Time	1 hour
Difficulty	★
Best Times	Year-round
Optional Map	USGS 7.5-min *Schonchin Butte*

Feel the cool inky darkness of a cave below a scorching volcanic desert.

Lava tubes are formed as the sides and surface of a lava flow solidify, covering with hardened basalt the liquid rock that still courses inside. Once the flow stops, the lava drains away and leaves a hollow tube with several distinctive features inside. *Lavicles* are formed when liquid rock drips from the ceiling and solidifies. *Benches* found on the tube walls represent decreasing surface levels brought on by reductions in flow volume. Roof collapse typically exposes the lava tubes, which can wind underground for miles through passages of varying widths.

The Hike is the only one in the book that goes underground, following spacious Valentine Cave to its terminus well beyond the reach of the sun's rays. It's a good introduction to more than 400 caves of Lava Beds, most of which are challenging to explore. It is short and easy but requires taking important precautions. Sturdy non-slip shoes are essential, and long pants and a warm pullover are recommended. Carry two sources of light with you at all times, but do not use gas or carbide lanterns. The visitor center provides flashlights free of charge during the day and sells simple, plastic hard hats, although Valentine Cave has ceilings sufficiently high for you to walk

upright. With its cool, constant, year-round temperature, Valentine Cave provides welcome respite from summer heat and winter chill, and is open all year long. No water is available at the trailhead.

To Reach the Trailhead, take the park road (Hwy. 10) 1.6 miles southeast of the visitor center and turn left toward Valentine Cave, reaching a substantial parking lot in 0.2 mile. Approaching from the south, the turnoff is 2 miles northwest of the park boundary. For general directions to Lava Beds National Monument, please see Hike 57.

Description: A paved trail leads 50 feet to the cave entrance, ringed by junipers and sage brush. The collapsed blocks preserve solidified *pahoehoe* (puh-HOY-hoy), a ropy type of lava flow formed by basaltic magma. The magma associated with Mt. Shasta and the Cascade Range forms blocky, slow-moving flows known as *aa* (ah-ah). After immediately splitting around a large pillar, the cave resumes its tube-like shape in increasing darkness. Lavicles cover the ceiling and benches. The cave narrows abruptly in the back, terminating in a small crawl space that continues a few feet farther. If the cave is empty of other visitors, turn out your lights to experience utter darkness.

Nearest Visitor Center and Campground: Please see Hike 57.

Hike 59—Obsidian

Location	Glass Mountain
Agency	Modoc National Forest
Highlights	A recent lava flow laced with volcanic glass.
Distance	1.0 mile or less round trip
Total Elevation Gain/Loss	50′/50′
Hiking Time	1 hour
Difficulty	★
Best Times	mid-June through September
Optional Map	USGS 7.5-min *Medicine Lake, West of Kephart*

Lava cooled so fast it turned to glass. Medicine Lake Volcano is larger in mass than nearby Mt. Shasta, yet its slopes are so gradual as to be almost unremarkable. It is a shield volcano formed from basaltic lava, an extremely broad mountain very similar to those of the Hawaiian Islands. Measuring 15 miles east-west by 25 miles north-south with a surface area greater than 900 square miles, it is a prominent landmark of the Modoc Plateau.

Unlike the towering stratovolcano of Mt. Shasta, Medicine Lake Volcano hardly appears intimidating. This is because the entire top of the mountain collapsed approximately 100,000 years ago in a block four miles wide by six miles long, forming a large depression, or *caldera*. Smaller volcanoes welled up along the circular fracture, spilling lava both into the caldera and down the slopes of the mountain.

Glass Mountain, the most recent flow in the Medicine Lake complex, spilled down the volcano's east flanks less than 1,000 years ago. Liquid magma is a soup of chemicals unformed and without structure. Most lava flows are extruded slowly enough for the assorted chemicals to gradually cool and form discrete crystals, but occasionally the molten rock cools so quickly that it hardens

unchanged, forming black glass, obsidian. It happened at Glass Mountain. Native Americans prized obsidian's sharp edges for knives and arrowheads; at least four different tribes collected here, trading to neighboring tribes more than a hundred miles away.

The Hike is an opportunity to wander around on a recent lava flow and see obsidian in its natural state. Small samples may be collected. This is a remote part of California and odds are that you won't encounter anybody else, regardless of when you come. This hike is at a relatively high elevation for the region—above 7,000 feet—and snow can fly as early as October. No water is available at the trailhead or on the lava flow.

To Reach the Trailhead, take Hwy. 97 west from Hwy. 139 for 18 miles to unpaved Forest Service Road 43N99 on the right, the first of three possible turnoffs for Glass Mtn. (Approaching from the west, the turnoff is 4.4 miles east of the Hwy. 49/97 junction. Don't be tempted by the GLASS MOUNTAIN signs you see at the first two turnoffs 1.0 mile and 3.6 miles from the junction.) As you head north on FS Rd. 43N99 astonishing views of the flow appear before you reach a small, posted pull-out at its base, 3.6 miles from Hwy. 97.

Description: From the trailhead (7050) head up the obvious path. The lava flow has been worked by heavy machinery and numerous paths wind this way and that. While none of them really go anywhere, they make for considerably easier walking than over the jagged piles of rock. Obsidian is visible everywhere, glinting in the sunlight, interlaid with enormous amounts of gray pumice. A few, scattered lodgepole and western white pine pioneer this moonscape. Mt. Hoffman (7913) is almost due west and Red Shale Butte (7834) is south, easily identified by the bare red nubbin at its summit. These mountains are two of the smaller volcanoes that welled up along the fracture zone after the mountaintop collapsed. Glass Mtn. (7622) is the bluff visible north, the highest point on the lava flow. Wander as much as you like, but don't lose your bearings in the maze of trails.

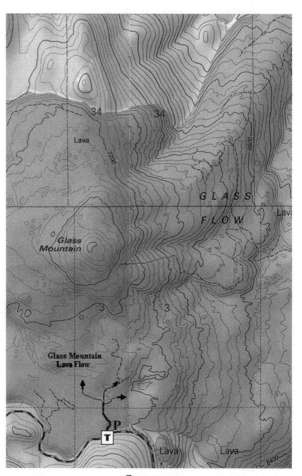

OBSIDIAN

Nearest Visitor Center: Doublehead Ranger District Office, (530) 667-2246, just southeast of the town of Tulelake on Hwy. 139. Open Monday through Friday 8 A.M.–4:30 P.M.

Nearest Campground: 4 campgrounds around Medicine Lake (72 sites total, $7).

Additional Information: *www.r5.fs.fed.us/modoc*

Hike 60—The Farthest Reaches

Location	Mt. Vida
Agency	Modoc National Forest
Highlights	A quiet mountaintop in the farthest corner of Northern California.
Distance	3.2 miles round trip
Total Elevation Gain/Loss	800´/800´
Hiking Time	2 hours
Difficulty	★★
Best Times	mid-June through October
Optional Map	USGS 7.5-min *Mount Bidwell*

Four miles from Oregon, twelve miles from Nevada. In this remote northeast corner of California, in the northern reaches of the Warner Mountains, on top of Mt. Vida, get away from it all.

The Hike climbs Mt. Vida (8224) via High Grade National Recreation Trail, an easy ascent along a disued jeep road that ends with a short off-trail jaunt to the summit. In this far corner of the state it is highly unlikely that you will encounter anybody regardless of when you come, although hunters travel the region in fall. Snow can linger here until late June. This is an extremely hot, dry area and summer months can be sweltering. Sun protection is always important. No water is available at the trailhead or anywhere along the hike.

To Reach the Trailhead, it is necessary to travel some rough roads. The final 2.6 miles climb 1,200 feet on a very rocky road, and should not be attempted if you are overly concerned about your low-clearance vehicle. To get there take Hwy. 395 to the Forest Service Road 2 turnoff, 0.8 mile south of the Oregon border. Head 5.1 miles east on mostly unpaved FS Rd. 2 to an unposted junction—0.4 mile after the posted turnoff on the right for Poison Lake and 0.6 mile before the Lily Lake Picnic Area. Those unwilling to drive the final section can park here and make the arduous walk to the trailhead. Otherwise, turn right (south) and begin climbing. After 1.1 miles, bear left at the fork and continue 0.6 mile before bearing right toward Little Lily Lake at the next fork. Continue straight 0.4 mile later, where a road branches right toward the Sunset Mine. You reach a sign for the High Grade Trail 0.5 mile farther where the forest opens up—park by the roadside. While the road continues, motor vehicles are prohibited beyond this point. It is also possible to reach the trailhead from the east by taking FS Rd. 2 west from Ft. Bidwell for 11.4 miles to the unposted junction described above. It is a rough and rocky option.

Description: From the trailhead (0.0/7600) continue on the road. Passing through dense fields of corn lilies, it offers good views of nearby Mt. Vida. The route briefly descends before climbing steeply back on the ridgetop—now with views west of giant Goose Lake. Continuing south, the road soon makes its closest approach to Mt. Vida (1.3/8000) before arcing away west. Leave the road here and proceed by the easiest off-trail route to the summit ridge of the mountain.

From the summit, look southeast and stare down the trinity of Upper, Middle, and Lower Alkali lakes, each encrusted with salt left by evaporating water. Enclosed on the east by the peaks of Nevada, they sit trapped in a *graben*, a valley formed through extension of the Earth's crust. Also known as a "pull-apart basin," Surprise Valley was formed when a large block dropped along parallel faults relative to the adjacent landscape, creating a basin hemmed in by sheer escarpments and covered with sediments washed down from the surrounding mountains. This is the defining geography of the Basin and Range Province, a distinct geologic region that essentially begins here and continues east to Utah. The valley floor is more than 3,500 feet beneath you on Mt. Vida and, presumably, still dropping.

On the skyline due south are the mountains of South Warner Wilderness (Hikes 61–62). Looking northeast below you, serene North Star Basin is a small piece of wonderful wilderness, with the long plateau of Mt. Bidwell (8290) rising beyond the basin. West beyond Goose Lake is the broad volcanic expanse of the Modoc Plateau, with the collapsed ring of Medicine Lake Volcano (Hike 59) clearly identifiable west-southwest. Back the way you came!

Nearest Visitor Center: Warner Mountain Ranger District Office or Modoc National Forest Supervisor's Office (see Hike 61).

Backpacking Information: A valid campfire permit is required. Because campsites are hard to find, this trip is better done as a dayhike.

Nearest Campground: Cave Lake Campground (6 sites, free), 0.3 mile past the Lily Lake Picnic Area (see above). Fishing is good at both lakes.

Additional Information: *www.r5.fs.fed.us/modoc*

THE FARTHEST REACHES

Hike 61—Welcome to the Warners

Location	South Warner Wilderness
Agency	Modoc National Forest
Highlights	Mill Creek Valley. The enigmatic Washoe pine.
Distance	3.8 miles round trip
Total Elevation Gain/Loss	750´/750´
Hiking Time	3–4 hours
Difficulty	★★
Best Times	mid-June through October
Optional Map	Forest Service *South Warner Wilderness* topographic map

Not many people have even heard of South Warner Wilderness, and even fewer have been there. A mountain range in miniature, it is remote, rugged, beautiful, and still largely untraveled.

The Hike provides an easy introduction to South Warner Wilderness, following Slide Creek Trail as it climbs a small rise to descend into wonderfully open Mill Creek Valley. With its large aspen groves, the valley could make an ideal fall hike—rustling golden leaves, perfect weather, and solitude. Colors peak in early to mid-October. The hike's only drawback is the grazing cattle in the valley from July through September. This region was used for cattle and sheep grazing long before it was designated an official wilderness; this was permitted to continue under the 1964 Wilderness Act—yet another reason to come in October. Snow usually flies by November. Water is available near the trailhead in Soup Spring Campground.

To Reach the Trailhead, take Hwy. 64 east from the town of Likely on Hwy. 395. In 9 miles, bear left on Hwy. 5 by a sign for Mill Creek Lodge. Proceed 2.7 miles to the turnoff for Mill Creek Campground. The paved road goes right but you continue straight on the unpaved but easily traveled gravel road. Continue 1.5 miles to an unposted **Y**-junction—

bear right. Take the turnoff for Soup Spring Campground 5.1 miles past this junction and proceed 0.4 mile to the trailhead parking lot on your left.

Description: After signing the register at the trailhead (0.0/6800), begin hiking along an old road lined with large gray boulders. Mule ears, white fir, and Jeffrey pine are all around. This is also a good place to begin looking for the rare Washoe pine. Closely related to ponderosa and Jeffrey pine, Washoe pine (*pinus washoensis*) was only recognized as a separate species in 1938. Its habitat is limited to only a few locations in northeastern California and western Nevada, with this region of the Warner Mountains nurturing the densest collection of specimens. It closely resembles its two relatives, possessing needles in bundles of three and developing yellowish plates on its trunk similar to those of ponderosa pines. Their cones identify them, however. Smooth to the touch, they look like Jeffrey pine cones but are noticeably smaller—only 2–4" long instead of 5–10". The wood resin produced by Washoe pine is also chemically distinct from that of Jeffrey pine and the two rarely hybridize. Genetically, it is more closely related to Rocky Mountain ponderosa pine; some experts speculate that it is a recent genetic offshoot from that population. Its exact origin remains unknown (Lanner 1999).

The wide road quickly reaches a fork by four wooden posts—go left through the posts. Now single-track, the trail alternately passes through thick forest and open areas populated with sage, rabbit brush, juniper trees, and more Washoe pines. Cresting the ridge (1.3/7150), you enter South Warner Wilderness and begin descending into Mill Creek Valley. Views of the rolling topography quickly open up as you leave the forest. Eagle Peak (9892), the highest peak in the wilderness, rises from the opposite side of the valley. Reaching mellifluous Mill Creek (1.9/6750) the path intersects Mill Creek Trail, which heads both upstream and down. Neither direction leads to any immediate destination but both are pleasant rambles. Go as far as you desire before returning the way you came.

Nearest Visitor Center: Warner Mountain Ranger District Office, (530) 279-6116, inconveniently located in Cedarville on the east side of the Warner Mountains. Open Monday through Friday 8 A.M.–4:30 P.M. Also try the Modoc National Forest Supervisor's Office, (530) 233-5811, located immediately west of Alturas on Hwy. 299. Open Monday through Friday 8 A.M.–5 P.M.

Backpacking Information: No wilderness permits are needed but a valid campfire permit is required. There are campsites along Mill Creek.

Nearest Campground: Soup Spring Campground (8 sites, $6 in summer but free after Labor Day).

WELCOME TO THE WARNERS

Hike 62—The Warners

Location	South Warner Wilderness
Agency	Modoc National Forest
Highlights	Patterson Lake. The heart of South Warner Wilderness.
Distance	10.2 miles round trip
Total Elevation Gain/Loss	2900´/2900´
Hiking Time	8–12 hours
Difficulty	★★★★
Best Times	mid-June through October
Optional Map	Forest Service *South Warner Wilderness* topographic map

Here's a hike to the heart of a small piece of mountain paradise.

The Hike climbs to Patterson Lake (9040) through Pine Creek Basin, a strenuous trip that packs in all the wilderness has to offer, from soaring raptors to crystalline creeks, from sweeping panoramic vistas to the largest lake in the wilderness. The hike's second half, climbing out of Pine Creek Basin, is steep, sustained, and shadeless—skin-frying conditions during the summer months. Those looking for a shorter excursion should make the 4.6-mile round trip to the Pine Creek crossing, a less demanding hike to a wonderful picnic spot. October is the nicest time to visit as aspens turn gold and weather is ideal. Snow can linger well into June along upper sections of the trail. While no water is available at the trailhead, Pine Creek is soon accessible.

To Reach the Trailhead, take Hwy. 64 east from the town of Likely on Hwy. 395. In 9 miles, bear left on Hwy. 5 by a sign for Mill Creek Lodge. Proceed 2.7 miles to the turnoff for Mill Creek Campground. The paved road turns right but you continue straight on the unpaved but easily traveled gravel road for 1.5 miles to an unposted Y-junction—bear left and continue on Hwy. 5 for 4.8 miles to the posted turnoff for the Pine Creek

Trail. Turn right, reaching the parking lot at the road's end in 1.3 miles. Approaching from the north, take Parker Creek Rd. (Hwy. 56) east from Alturas for 13 miles to the Hwy. 31/5 split. Head south on Hwy. 5 for 9.7 miles to the Pine Creek Trail turnoff.

Description An information sign and register marks the start of the trail. From the trailhead (0.0/6800) the single-track trail passes through thick white fir where babbling Pine Creek can be heard unseen below you. The firs increase in size and are joined by large ponderosa pines as you cross into the wilderness by an idyllic stream confluence. Fill your water bottles here because the trail next travels away from the creek, seldom approaching it.

Becoming progressively steeper, the trail passes near several, shallow, swampy lakes before reaching the open meadows of Pine Creek Basin (2.3/7400). While the trail crosses the creek and reenters the trees, you should continue a short distance ahead to an ideal picnic spot by a small bend in the creek. Of volcanic origin, Warner Mountains' rocks were formed from ash and lava flows extruded on the landscape roughly 30 million years ago. Within the past two million years, glaciers carved the upper mountain reaches and formed the broad bowl of Pine Creek Basin.

Back on the main trail, you begin the long brutal climb to the ridgecrest above. Views become increasingly expansive as the exposed path climbs through sage, mule ears, and spring-fed patches of corn lilies. A few isolated whitebark pines dot the slopes. Mt. Shasta's distinct cone more than 100 miles west becomes visible near the top before you reach the ridge and the junction with the Summit Trail (4.2/9000).

Views east suddenly open up and the deep basin of Surprise Valley lies below you, brimming with the salt-encrusted trinity of Upper, Middle, and Lower Alkali lakes. Enclosed by Nevada peaks to the east, the lakes fill depressions in a *graben*, a valley formed through extension of the Earth's crust. Also known as a "pull-apart basin," it occurs when a large block of crust drops along parallel fault lines relative to the adjacent landscape. This is the defining geography of the Basin and Range Province, a distinct geologic region that essentially begins here and continues east to Utah. Surprise Val-

ley is more than 4,000 feet below you on the Summit Trail and, presumably, still dropping. Eagle Peak (9892), the highest peak in the Warner Mountains, is visible almost due south.

Turning north, the trail continues to climb before finally cresting a rise and dropping 300 feet to Patterson Lake (5.1/9715). Exceedingly deep and green, Patterson Lake was formed 1.8 million years ago through glacial erosion. Backed by the sheer layered cliffs of Warren Peak (9710), it boils with rainbow trout and is excellent for fly fishing. Rest and rejuvenate here before returning the way you came.

Nearest Visitor Center: Warner Mountain Ranger District Office or the Modoc National Forest Supervisor's Office (see Hike 61).

Backpacking Information: No wilderness permit is needed but a valid campfire permit is required. Campsites are located around Patterson Lake and in the Pine Creek Basin.

Nearest Campground: Soup Spring Campground (see Hike 61).

THE WARNERS

Hike 63—Burney Man

Location	Burney Falls
Agency	McArthur-Burney Falls Memorial State Park
Highlights	A perennial waterfall unlike any other.
Distance	1.2 miles
Total Elevation Gain/Loss	200´/200´
Hiking Time	1 hour
Difficulty	★
Best Times	April through November
Optional Map	USGS 7.5-min *Burney Falls*

Imagine a volcanic cliff 129 feet high. Over its lip twin waterfalls cascade into an iridescent pool. Springs gush from its face, showering lush vegetation with spray while birds dart through rainbow refractions of light. This is Burney Falls.

The unusual multitiered falls result from two distinct geologic layers stacked on top of each other. The upper layer is the porous Burney Basalt, which allows water to easily percolate to the non-porous formation underneath. Both layers are exposed in the cliff face, where water pours forth in a constant year-round flow. The volume of Burney Creek, spring fed less than a mile above the falls, varies little with season; the entire system gushes a steady 100 million gallons of water a day. The moist corridor below the falls is an ecologic oasis, harboring species not normally seen in the Modoc Plateau. Oregon oak, Douglas-fir, vine maple, flowering currant, and bear clover are at the far limit of their respective ranges, accompanied by the more typical assortment of Jeffrey pine, black oak, and manzanita. The fish of nearby Lake Britton attract osprey and bald eagles, sometimes seen soaring overhead.

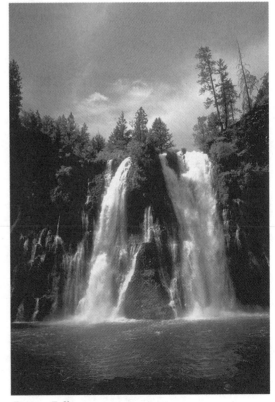

Burney Falls

The Hike is an easy loop that descends to viewpoints of Burney Falls and explores the ecology of Burney Creek with the help of interpretive placards. The park is open year-round but snow may cover the trail from Thanksgiving until April. Crowds are extremely heavy from Memorial Day through Labor Day. Fishing is popular (but challenging) in Burney Creek, although strict regulations govern the stretch of water below the falls. Above the falls, standard regulations apply and the fishing is just as good. Water is available at the trailhead.

To Reach the Trailhead, take Hwy. 89 north for 5 miles from the Hwy. 89/299 junction to the park entrance. There is a day-use fee of $5 per vehicle. Park in the lot across from the visitor center.

Description: From the parking lot, descend to the falls along the wide paved path, enjoying the cool 65°F temperature near the bottom. Continue downstream on the paved trail below large piles of broken Burney Basalt. Notice the springs that continually gush from the opposite stream bank, indicating surface exposures of the geologic formation below the basalt. Cross the first bridge and continue on the dirt trail that heads an additional 50 yards downstream and splits—go left on the Falls Trail. Heading uphill away from the creek, the trail quickly reaches the level of the falls. Although unseen, the falls sound louder and more powerful here. Cross the river above the falls on a bridge (memorialized by visitors' chisel marks) to where the trail once again divides. Head left (downstream) to another parking lot where a rock-lined pedestrian path paralleling the road gets you back to the starting point. A half mile upstream from the bridge, the riverbed springs make an interesting side trip.

Nearest Visitor Center: Park visitor center, (530) 335-2777. Open daily 10 A.M.–4 P.M.

Nearest Campground: McArthur-Burney Falls Memorial State Park Campground (128 sites, $16). Reservations are recommended in the summer.

Hike 64—It's All About the Trout

Location	Eagle Lake
Agency	Lassen National Forest
Highlights	Eagle Lake. Osprey.
Distance	0.7 mile
Total Elevation Gain/Loss	200´/200´
Hiking Time	1 hour
Difficulty	★
Best Times	June through October
Optional Map	USGS 7.5-min *Pikes Point*

Enormous Eagle Lake occupies a natural basin, drained by no stream. Water can only escape by evaporation, leaving dissolved solids behind that increase the lake's alkalinity to almost inhospitable levels. But one fish thrives in these unfriendly waters, growing to impressive size, the dream of any angler. It is the Eagle Lake trout.

Eagle Lake (5100) began some 7,000 years ago as Lake Acapsukati, a shallow body of water with approximately twice the current surface area. Initially Lake Acapsukati drained to Lake Lahontan, an enormous water system that covered vast areas of Nevada, Utah, southern Oregon, and eastern California after the end of the last Ice Age about 17,000 years ago. Subsequent volcanic activity cut off this outlet, with lava flows shaping the irregular lakeshore as recently as 1,000 years ago. Geologic activity continues today—an earthquake in 1889 lowered the lake by 2 feet! With its deepest point only 95´, Eagle Lake is still relatively shallow. The average depth of 60´ at its deepest southern end gets progressively shallower as you go north. It is the second largest natural lake entirely contained within California after Clear Lake.

Straddling a distinct ecological divide between pine forest and sage desert, the Eagle Lake basin hosts a remarkable number of plant species (280), and exhibits increasingly dry conditions going from south (with a 30" annual precipitation) to north (12"). Wildlife also abounds—especially birdlife—and bald eagles and osprey both soar above the lake. Due to the water's high alkalinity, all introduced species of fish have not survived, leaving its original five inhabitants—the speckled dace, Tahoe sucker, Eagle Lake tui chub, Lahontan redside, and Eagle Lake trout.

Eagle Lake Trout are an evolutionary mystery. Although originally thought to be related to the Lake Lahontan cutthroat trout that once populated Lake Lahontan and still exist in Pyramid Lake, Eagle Lake trout are currently considered a subspecies of rainbow trout (*oncorhyncus mykiss aquilarum*—"hooked snout trout eagle"). They grow rapidly to great size, reaching lengths of 20 inches and weights of 4 pounds within three years, and are unusually long lived. The oldest trout on record here clocked in at eleven years! Their primary historic spawning ground is Pine Creek, the largest tributary to Eagle Lake, flowing 38 miles from its headwaters in the Caribou Wilderness. During periods of drought this creek can run dry before reaching the lake, and it is possible that Eagle Lake trout developed their longevity as a response to these breeding limitations. Only the longest-lived trout survived to reproduce during episodes of multi-year drought. Today up to 200,000 one-year-old Eagle Lake trout are planted annually for anglers. Fishing is best in the fall after the lake's water has turned over, bringing the colder bottom water to the surface. This usually occurs in early October, when it is possible to catch fish from shore by casting juicy night crawlers beyond the tule reeds. The faster the lake bottom drops off from shore, the better. One catch: the worse the weather, the better the fishing. Hard-core anglers will be out at sunrise on bitterly cold mornings. Summer fishing is barely worth it.

The Hike follows the only existing hiking trail around Eagle Lake, a short and very easy path called the Osprey Trail. Hiking weather is best in the summer and osprey can often be seen during nesting season, which lasts from March until October. Snow flies by November. No water is available at the trailhead.

To Reach the Trailhead, take Hwy. A1 (Eagle Lake Rd.) north from Hwy. 36—the turnoff is 2 miles west of Susanville. After 13.1 miles, turn right onto Gallatin Rd., heading toward the marina. In 1.5 miles turn right again, staying on Gallatin Rd. where the main road continues to the marina. Ronald McDonald Camp is 1.0 mile farther, and the parking lot is just beyond it on the left where the pavement ends.

Description
Throughout this hike, scan the trees for osprey nests and the skies for the birds' telltale white undersides. These large raptors feed in the lake, swooping

fish from the water with their talons. From the trailhead the path passes beneath platy ponderosa pine but soon deposits you in a maze of old roads—head left to reach the lakeshore. Whaleback Mtn. (6924) is visible across the lake, as is evidence of the plentiful logging activity in Lassen National Forest. Walk north along the sandy beach bordered by rabbit brush and a few pioneering pines. Note the volcanic rocks scattered around you, remnants of flows that shaped the landscape here. Air bubbles solidified in the rock as it quickly cooled. The trail narrows as it continues along the rocky shores; white fir and incense cedar appear as you turn away from the lake and begin climbing. After 100 feet of elevation gain, you reach an overlook where the Pine Creek drainage can be discerned northwest. An access road continues to this overlook and you can return along it for the shortest return to the trailhead.

Nearest Visitor Center: Eagle Lake Visitor Center, (530) 257-4188, located on Eagle Lake Rd. 0.2 mile north of the Hwy. A1/36 junction. Open Monday through Friday 8 A.M.–4:30 P.M.

Nearest Campground: Eagle Campground, located on Gallatin Rd. (45 sites).

It's All About the Trout

Hike 65—Thousand Lakes Volcano

Location	Thousands Lakes Wilderness
Agency	Lassen National Forest
Highlights	The remote rim of an extinct volcano. Backcountry lakes.
Distance	12.0 miles round trip
Total Elevation Gain/Loss	3200´/3200´
Hiking Time	5–7 hours
Difficulty	★★★★
Best Times	July through September
Optional Map	Forest Service *Ishi, Thousand Lakes,* and *Caribou Wildernesses* topographic map

Thousand Lakes offers a less-traveled wilderness in the Modoc Plateau, complete with alpine lakes and sweeping mountain summits. Here you can contemplate the construction and destruction of a volcano from atop an eroding crater rim.

Spawned from the same volcanic activity that created Lassen Peak, Thousand Lakes Volcano has not been active in historical times. Although it was likely created within the past million years, it has been dormant long enough for a glacier to eat away its northeastern slopes and leave a horseshoe of peaks around the former crater. One of them, Crater Peak (8683), is the highest point in Lassen National Forest. Thousand Lakes Wilderness is small, only 16,335 acres, and does not have one thousand lakes—more like a dozen.

The Hike ascends Magee Peak (8549), one of the peaks along the volcano's summit rim, passing several lakes along the way. Two of them, Everett and Magee, are located roughly midway and make a worthwhile destination for those unprepared for the full ascent. Our approach from Cypress trailhead in the northwestern corner of the wilderness receives lighter use than Tamarack trailhead farther east. While this approach adds about 500 feet of elevation gain, it avoids the popular but less exciting Lake Eiler area. You are more likely to encounter equestrians than hikers on this trail. Fishing is worthwhile throughout the wilderness. No water is available at the trailhead and none can be easily obtained for the first 3.5 miles and 1,600 feet of ascent.

To Reach the Trailhead, prepare yourself to cover some dirt roads. Take Hwy. 89 north from the Hwy. 89/44 junction in Old Station for 10.7 miles to the turnoff for Forest Service Road 26, located 0.2 mile past the Hat Creek Work Center. Approaching from the north, the turnoff is located 1.5 miles south of the Hat Creek Fire Station and post office. Reset your odometer at the turnoff and head west on the unpaved road to the first junction (mile 3.3)—bear right to continue on FS Rd. 26. Turn left at the next junction (mile 4.8), still continuing on FS Rd. 26. At mile 7.6, turn left onto FS Rd. 34N60 and follow it to the road's end at mile 10.0. The information sign at the head of the parking area marks the trailhead.

Description: From the trailhead (0.0/5520), you pass through stands of sugar pine, red and white fir, juniper, and Jeffrey pine before quickly crossing

THOUSAND LAKES VOLCANO

rocky and seasonally dry Eiler Gulch. From here, a steady climb brings you into the wilderness. Shortly after the weathered boundary sign (1.0/6240) the trail levels out and reaches a junction (1.2/6330)—go right toward Barrett and Magee lakes. A left turn would bring you to large but shallow Lake Eiler, a side trip not recommended unless you are desperate for water. Crossing Eiler Gulch, bear right again at two, subsequent, nearby junctions and stay on the trail (3E04) toward Magee Peak.

The trail switchbacks steeply southwest before leveling out in a forest where western white and lodgepole pine enter the mix. Mountain hemlock can also be identified near the lakes. After a long, level stretch and a brief climb, you pass dried-up Upper Twin Lake and soon reach Everett Lake (3.6/7180). Magee Lake is next, accessed by going left on the unposted spur trail after Everett Lake. Both lakes are pretty and deep, good for relaxing and swimming.

Now climbing again, you enter the heart of the ancient volcano with Crater Peak towering above to the west. The trees are now almost exclusively mountain hemlock, although a smattering of whitebark pine can also be seen. The views become more expansive as you ascend up-canyon past the prominent red outcrops to the east, climbing nine steep switchbacks on the loose upper slopes to finally reach the summit ridge (5.3/8400). Traverse west along the ridge to stand on top of Magee Peak (5.5/8549).

As you look northeast, the scouring force of the glacier that carved this volcano is obvious. The broad valley formed by the glacier turns east below Freaner Peak (7485), a satellite vent of the same volcanic complex. Fredonyer Peak (8054) is the summit on the ridge extending due east from the crater rim. Lassen Peak (10457) is an easy landmark to the south, and Chaos Crags (Hike 66) are visible below its northern flanks. The ridge extending west from Lassen Peak ends in Brokeoff Mtn. (9235, Hike 67), the highest remnant of Mt. Tehama. This ancient volcano once rose above present-day Lassen Volcanic National Park and was probably contemporary with Thousand Lakes Volcano. Return the way you came.

Nearest Visitor Center: Hat Creek Visitor Center, located in Old Station at the Hwy. 89/44 junction. Open mid-June through mid-September daily 9:30 A.M.–5 P.M., mid-September through mid-December Friday through Sunday 10 A.M.–4 P.M. The Hat Creek Ranger District Office, (530) 336-5521, is located in Fall River Mills on Hwy. 299.

Backpacking Information: No wilderness permit is required but a valid campfire permit is necessary. Both Everett and Magee lakes have good campsites.

Nearest Campground: Honn Campground, 2.1 miles south of the turnoff for FS Rd. 26 on Hwy. 89 (6 sites, $8).

Hike 66—Chaos

Location	Chaos Crags
Agency	Lassen Volcanic National Park
Highlights	An ephemeral frog pond below a 2,000′-high jumble of volcanic rock.
Distance	4.0 miles round trip
Total Elevation Gain/Loss	1050′/1050′
Hiking Time	2–3 hours
Difficulty	★★
Best Times	mid-June through September
Optional Map	USGS 7.5-min *Manzanita Lake*

Roughly 1,000 years ago, lava was extruded from Lassen Peak's northern flank. Too viscous to flow downhill, it piled up as giant domes of solid rock covered in loose rubble—Chaos Crags. A minor explosion about 300 years ago along Chaos Crags' northwestern slope triggered a huge landslide that traveled more than two miles to dam Manzanita Creek and form Manzanita Lake. Dubbed the Chaos Jumbles, the chaotic remains of the slide are plainly evident today.

The Hike climbs from the northwest corner of the park to tiny Crags Lake at the base of Chaos Crags. The "lake" is really a small pond fed only by snowmelt, which slowly evaporates over the course of the summer. Although largest in late June, it's never really big enough to be nice for swimming. Depending on conditions, it can be completely dry by August or remain as a tiny puddle throughout the season. Visitation here is relatively light, especially compared to other national parks. No water is available at the trailhead.

To Reach the Trailhead, take Hwy. 89 to the Loomis Museum in the northwest corner of the park, located 0.4 mile east of the Manzanita Lake Entrance Station. There is a $10 entrance fee for

Lassen Volcanic National Park, valid for seven days. At the east end of the museum parking lot, turn south on the road to Manzanita Lake. The trailhead is almost immediately on the left in 0.1 mile. If there is no space for your vehicle here, park in the museum lot and walk to the trailhead.

Description: The path, running within earshot of rushing Manzanita Creek, is initially outlined with large volcanic boulders. Jeffrey pine and white fir compose this open forest. The trail soon arcs away from the creek into dense trees and shortly passes a lush spring, which feeds a brook lined with alder trees. Sugar pine and red fir begin to appear. A few scattered Douglas-fir can be identified, too, by their distinctive cones around you on the ground. The trail next ascends adjacent to the hummocky moonscape of Chaos Jumbles, occasionally visible through the trees. Chaos Crags increasingly loom east above the treetops, where the trail enters more open terrain carpeted with manzanita scrub. You pass through lodgepole pine a few hundred feet before breaking out into a rough boulder field with epic views of Chaos Crags.

The final stretch to Crags Lake (6630) is the most challenging, a 100-foot descent through sand and loose rock. Hundreds of tadpoles inhabit the lake and many mature frogs lurk along the moist shore, hurtling themselves into nearby rocks at the approach of the curious hiker. Most trees here are sugar pine, although a few white fir and Jeffrey pine can be seen. A small chokecherry sits above the east end of the pond. Also known as Chaos Crater, this basin was created from the blast that triggered the massive landslide of Chaos Jumbles. Above, the pink scree slopes of Chaos Crags are deceptively high (not recommended for exploration); it's 1,900 feet from the lake to the top of the highest promontory (8530).

Nearest Visitor Center: Loomis Museum and Visitor Center, (530) 595-4444 ext. 5187. Open mid-June through September daily 9 A.M.–5 P.M., open weekends only Memorial Day until mid-June.

Nearest Campground: Manzanita Lake Campground, located on the south side of Manzanita Lake (179 sites, $14).

Additional Information: *www.nps.gov/lavo*

CHAOS

Hike 67—Broke Off

Location	Brokeoff Mountain
Agency	Lassen Volcanic National Park
Highlights	The eroded lip of an ancient volcano. Far-reaching views of modern volcanoes.
Distance	7.4 miles round trip
Total Elevation Gain/Loss	2600´/2600´
Hiking Time	4–6 hours
Difficulty	★★★★
Best Times	July through September
Optional Map	USGS 7.5-min *Lassen Peak*

While everybody likes to climb Lassen Peak, try Brokeoff Mountain instead—a less-traveled peak with views every bit as exceptional.

Brokeoff Mountain (9235) is the highest remnant of the former Mt. Tehama, a huge stratovolcano, which began erupting 600,000 years ago and grew to be over 11 miles wide at its base. Erosion and structural collapse wasted the volcano core once major activity stopped 200,000 years ago, leaving only the volcanic slopes. Lassen Peak (10457) was formed from more recent eruptions along the eroded eastern flanks of Mt. Tehama some 11,000 years ago.

The Hike climbs Brokeoff Mountain from the park road near the south entrance station, a strenuous trip flush with wildflowers in July and early August. Snow can linger a long time in Lassen Volcanic National Park, and usually does not disappear on this trail until very late June or early July. While less popular than the Lassen Peak Trail, this hike still receives ample use during the summer. No water is available at the trailhead but sources are plentiful along the first half of the hike.

To Reach the Trailhead, take Hwy. 89 to the park's southwest edge. The trailhead is 0.4 mile south of the entrance

station on the west side of the road. Parking is opposite the trailhead. There is a $10 entrance fee for Lassen Volcanic National Park, valid for seven days. Those approaching from the south are still required to pay at the entrance station.

Description From the trailhead (0.0/6600), you immediately start climbing through dense alder thickets. After crossing a small stream, the trail breaks out into a more open forest of red fir, incense cedar, and western white pine. The rocky pyramid of Brokeoff's summit is a beacon already visible northwest above the trees as you continue upward to rejoin the earlier stream. Paralleling the water, the trail crosses a small creek outlet (1.2/7460) from tiny, unseen Forest Lake, and then starts to climb more rapidly. As you gain elevation, mountain hemlock appear and soon views open up—Lake Almanor is visible southeast and Forest Lake just below you. Leaving the creek (and your last water source), you traverse below the imposing southeast face of Brokeoff Mtn., making a few switchbacks among dense mats of lupine before cresting the mountain's south ridge (2.4/8400). On a steady ascending traverse northwest, you have good views west across the

Great Central Valley. All the trees here are mountain hemlock, most bursting with tiny cones. Near the ridgetop, the trail cuts back east, passing below a satellite summit before finally reaching the top (3.7/9235). A few scraggly whitebark pines and an anomalous, krummholz Jeffrey pine are growing from the rocky hillside just below the summit.

Grab a seat on the flat summit and admire the view. Looking northeast, Mt. Diller (9087) is the highest peak between you and imposing Lassen Peak. Mt. Diller is another remnant of Mt. Tehama; the bands exposed below its western ridge are hardened flows that once coursed down the western flanks of the long-gone volcano. North beyond these bands are Chaos Crags (Hike 66) and more distant Thousand Lakes Volcano (Hike 65). Turning east-southeast, Mt. Conard (8204) is the bare sandy looking ridgetop across the deep valley of Mill Creek. Some 200,000 years ago, the towering summit of Mt. Tehama rose between you and Mt. Conard directly above today's Sulphur Works, the park-

ing lot of which is visible more than 2,000 feet below. Back down you go!

Nearest Visitor Center: Southwest Information Station, (530) 595-3308, located by the Lassen Chalet just north of the southwest entrance station. Open mid-June through Labor Day daily 9 A.M.–4 P.M. Park headquarters is in Mineral, (530) 595-4444, located on Hwy. 36 five miles west of the Hwy. 89/36 junction south of the park. Open Monday through Friday 8 A.M.–4:30 P.M.

Backpacking Information: While backpacking is allowed on this hike, the lack of good campsites makes it less appealing than dayhiking. A wilderness permit is required and can be obtained at the visitor centers, as well as at the southwest entrance station and the Loomis Museum (see Hike 66).

Nearest Campground: Southwest Campground, a walk-in campground by the southwest entrance station (21 sites, $12). The Summit Lake campgrounds in the center of the park are the closest drive-in options.

Additional Information: *www.nps.gov/lavo*

BROKE OFF

Hike 68—Baking with the Devil

Location	Devils Kitchen
Agency	Lassen Volcanic National Park
Highlights	Geothermal action away from the crowds.
Distance	5.0 miles round trip
Total Elevation Gain/Loss	700´/700´
Hiking Time	2–3 hours
Difficulty	★★
Best Times	mid-June through September
Optional Map	USGS 7.5-min *Reading Peak*

California lives, breathing outward in hissing fumaroles and fetid mudpots! While most experience bubbling volcanic activity along the mobbed trail to Bumpass Hell, you should come—away from the crowds—to Devils Kitchen.

Underneath Lassen Volcanic National Park, at least 6 miles deep, is a large body of molten rock. Groundwater encountering it is heated to extraordinary temperatures sometimes in excess of 500°F. Kept in liquid form by intense pressures found at such depth, the super-heated water rises and flashes to steam near the surface. Boiling pools and billowing fumaroles are the result. Most of the hot water rises vertically to Bumpass Hell but several substantial lateral flows exist, including the one spewing out at Devils Kitchen.

The Hike is an easy one, following Hot Springs Creek to a substantial area of geothermal activity. It is a quieter section, accessed far from the main park road and receiving light use. A great early summer hike for wildflowers, it generally receives light use in the fall. While no water is available at the trailhead, Hot Springs Creek is accessible early on.

To Reach the Trailhead, take Hwy. 36 to Chester and turn north on Feather River Drive—the turnoff is across from Plumas Bank in the east end of town. In 0.7 mile, bear left at the fork to stay on Feather River Rd. Drive 5.2 miles to another fork. Bear right and follow Warner Valley Road 9.7 miles to the trailhead parking lot, located on the left immediately past Warner Valley Campground. The last 2.8 miles are unpaved. A $10 entrance fee is due at the self-pay entrance station just inside the park boundary.

Description At the trailhead (0.0/5670), brochures are available for Boiling Springs Lake Nature Trail, a 3-mile interpretive trail to Cold Boiling Lake that parallels this hike for a short distance to stop 9. Our trail begins on the PCT and immediately heads to Hot Springs Creek, briefly following it before crossing a rusting metal bridge and heading slightly upslope. A hot spring can be seen flowing directly out of the ground at stop 8, the water almost too hot to touch. This water, along with that from other nearby hot springs, flows into the baths at Drakesbad Guest Ranch visible across the broad meadow. Unfortunately, the baths are for guests only.

At stop 9 the trail reaches a four-way junction (0.3/5730) by a large incense cedar. The Cold Boiling Lake Nature Trail and PCT head left, straight leads to Drake Lake, but you turn right and head back downslope. You reach another junction immediately prior to recrossing the creek. Turning left here leads to Dream Lake, a nearby shallow pond where beaver can sometimes be spotted, but you continue straight across the alder-choked stream and enter the wide, open meadow. A few paths from the ranch join your trail, now winding along the north side of the meadow. You reenter a dense forest of predominantly white fir (1.1/5760) and soon reach another junction. An optional return trail splits left to join the trail leading to Drake Lake. A slow and gentle climb ahead toward Devils Kitchen ends by a hitching post atop a small rise, where the sulfuric stench of geothermal activity first assaults your nose.

A 0.5-mile loop trail runs through Devils Kitchen, with informative placards and a stern warning not to go off the trail. Enjoy the fantastic hues of technicolor rock, accompanied by the dull roar of venting fumaroles and the musical bass of bubbling mudpots.

Nearest Visitor Center: Warner Valley Ranger Station, located just east of Warner Valley Campground, open sporadically—try knocking on the door. See Hike 67 for other park information centers.

Nearest Campground: Warner Valley Campground, located 0.5 mile east of the trailhead (18 sites, $12).

Additional Information: *www.nps.gov/lavo*

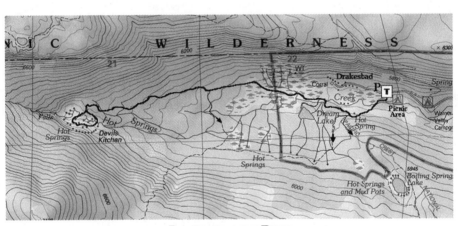

BAKING WITH THE DEVIL

Hike 69—Ridge World

Location	Keddie Ridge
Agency	Lassen National Forest
Highlights	A remote ridge with lakes along the Sierra's northern frontier.
Distance	5.2 miles round trip
Total Elevation Gain/Loss	900′/900′
Hiking Time	3–4 hours
Difficulty	★★
Best Times	mid-June through September
Optional Map	USGS 7.5-min *Greenville*

Keddie Ridge marks the northern limit of the Sierra Nevada. It is here—on this last exposure of ancient rock, in these beautiful alpine lakes—that the Sierra Nevada makes its final appearance before diving below the Modoc Plateau.

The rocks of Keddie Ridge are old, far older than the young rocks of the Modoc Plateau, and even more ancient than all the Sierra Nevada granite. They are the remnants of volcanic activity 350 million years ago in what was once a great island arc of volcanoes far offshore from ancient North America. Accreted to the continent some 250 million years ago, the rocks were tilted on end and exposed in broad bands that stretch for miles. Condensed ash and lava flows formed primarily from submarine eruptions, the rocks were altered by distinctive metavolcanics of the present-day ridge (Durrell 1987).

The Hike is a gentle traverse from Homer Lake to Deerheart Lake along the upper northeast slopes of Keddie Ridge, with a worthwhile side trip to small Hidden Lake halfway along. A rough, 12-mile-long dirt road together with an unposted destination deters most people. Bears are reportedly numerous in this isolated ridgetop ecosystem—take bear precautions. Fishing is possible in Homer and Deerheart lakes. No water is available at the trailhead but Homer Lake is immediately accessible.

To Reach the Trailhead, take Hwy. 89 west from Main St. in Greenville for 2.5 miles to an unposted turnoff on the right, directly across from Wolf Creek Rd. Approaching from the west, the turnoff is 6.3 miles east of the Hwy. 147/89 junction. Reset your odometer. From the turnoff (mile 0.0), the paved road soon becomes dirt after a SNOW NOT REMOVED BEYOND THIS POINT sign. At mile 1.9, bear right at the junction toward Homer Lake. Climbing steadily to the saddle above Indian Valley, you get great views. At the junction here (mile 7.8), go left on FS Rd. 28N60. You reach an unposted fork after 2.9 miles (mile 9.7). Turn left and follow this road 2.1 miles to its end at a large cul-de-sac (mile 11.8).

Description: From the parking lot (0.0/6700), the trail drops down among Douglas-fir and Jeffrey pine to immediately reach Homer Lake at a level clearing. The circular lake, which provides deep swimming and fishing holes, is flanked to the south by the towering jumble of Keddie Peak (7499). The trail follows the northeast lakeshore to cross the small outflow creek, where it is possible to continue around the lake. The hike goes right, however, descending four quick switchbacks through dense tree cover; you emerge on a short, open traverse beneath huge rock piles. Glacial polish is in evidence before you cross a small but pretty stream cascading across the trail. Mountain Meadows Reservoir is visible north.

After a gentle ascent, you soon encounter an unposted junction (1.5/ 6270), where a trail flanked by two, small incense cedars strikes left uphill. This is the trail to Hidden Lake 300 feet above you, accessed via seven steep switchbacks along a somewhat overgrown trail. It is a very worthwhile side trip.

As you continue on the main trail, the forest becomes thick and the path overgrown in places. With forest debris

everywhere, it is obvious that no wildfire has occurred here recently. After a stretch of mostly level walking, you drop down to Deerheart Lake (2.6/6319), another deep-blue lake good for fishing, swimming, and relaxing.

Nearest Visitor Center: Chester-Almanor Ranger Station, (530) 258-2141, located on Hwy. 36 just west of Chester. Open Monday through Saturday 8 A.M.–4:30 P.M.

Backpacking Information: Campfire permit required. The only campsites are at Homer and Deerheart lakes.

Nearest Campground: Greenville County Park Campground, located 1 mile north of Greenville on Hwy. 89.

Additional Information:
www.r5.fs.fed.us/lassen

RIDGE WORLD

Hike 70—Ishi

Location	Ishi Wilderness
Agency	Lassen National Forest
Highlights	A remote world of rugged cliffs and canyons.
Distance	2.0 miles
Total Elevation Gain/Loss	750´/750´
Hiking Time	1–2 hours
Difficulty	★★★
Best Times	Spring and Fall
Optional Map	Forest Service *Ishi, Thousand Lakes,* and *Caribou Wildernesses* topographic map

Here, dark basalt cliffs compose inaccessible canyons—a place that once sheltered Ishi, the last of the Yahi Indians. Before the Gold Rush, the Yahi occupied a vast region in the foothills southwest of Lassen Peak. By 1865 nearly the entire Yahi nation had been wiped out, the victim of disease, atrocity, and ruthless extermination by encroaching settlers. Only a tiny band survived, disappearing into the rugged terrain around Mill and Deer creeks in 1872. They lived in traditional fashion—hunting with bow and arrow and gathering what the land provided—but their numbers slowly dwindled. By the early 1890s Ishi and only four others remained, living in a tiny settlement perched on a narrow ledge 500 feet above the creek. When surveyors stumbled across Ishi fishing with a harpoon in the river in 1908, the Yahi survivors fled into the surrounding hills. But by the year's end only Ishi still lived.

The Hike is a short exploratory loop of Deer Creek, once the center of the Yahi people and later Ishi's final refuge. In order to complete the loop, it is necessary to ford Deer Creek—be prepared for waist-deep water on the crossing year-round. The creek swells with snowmelt and can be impassable during spring and early summer—try the easier out-

and-back adventure along the more scenic north side during these times. Spring is the best time to visit, when wildflowers and pleasant temperatures are common. Summers are brutally hot and should be avoided, but mild weather returns in the fall. Fishing is possible in Deer Creek but special restrictions apply—check current regulations. Beware poison oak and ticks in the brush. Due to the difficulty of access, crowds are light here. Water is available from Deer Creek.

To Reach the Trailhead it is important to have a high-clearance vehicle, because the final 13 road miles are unpaved and rough. From Hwy. 99, take the Cohasset Rd. off-ramp just north of Chico and follow Cohasset Ridge Rd. northeast. The pavement ends 16 miles from the freeway. Continue on 7.2 miles of dirt and gravel to reach a Y-junction—bear right toward Deer Creek (a painted rock by the roadside indicated it in 1999). Forest Service Rd. 24OH goes right 1.1 miles past this junction, but you continue straight another scant 0.05 mile. Go left at the unposted fork and descend 5.0 miles to the Deer Creek bridge. The southern trailhead is located by the Ishi Wilderness information signs just before the bridge. The northern trailhead is immediately across the creek. Approaching the wilderness by road from the northeast is possible but not recommended.

Description From the southern trailhead (0.0/1700), the hike begins on Devils Den Trail and immediately crosses a small creek. In 0.1 mile, you pass a small wilderness boundary placard hammered to a ponderosa pine; the trail stays left, away from the creek. Douglas-fir, canyon live oak, black oak, incense cedar, California bay, ponderosa pine, and alder compose this low-elevation forest, with a thick undergrowth of blackberries, wild grape vines, toyon, and poison oak. On this north-facing slope, plants are protected from the heat of the sun's rays, and even delicate ferns survive in the dribbling stream gullies.

The river remains largely inaccessible where the trail climbs two switchbacks, traversing briefly 100 feet above the river before descending steeply to cross Little Pine Creek. After this crossing, Devils Den Trail turns abruptly up-slope away from the water, but you follow the faint path that heads toward Deer Creek. Reaching the river by a pleasant swimming hole, continue downstream to the long riffle located above the next pool. This is the crossing (1.3/1550).

Once on the other side of Deer Creek, follow the grassy clearing uphill to find the trail. On these drier south-facing slopes, the vegetation changes dramatically. Juniper, blue oak, and gray pine are common away from the river. California buckeye, redbud, and live oak grow closer to the water. While the trail continues 12 miles downstream, your route turns up-canyon and immediately begins climbing above the river through a bizarre world of volcanic cliffs and pillars.

Over the past million years, ancient volcanoes near today's Lassen Volcanic National Park sent periodic mudflows coursing across the land. A jumble of rocks, mud, and ash, the mudflows solidified in layers, which were later exposed as Deer Creek eroded through them. Threading two impressive pillars, the trail descends briefly and then climbs, making a long traverse through a dense forest of ponderosa pine, black oak, and manzanita before descending abruptly to the trailhead.

As you soon will, Ishi left this wilderness and entered the modern world. Found in a corral outside of Chico, he became an overnight sensation and attracted the attention of anthropologists at the University of California. Brought to San Francisco on August 9, 1911, Ishi lived a mostly private life in the Museum

Ishi's World

of Anthropology until his death in March 1916 from tuberculosis. Under the genuine care of many benefactors, Ishi adapted surprisingly well to civilization and contributed valuable information about an ancient way of life now completely extinct (Kroeber 1961).

Nearest Visitor Center: Very distant Chester-Almanor Ranger Station, (530) 258-2141, located on Hwy. 36 just west of Chester. Open Monday through Saturday 8 A.M.–4:30 P.M.

Backpacking Information: No wilderness permit is needed but a valid campfire permit is required. There are numerous campsites down-river along Deer Creek.

Nearest Campground: Gaither Camp, located 0.5 mile north of the Deer Creek bridge at the end of an unposted turnoff (free, river water only).

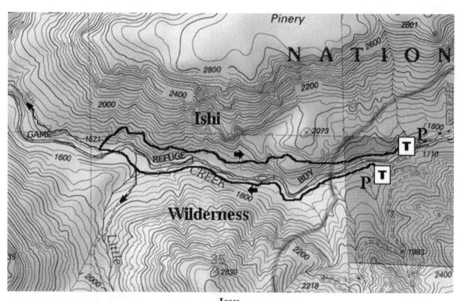

ISHI

Hike 71—Bidwell Did Well

Location	Bidwell Park
Agency	City of Chico
Highlights	Bountiful valley woodlands. A basalt gorge.
Distance	3.5 miles round trip
Total Elevation Gain/Loss	600´/600´
Hiking Time	3–5 hours
Difficulty	★★
Best Times	Spring and Fall
Optional Map	USGS 7.5-min *Richardson Springs, Paradise West*

Bidwell Park provides a living diorama—a glimpse of the bounty and rich diversity of life that once flourished in the Great Central Valley. It's also good for swimming.

In 1905 John and Annie Bidwell donated this land to the city of Chico for the public's use and enjoyment. The third largest municipal park in the country after New York's Central Park and Portland's Forest Park, it is a beautiful tract along Big Chico Creek, a lush riparian alley winding through dry oak woodlands. Fremont cottonwood, California bay, willow, Oregon ash, white alder, California box elder, big leaf maple, and California sycamore line the creek; their trunks are interwoven by the twisting tendrils of wild grape vines. Valley oak, blue oak, interior live oak, canyon live oak, gray pine, California buckeye, black walnut, and the Chinese stink tree thrive on the dry slopes away from the creek (Boze 1998). Flowers and some trees offer seasonal displays of color, and birdlife abounds year-round. In Upper Bidwell Park, sheer canyons carved through erosion-resistant basalt result in wild formations of rock, stripped clean of soil and plant life for long sections.

The Hike winds along Big Chico Creek in upper Bidwell Park, passing through lush creekside vegetation before threading up through basalt outcroppings to the canyon rim and park road. (A bicycle or vehicle left at parking lot P would facilitate an easy return to the trailhead.) While the hike can be done year-round, it is sizzling in the summer months with daily highs hovering around 100°F. Fall and spring provide the most ideal temperatures. Sun protection is always worth having. Fishing is prohibited in Big Chico Creek. No water is available at the trailhead.

To Reach the Trailhead, take Hwy. 99 in Chico to the East 8th St./Hwy. 32 off-ramp and head east on E. 8th St. for 1.8 miles to Chico Canyon Rd. Turn left and go 0.6 mile to Centennial Ave. Turn right, and 0.5 mile farther turn right again onto Wildwood Ave., immediately beyond the sign for Upper Bidwell Park. After 1.7 miles of road, with speed bumps by the golf course, you reach a gate closed Sunday and Monday. If you're here on those days, park and walk the short distance to the trailhead. The trailhead is in parking lot F, 0.6 mile past the gate on the right. The last 0.4 mile is unpaved.

Description From the parking lot (0.0/300), take the widest, most obvious trail down to the creek and begin heading upstream. Throughout this hike numerous use paths branch this way and that, but the main trail close to the stream is generally obvious. A posted spur trail soon leads down to the Day Camp swimming area, overshadowed by layered basalt—a pancake stack—exposed near the top of the opposite cut bank.

Known as the Lovejoy Basalt, it's a result of volcanic flows 18 million years old that originated somewhere east of present-day Susanville. With no intervening mountains present at the time, the flows coursed southwest, nearly reaching the present site of Winters in the middle of the Great Central Valley. Existing rocks in what is now Bidwell Park were coated with a thick layer of erosion-resistant basalt. The underlying rocks compose the Chico Formation, formed approximately 75–100 million years ago just offshore from the continental edge. Sediments washed into the sea were deposited in beds thousands of feet thick, becoming shale and sandstone over time. Where exposed by the downcutting of Big Chico Creek, this formation provides good soil for the rich plant life around you.

Continuing upstream, you soon reach Bear Hole (0.7/300), where there's a remarkable change in scenery. Here the creek has not eroded through the Lovejoy Formation and instead flows through surprising basalt formations bare of most vegetation. Numerous signs warn of the swimming hazards in this treacherous section. From here, it is possible to walk along the creek a short distance on the remains of an old cement flume. Passing through a narrow basalt gorge with sheer, 40-foot walls, the flume ends at an old diversion dam. A mildly precarious stairway requires a bit of scrambling to get to here. An alternative stretch of trail skirts this section along the canyon rim.

Now at the top of the stairs, follow the shadeless trail along the canyon rim to an overlook of Salmon Hole (1.6/530), a deep, accessible swimming spot in the gorge below. Beyond this point, the canyon below becomes wider and difficult to access. It is possible to continue to the northern reaches of upper Bidwell Park, but this hike—having sampled what the park offers—ends where the trail rejoins the park road at parking lot

BIDWELL DID WELL

P. Return the way you came or via the park road.

Nearest Visitor Center: Chico Creek Nature Center, (530) 891-4671, located on E. 8th St. 1 mile east of the Hwy. 99 off-ramp. Open Tuesday through Sunday 11 A.M.–4 P.M.

Nearest Campground: None close to Chico. The closest Forest Service campgrounds are more than 40 miles northeast of Chico along Hwy. 32.

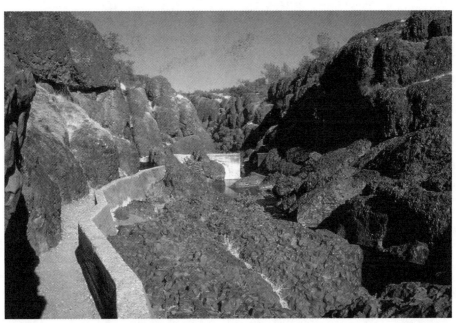

Above Bear Hole on Big Chico Creek

Hike 72—Wild Feather

Location	Middle Fork Feather River
Agency	Plumas National Forest
Highlights	Deep wilderness. Untouched forest. Crystalline river.
Distance	7.0 miles round trip
Total Elevation Gain/Loss	2900´/2900´
Hiking Time	4–6 hours
Difficulty	★★★★★
Best Times	mid-July through September
Optional Map	USGS 7.5-min *Haskins Valley*

Not an easy hike, this is an introduction to Middle Fork Feather River country, perhaps the deepest, least hospitable wilderness in California.

Below the bridge on Quincy-La Porte Rd., the Middle Fork Feather flows inaccessible to vehicles for over 30 miles, as it rushes below steep canyon slopes 2,000–3,000-feet high. Numerous mines dotted the region in the past, and many of today's trails (including this one) are their former access roads. The geology of the Feather River region is incredibly complex. Exposed rocks range in age from approximately 150 million years to over 400 million years, making the mix far older than the typical Sierra Nevada granite. This hike descends into one of the most poorly understood geologic provinces in California, a jumble of metamorphosed blocks accreted to North America approximately 250 million years ago.

The Hike follows Little California Trail, which drops 2,450 feet along a seldom-used jeep road to a point just above the river. The remaining 300 feet of descent is a harrowing bushwhack. It is highly unlikely that you will see anybody else, regardless of when you go. Fishing is excellent with native rainbows particularly abundant. There is no water at the trailhead or anywhere before the bottom.

To Reach the Trailhead, take Bucks Lake Rd. west from Quincy (the turnoff is downtown by the courthouse) toward Meadow Valley. In 8.7 miles turn left onto Big Creek Rd. and proceed 6.2 miles to Forest Service Road 60. This is the end of the pavement. Reset your odometer and turn left. Reaching a fork at mile 1.7, bear left on FS Rd. 23N19. Beyond the Lookout Rock trailhead, the road reaches a T-junction at mile 3.9—go right on FS Rd. 23N55. You reach an unposted four-way junction at mile 6.0; those with low-clearance vehicles should park here and walk to the trailhead. The rest can turn left and go 0.7 mile to the trailhead, in a small lot where the road narrows. A sign warns would-be motorists that the road beyond this point is steep, narrow, and 4WD only.

Description From the trailhead (0.0/5330), follow the jeep road, briefly passing through a thick forest of dogwood, red fir, and sugar pine, and then along a level, more-open stretch lined with manzanita. You get the best views of the hike along this early section. Curving east into tree cover, the trail passes several large ponderosa pines and Douglas-firs, and soon begins its steep, unrelenting descent. As the elevation drops switchback by switchback, the vegetation slowly changes. Sugar pine and red fir quickly disappear, replaced by increasing numbers of incense cedar, ponderosa pine and, especially, black oak. Canyon live oak can be seen near the bottom.

The jeep road abruptly terminates in a forest of black oak, where there's a table hammered to a tree (3.2/2750). The barely discernible trail continues beyond the washout gully that blocks the road. With a keen eye pick out the path traversing slowly downward through thick brush. Watch your footing on the steep slopes in this section. Before long, a discernible path bears off, dropping more directly down toward the river (3.5/2450). Although challenging, it's rewarding to explore the Middle Fork Feather River both up- and downstream...at least for a little bit.

Nearest Visitor Center: Mt. Hough District Ranger Station, (530) 283-0555, located 3 miles north of Quincy on Hwy. 70. Open Monday through Friday 8 A.M.–4:30 P.M.

Backpacking Information: Valid campfire permit required. There are a few campsites where the jeep road ends.

Nearest Campground: Numerous campgrounds around Bucks Lake.

WILD FEATHER

Hike 73—Look Out

Location	Sierra Buttes
Agency	Tahoe National Forest
Highlights	Sierra Buttes. The fire lookout on top.
Distance	11.0 miles round trip
Total Elevation Gain/Loss	3200´/3200´
Hiking Time	8–10 hours
Difficulty	★★★★
Best Times	July through September
Optional Map	USGS 7.5-min *Sierra City*

Sierra Buttes soar, powerful monoliths of naked rock that burst from the sylvan terrain of the North Fork Yuba River. Atop their highest peak a tower perches—a lookout for wildfire with commanding views.

Part of a complicated geologic puzzle, the rocks of Sierra Buttes were probably formed during the eruptions of ancient undersea volcanoes some 350 million years ago. Accreted to North America more than 200 million years ago, their resistance to erosion has left them exposed as naked mountains today.

The Hike is a long, challenging ascent of Sierra Buttes from Lower Sardine Lake and provides the full Sierra Buttes experience of scenery, lakes, and summit vista. Two alternative access trails—one via the Pacific Crest Trail, one via Tamarack Lakes—offer shorter routes to the summit. Both these trails miss out on the exceptional views of Sierra Buttes above Sardine Lakes, however. Via the Pacific Crest Trail, the round trip to the summit is 4.6 miles with an elevation gain/loss of 1,600 feet. Via the Tamarack Lakes, the round trip is 6.2 miles with an elevation gain/loss of 2,300 feet. With two vehicles or one vehicle and a bicycle, you can begin at Lower Sardine Lake and exit via the PCT, sparing your knees considerable downhill compression. Snow can linger deep into June and the trail is usually not snow-free until July. While the Sardine lakes are an extremely popular fishing destination with heavy crowds all summer long, only a small percentage of people are on the trail. Fishing is possible at the Tamarack lakes and both are planted annually with fingerling trout. Water is available near the Lower Sardine Lake trailhead but not at the two alternative trailheads. Sources are scarce along the trail—Tamarack lakes near that trailhead are your only sure bet.

To Reach the Trailhead, take Hwy. 49 to Bassetts Station, located 5 miles east of Sierra City and 14 miles west of Sattley. Turn north onto Gold Lake Rd., proceed 1.2 miles, and turn left toward Sardine and Packer lakes. In 0.3 mile the road forks—left leads to the lower trailhead, right to the two upper trailheads. Going left, the trailhead is 0.1 mile farther on the right just before Lower Sardine Lake Campground, and is signed TAMARACK CONNECTION TRAIL 12E08. Going right at the fork, you reach a Y-junction in 2.5 miles by the Packer Lake day-use area—go left and stay on Forest Service Road 93. The Tamarack Lakes trailhead is a short 0.2 mile ahead and the PCT trailhead a steep and winding 1.9 miles farther.

Description: From the Lower Sardine Lake trailhead (0.0/5770), the wide and rocky trail begins climbing through manzanita, Douglas-fir, Jeffrey pine, white fir, and incense cedar. The lookout tower is barely discernible to the naked eye, perched on top of the mountain's highest point. The trail soon climbs a ridge, crossing briefly to the eastern side before returning to begin the fabulous traverse above Sardine lakes. Dazzling Sierra Buttes overshadow the emerald waters of Upper and Lower Sardine lakes, lending inspiration to your feet as you approach the grueling ridgetop ascent. Along the way, you pass the junction for the Sardine Lakes Overlook Trail (1.7/6500). After powering up the steep switchbacks to attain the ridge (2.3/7050), you descend briefly and pass two small ponds before reaching the junction with the Lookout Trail (3.2/6720). Those approaching from **Tamarack Lakes trailhead** join here; you turn left (southwest) on the wide 4WD road to immediately reach Lower Tamarack Lake. The trail forks just past the lake—left leads down to nicer Upper Tamarack Lake, right is the continuation of the hike. The upper lake is good for some very brisk swimming.

Now on posted Tamarack Connection Trail 12E30, you climb steadily southwest and cross a wide logging road halfway to the ridgetop. The lookout becomes visible southeast between the

Look Out

peaklets before three switchbacks bring you to the ridgetop. The junction with the PCT (4.0/7350) is located by a large, twisted western white pine. Those approaching from the **PCT trailhead** join here, where your trail continues southeast up toward the summit. Winding steeply through large boulders, you stay near or along the ridgecrest and begin the final push to the top. Note your route as it can be difficult to spot on your return, especially when lingering snow obscures the track. The icy, turquoise water of Little America Lake lies below, the lookout sits above, and mountain hemlock grows all around you, climbing the 4WD access road to the top. Following it up eight switchbacks, you reach the stairs. The stairs. As if you weren't tired enough—141 steps later you reach the top (5.5/8591).

The interior of the seasonally staffed lookout is off-limits, but the walkway that surrounds it is open for 360° views. The northeast corner of this precarious roost actually juts out into the void beyond the summit cliffs! On a reason-ably clear day, Lassen Peak (10457) is visible more than 70 miles away on the northwest horizon, the peaks of Desolation Wilderness appear far to the south-southeast, and the Coast Ranges rise beyond Sutter Buttes and the Great Central Valley (a distance of more than 100 miles). Return as you came, or by one of the two alternate routes.

Nearest Visitor Center: North Yuba Ranger Station, (530) 288-3232, located 7 miles north of North San Juan and 23 miles south of Downieville on Hwy. 49. Open Monday through Saturday 8 A.M.–4:30 P.M. Closed Saturdays in winter.

Backpacking Information: A campfire permit is required. The only campsites along this hike are around Tamarack Lakes and receive heavy use.

Nearest Campground: The campgrounds at Lower Sardine and Packer lakes are developed and charge a fee. Primitive Berger and Diablo campgrounds are on the road to Packer Lake (free, no water).

Hike 74—The Middle Yuba

Location	Middle Fork Yuba River
Agency	Tahoe National Forest
Highlights	The peaceful Yuba watershed.
Distance	2.0 miles round trip
Total Elevation Gain/Loss	1200´/1200´
Hiking Time	3–4 hours
Difficulty	★★★
Best Times	May through mid-November
Optional Map	USGS 7.5-min *Alleghany, Graniteville*

Difficult to access, this diminutive fork of the larger Yuba system was once swarming with miners during the height of the California Gold Rush. Ditches were dug, the river dammed, flumes constructed, lumber milled, towns built, and not a stone left unturned in the fervent quest for gold. Today only the gurgling river remains.

The Hike descends steeply to the river via a spotty, overgrown, and unmaintained trail. The river can be shallow, but numerous deep pools provide opportunities for swimming and fishing. It is very unlikely that you will encounter anybody regardless of time of year. No water is available at the trailhead or anywhere before the river itself. **WARNING:** This is an area rife with abandoned mine shafts and tunnels. Be cautious when traversing cross-country on the slopes as collapsed mines can create pitfalls beneath the litter of the forest floor. **Never, ever go into an abandoned tunnel!**

To Reach the Trailhead, take Hwy. 49 north from Nevada City. After driving 3.8 miles beyond the South Fork Yuba's crossing, turn right onto Tyler Foote Rd. going toward North Columbia and Malakoff Diggins State Park. In 7.9 miles the road reaches a Y-junction—continue straight on Cruzon Grade Rd.

for another 5.0 miles. Leave the paved road where it swings south at the posted turnoff for Malakoff Diggins, and proceed straight ahead on the washboard surface of Backbone Rd. Bear right on Snow Tent Rd., where Backbone Rd. quickly forks left, and go 10 miles to the (easily missed) fenced Graniteville cemetery on the road's south side. Directly across the road from the cemetery is an unmarked 4WD road. If you have a low-clearance vehicle, park here and walk the short distance to the trailhead. Otherwise, turn left on the road and proceed for 0.3 mile to a fork—bear right to immediately reach a four-way intersection. Turn left down the very steep, rocky, and overgrown path, which terminates in a small lot after 0.3 mile. Be aware that the final section of road crosses private property.

Description From the lot (0.0/4530), the trail is almost indiscernible. It descends north—straight down—along the ridge below you for 600 feet. Although sketchy in spots, the trail becomes somewhat more distinct as you go—just stay on top of the ridge. Without a turn the trail plummets downward, soon reaching a small stand of Douglas-firs on a ridge bump (0.3/4200). Clear views southwest reveal the undeveloped Middle Yuba drainage. The trail veers

obviously west 300 feet farther down—keep your eye
out. Passing through dense
forest, this overgrown section of trail is, nonetheless,
generally easy to spot. If
you find yourself off-trail,
retrace your steps to find
the path; the slopes are dangerously steep. Look for a
few, particularly large
sugar pines before you
finally reach the river (1.0/
3340). Douglas-fir, pon-
derosa pine, black oak, big
leaf maple, and canyon live
oak line the riverbanks.
Exploratory adventures
await upstream and down.
Return the way you came.

Nearest Visitor Center:
North Bloomfield Ranger
Station, (530) 265-2740,
located in Malakoff Diggins
State Historic Park. North
Yuba Ranger Station, (530)
288-3232, located 7 miles
north of North San Juan
and 23 miles south of
Downieville on Hwy. 49.
Open Monday through Sat-
urday 8 A.M.–4:30 P.M.
Closed Saturdays in winter.

**Backpacking Informa-
tion:** A valid campfire permit is required. Campsites
exist along the river.

Nearest Campground:
Shooter Hill Campground
in Malakoff Diggins State
Historic Park (30 sites, $10).

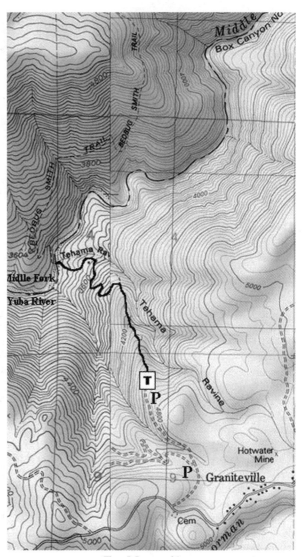

THE MIDDLE YUBA

Hike 75—The Mother Lode

Location	North Fork American River
Agency	Tahoe National Forest
Highlights	Gold Rush echoes. The North Fork chasm.
Distance	8.5 miles one way
Total Elevation Gain/Loss	2300´/2600´
Hiking Time	5–7 hours
Difficulty	★★★★
Best Times	May through October
Optional Map	USGS 7.5-min *Duncan Peak*

The North Fork American River tumbles west through the Sierra foothills, slicing through the heart of California's Gold Country. Despite running parallel to the busiest highway in the Sierra Nevada (I-80), this stretch of river receives surprisingly light use. The fact that it rushes through a precipitous canyon a half mile deep may have something to do with it.

In 1848, gold was discovered at Sutters Mill on the South Fork American River above Sacramento. Within two years, thousands of gold-seekers were poking and prodding every unturned rock in the American River drainage. The surrounding slopes were denuded, mines dug; fortunes were made, fortunes lost. After the gold petered out, the remote canyons were left to Nature. Mine shafts and memories are all that remain along this hike.

The Hike approaches the North Fork from the south on Beacroft Trail, descends steeply to reach the river, follows it 2.2 miles downstream to Mumford Bar, and then climbs just as steeply to Mumford Bar trailhead. Since the two trailheads are separated by 4.6 miles of paved road, leave either a car or a bicycle at the end trailhead. While the hike can be completed in either direction, beginning on Beacroft Trail, described below, spares you an extra 100 feet of climbing.

Due to the easy trailhead access and close proximity to major population centers, you will likely see a few people (though not many). Fishing is good. No water is available at either trailhead and none is available before canyon bottom. **WARNING:** This is an area rife with abandoned mine shafts and tunnels. Be cautious when traversing the slopes cross-country, as collapsed mines can create pitfalls beneath the litter of the forest floor. **Never, ever go into an abandoned tunnel!**

To Reach the Trailhead, take the Forest Hill Road exit from I-80, just east of downtown Auburn. Proceed east on Forest Hill Rd. for 31 miles to the substantial Mumford Bar trailhead lot—your terminus. The hike begins at the smaller (and more easily missed) Beacroft trailhead lot 4.6 miles farther along the road.

Description: The posted trailhead (0.0/5450) is at the end of the very rough road that strikes north from the main Beacroft parking area. Climbing very briefly, the trail then begins its descent into the canyon. If thick vegetation obscures views for most of the drop, it allows passage through two distinct plant communities. Above 4,000 feet is the coniferous woodland community, where red fir, sugar pine, and Douglas-fir are the dominant trees. Below 4,000 feet, the vegetation changes to that of the foothill woodlands community. Incense cedar and ponderosa pine replace the higher elevation conifers, and black oak, manzanita, California bay, big leaf maple, and canyon live oak appear everywhere. This ecological transition zone extends the length of the western Sierra Nevada between roughly 3,000 and 5,000 feet.

Almost exactly 1,000 feet down (1.0/4400), the trail passes through an open area with dizzying views up-canyon. The geology of the area is extremely complex, resulting from the accretion of an offshore landmass to North America approximately 250 million years ago. Part of this landmass likely contained the gold of California's Mother Lode, redistributed throughout the region in the scattered pockets so fervently hunted by prospectors.

Continuing to the bottom, the trail reaches a junction (2.4/2860), where the river is readily accessible as it races through a chute 10 feet deep—a great swimming hole. From here, head downstream 2.5 miles to the junction for Mumford Bar Trail. The trail runs among trees parallel to the broad riverbed. The river can be accessed at various points; it is possible to walk along the river itself for stretches to rejoin the trail later on.

Immediately prior to reaching the junction (4.9/2650), you pass the Mumford Bar Cabin, built around 1900 and currently being repaired by the Forest Service. From here, the Mumford Bar trailhead is only a few thousand feet above and a couple dozen switchbacks away. Once trailside views into the canyon disappear, it's only 500 more feet of gain to the parking lot (8.5/5250).

Nearest Visitor Center: Forest Hill Ranger Station, (530) 367-2224, located 15 miles east of I-80 on Forest Hill Rd. Open in summer daily 8 A.M.–5 P.M., the rest of the year from Monday through Friday 8 A.M.–4:30 P.M.

Backpacking Information: This is an excellent overnight trip with numerous campsites along the river. A valid campfire permit is required.

Nearest Campground: Secret House Campground, located on Forest Hill Rd. between the trailheads (2 primitive sites, no water); Robinson Flat Campground, 5 miles east of the Beacroft trailhead on Forest Hill Rd. (5 sites).

THE MOTHER LODE

Hike 76—Gone on the Rubicon

Location	Rubicon River
Agency	Eldorado National Forest
Highlights	The crystalline Rubicon River.
Distance	6.0+ miles round trip
Total Elevation Gain/Loss	1200´/1200´
Hiking Time	1–5 hours
Difficulty	★★
Best Times	May through October
Optional Map	USGS 7.5-min *Bunker Hill, Robbs Peak*

Originating in Desolation Wilderness, Rubicon River flows through beautiful, unspoiled Sierra foothills on its way to join the Middle Fork American River. Hiking beside this river—clear as glass and emerald green—is a peaceful experience.

The Hike is an exploration of a small stretch of Rubicon River that flows for 10 miles without road access. Running along slopes parallel to the river, the trail provides views into some deep gorges, as well as opportunities to scramble down and explore along the river. There is no end destination for this hike—this description goes 3 miles upstream but you can continue past this point, or turn around earlier without missing any sights. The first 1.5 miles of trail are the most dramatic. This hike can be done virtually year-round as snow usually does not fall here until January. Fishing is fair to good, with the water clarity often making for challenging conditions. No potable water is available at the trailhead but the river is easily accessible.

To Reach the Trailhead, take Hwy. 49 south from Auburn for 6 miles to the Hwy. 193 junction in Cool and turn east. Proceed 11.6 miles to the Georgetown stop sign and turn left on Main St., which becomes Forest Service Road 1 on the other side of town. Follow FS Rd. 1

for 18.1 miles to the junction with FS Rd. 2 and turn left. The road descends and crosses the Rubicon River in 4.5 miles. Immediately past the bridge, there is a small unmarked dirt road on the right. Those with low-clearance vehicles should park here by the paved road. The others can take the rough road 0.4 mile to a parking area by the river. The unposted trailhead is halfway down this road, marked by five 1´-high wooden posts.

Description From the trailhead (0.0/3390), climb past an angler's survey box and begin your hillside traverse among black oak, canyon live oak, ponderosa pine, incense cedar, and Douglas-fir. Fragrant bear clover fills in the understory. The early section also crosses a geologic divide, passing briefly over metamorphic rocks before reaching the more typical granite of the Sierra Nevada. Early on look for schist and other metamorphic rocks in the creekbeds that the path crosses.

Climbing high above the river, the trail peaks at a clearing (1.0/3710), which offers views up-canyon and of the opposite slopes rising more than 2,000 feet above the river. It then drops back down; where the trail bottoms out you pass a spur trail to the river (1.7/3600), one of only two, good access points. A few, small white fir can be spotted as you continue along the more level trail and the canyon slopes become more gradual. Near a significant creek gully where the riverbed is clearly visible, you pass the next river access point. Large, healthy representatives of incense cedar, Douglas-fir, and ponderosa pine grow along the trail's upper section; it is possible to continue all the way to Hell Hole Reservoir, a 10-mile one-way journey from the trailhead. Or you could turn around.

Nearest Visitor Center: Georgetown Ranger Station, (530) 333-4312, located 3.6 miles east of the Georgetown stop sign on FS Rd. 1. Open daily 8 A.M.–4:30 P.M. until winter arrives, then from Monday through Friday only.

Backpacking Information: While it is legal to backpack on this hike (valid campfire permit required), finding good campsites can be a challenge.

Nearest Campground: Stumpy Meadows Campground, located 12 miles east of Georgetown on FS Rd. 1 (39 sites). There are a few, primitive use sites near the trailhead parking area.

Gone on the Rubicon

Hike 77—Tallac Attack

Location	Mt. Tallac
Agency	Desolation Wilderness
Highlights	Views encompassing all of Lake Tahoe and much of Desolation Wilderness.
Distance	9.2 miles round trip
Total Elevation Gain/Loss	3400´/3400´
Hiking Time	6–8 hours
Difficulty	★★★★
Best Times	July through September
Optional Map	Forest Service *Desolation Wilderness* topographic map; Wilderness Press *Desolation Wilderness* map, 2000.

Mt. Tallac soars above Lake Tahoe's southwest shore, a landmark peak beckoning fit hikers to its lofty summit. From the top, Lake Tahoe and the heart of Desolation Wilderness spread out below you.

In this land of exposed granite, Mt. Tallac (9735) is a dark, metamorphic anomaly. A *roof pendant,* the mountain is a remnant of the landscape that existed prior to the intrusion of the Sierra Nevada granite. Formed near the ancient continental margin of North America 200–120 million years ago, the rocks of Mt. Tallac are a complex mix of volcanic flows above metamorphosed sea-floor sediments. While these rocks once covered the surrounding landscape, erosion has exposed the underlying granite,

Thunderhead over Desolation Wilderness

leaving only a few small remnants on the highest peaks.

The Hike quickly and steeply ascends Mt. Tallac via the most direct route from Lake Tahoe's southwest shore, passing Floating Island and Cathedral lakes along the way. Mt. Tallac is in Desolation Wilderness, an incredibly popular area that is heavily traveled all summer long until Labor Day. In September, the weather remains delightful and crowds all but disappear—the optimal time for your "Tallac Attack." Snow lingers well into June on the trail's upper reaches and can return as early as October. No water is available at the trailhead. Cathedral Creek, about halfway up the mountain, provides a reliable trailside source.

To Reach the Trailhead, take Hwy. 89 north of the Hwy. 50/89 junction in South Lake Tahoe for 3.5 miles to the posted turnoff for the Tallac trailhead on the left. Approaching from the north on Hwy. 89, the turnoff is 2 miles south of Eagle Point Campground. From Hwy. 89, it is a short 1.1 miles on the access road to the large trailhead parking lot—bear left at the first fork and right at the second.

Description: All dayhikers are required to obtain a wilderness permit, available free at the big information sign by the start of the trail (0.0/6500). Immediately climbing, the trail ascends through Jeffrey pine, white fir, and manzanita to quickly obtain the top of the ridge that hems in Fallen Leaf Lake, visible below you to the east. As glaciers advanced from the mountains toward Lake Tahoe in the recent geologic past, they pushed rocky debris in front of them like giant bulldozers, depositing it alongside to form *lateral moraines*, parallel ridges along the glacier edges; and *terminal moraines* at the points of farthest advance. Remaining after a glacier melted, moraines formed natural basins that filled with large lakes. Fallen Leaf Lake is an outstanding example, as is Emerald

Bay, joined to Lake Tahoe because its terminal moraine is slightly lower than Tahoe's current water level.

Views of Mt. Tallac's eastern flanks are constant until the trail drops west below the ridgetop, briefly parallels Tallac Creek, and enters Desolation Wilderness a few hundred yards before reaching Floating Island Lake (1.4/7230). Named for the large grassy mats that occasionally break off from its shores and float about, the shallow lake once contained a floating island buoyant enough to float six men (Lekisch 1988).

The trail crosses Cathedral Creek before reaching a junction (2.3/7580) where a steep trail climbing from Stanford Sierra Camp on Fallen Leaf Lake joins from the left. Cathedral Lake (2.5/7620) makes a wonderful rest stop, and good views can be had from its eastern rim. Continuing, the rocky trail steepens and makes a few switchbacks on the way to a glacial cirque dotted with drooping mountain hemlocks (2.9/8200). A tall, wizened western white pine stands between you and the rocky slopes of Mt. Tallac. The small creek here is your last opportunity to obtain water.

Snow can remain on the east-facing headwall late in the season and obscure the already difficult-to-distinguish track—the correct route runs along the headwall's northwest side. Once you're on top of the slope (3.2/8550), the broadly sloping southwestern flank of the mountain is revealed. Pink phlox hug the ground as the trail veers northwest parallel to the ridge, reaching the summit via a short, posted trail (4.6/9715).

The jagged summit makes for difficult seating but get comfortable, you'll want to savor the view. The stretch of land from Emerald Bay (Hike 78) to the Stateline casinos was once filled with rivers of ice, a spectacular scene to imagine. As you look southwest down into Desolation Wilderness, the irregular shape of island-studded Lake Aloha (8116) sits below the peaks of the Crystal Range, and perfectly round Gilmore Lake lies immediately below you. Return the way you came.

Nearest Visitor Center: Lake Tahoe Visitor Center, (530) 573-2674, located 2.7 miles north of the Hwy. 50/89 junction in South Lake Tahoe on Hwy. 89. Open daily in summer 9 A.M.–5:30 P.M.

Backpacking Information: Campsites are extremely limited on this hike—neither lake visited has a legal site; and your best options are the broad southwest shoulder of Mt. Tallac above the headwall or the somewhat more distant Gilmore Lake. Wilderness permits are required for all overnight stays and, as part of a Forest Service pilot program,

there is a $5 per person fee. Permits can be obtained at the Lake Tahoe Visitor Center or the Eldorado National Forest Information Center, located 5 miles east of Placerville on Hwy. 50. The Tallac trailhead has a daily quota of 32 people. Half the spots are first-come, first-served; the other half can be reserved by calling (530) 644-6048 ($5 reservation fee).

Nearest Campground: Campgrounds line Lake Tahoe's shore. The closest are Eagle Point Campground (100 sites, $16) and Fallen Leaf Campground (205 sites; $15).

Additional Information:
www.r5.fs.fed.us/ltbmu

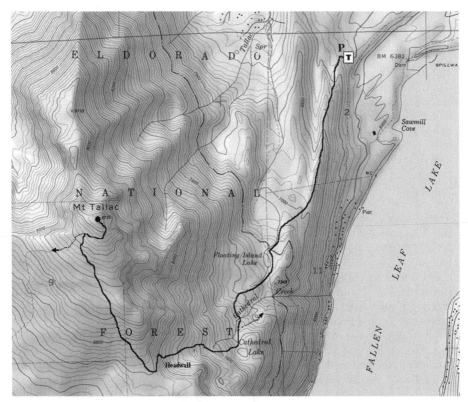

TALLAC ATTACK

Hike 78—Tahoe Bliss

Location	Lake Tahoe
Agency	D.L. Bliss & Emerald Bay State Parks
Highlights	Tahoe shores. Emerald Bay. Vikingsholm.
Distance	6.6 miles one way
Total Elevation Gain/Loss	1150′/850′
Hiking Time	3–5 hours
Difficulty	★★
Best Times	mid-June through September
Optional Map	USGS 7.5-min *Emerald Bay*

Lake Tahoe needs no introduction. Despite the thick development elsewhere, this pristine shoreline allows us to experience the majesty of what Tahoe must have once been.

The Hike is a one-way journey along Lake Tahoe's shoreline from D.L. Bliss State Park to Emerald Bay State Park along the Rubicon Trail. Swimming, sunning, and fishing are all possible diversions, and fairy-tale Vikingsholm awaits in enchanting Emerald Bay. While it can be completed in either direction, the hike description proceeds south from D.L. Bliss, saving Emerald Bay for the latter half of the day. Either a car shuttle is required for this hike, or you take public transportation (see below) back to the entrance of D.L. Bliss. Be aware that the trailhead is a 2.3-mile road walk from the D.L. Bliss park entrance. This trail is very crowded in summer, so arrive before 10 A.M. to get a spot in the small trailhead parking lot. After the lot has filled, check the small, unposted parking spaces 1.1 miles from the entrance—you can easily connect with the trail from there. If they too are full, the only available parking is along Hwy. 89. Water is available at the trailhead.

To Reach the Trailhead, take Hwy. 89 to the entrance for D.L. Bliss State Park. Approaching from the south, it is

10.7 miles from the Hwy. 50/89 junction in South Lake Tahoe, and 3.8 miles past Eagle Point Campground. From the north, it is 5.1 miles past Meeks Bay Campground. From the entrance station, follow signs toward CAMPS 141–168 and, at the final intersection, bear right toward the Rubicon Trail parking lot. There is a $5 day-use fee.

Public Transportation is available from mid-June through mid-September on The Emerald Bay Shuttle (530) 541-7548. From around 10 A.M. until 5 P.M., buses run a regular hour-long loop from Camp Richardson Resort to D.L. Bliss State Park and back, stopping at the Eagle Point Campground entrance and Vikingsholm parking area. Connections to and from South Lake Tahoe can be made at Camp Richardson.

Description From the parking lot (0.0/6260), the single-track trail strikes south among white fir, huckleberry oak, and manzanita. At the immediate junction for the lighthouse trail continue straight to quickly obtain your first views of Tahoe's distinctive, clear, aquamarine-tinted water below you. While reduced from its historic clarity of 120 feet deep, objects can still be seen to 75 feet in places! Along this early section of trail, numerous use paths branch down toward the lake. Lake access ends after the trail reaches a mildly precariously section protected by a chain fence (0.3/6330) and slowly begins climbing. Osprey nest along this stretch and can occasionally be spotted until their departure in mid-August. By the time you reach the second junction for the lighthouse trail (0.4/6430), the lake is 200 feet below. Resembling a modified outhouse, the lighthouse makes for an easy 0.1-mile side trip.

Turning inland, the trail continues to climb and suddenly offers magnificent views southwest of snow-frosted Mt. Tallac (Hike 77). Two large spur trails from the alternate parking lot in D.L. Bliss soon join the route in a dense forest of white fir (0.9/6520), just before the trail crests at 350 feet above the lake. From here the trail slowly descends, passing among the bleached debris of a 1982 avalanche before reaching the lake-shore near Emerald Point (2.5/6230). The trail forks—left goes around the small peninsula's perimeter to worthwhile Emerald Point and the mouth of Emerald Bay, while right short-cuts to the bay proper. The flat peninsula is the terminal moraine of the glacier that carved Emerald Bay and pinedrops,

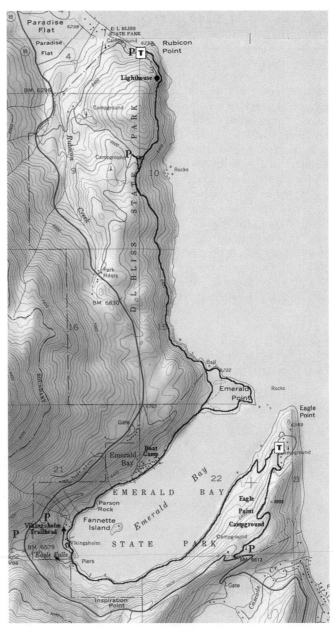

TAHOE BLISS

horsetails, ferns, and large Jeffrey pines sprout in the lush, sandy soil.

Veering southwest along the shores of Emerald Bay, the trail widens, passing Boat Camp before winding through the jumbled remains of a 1980 landslide (stay along the lake) to reach the Viking-sholm complex at the head of the bay (4.4/6230). Considered the most authentic reproduction of Scandinavian architecture in the United States, Vikingsholm was completed in 1929 without damaging any of the site's beautiful trees. Mrs. Lora J. Knight spent summers here until her death in 1945, entertaining guests both onshore and in the teahouse on Fannette Island, in the middle of Emerald Bay. Donated to the state in 1958, the site now houses a visitor center, ferry dock, and other tourist-friendly facilities. The sod roof still sprouts flowers and regular tours inside Vikingsholm are offered daily ($3). A steep trail climbs 1.0 mile and 800 feet to the Vikingsholm parking lot on Hwy. 50. From here, con-tinue on the newly-constructed trail running along the bay's southeast shore.

This quiet section is almost entirely level, climbing 300 feet only at the end to terminate at the campfire circle in upper Eagle Point Campground (6.3/6500). It is an easy uphill through the campground to the parking spaces on Hwy. 50.

Nearest Visitor Center: D.L. Bliss Visitor Center, (530) 525-7277. Open May through mid-October daily 9 A.M.–4 P.M. Vikingsholm Visitor Center, (530) 525-7277. Open Memorial Day through September daily 9 A.M.–4 P.M.

Nearest Campground: Eagle Point and D.L. Bliss campgrounds ($12–20). Though large, both regularly fill during the summer.

Emerald Bay

Hike 79—Muh-KULL-uh-mee

Location	Mokelumne Wilderness
Agency	Eldorado National Forest
Highlights	Splitting granite gorges. Remote Grouse Lake.
Distance	11.0 miles round trip
Total Elevation Gain/Loss	2500´/2500´
Hiking Time	6–8 hours
Difficulty	★★★★
Best Times	Mid-June through September
Optional Map	Forest Service *Mokelumne Wilderness* topographic map

Unlike most of the High Sierra, little-traveled Mokelumne Wilderness is a land more renowned for its deep river gorges than its soaring mountains. Experience here the sweep and variety of a rolling granite landscape topped with volcanic peaks and sliced by canyons thousands of feet deep.

The Hike follows a ridge west from the popular Blue lakes to isolated Grouse Lake, perched in a magnificent granite bowl near the chasm formed by Summit City Creek. The trail passes Granite Lake in 1.8 miles, a somewhat traveled fishing destination for the numerous anglers that ply the waters of the Blue lakes area. Fishing is possible at both lakes. Snow usually clears by late June, with July and August the best months for wildflowers. While no water is available at the trailhead, faucets can be found in the nearby campgrounds around the Blue lakes.

To Reach the Trailhead, take Blue Lakes Rd. (FS Rd. 015) south from Hwy. 88—the posted turnoff is 6.0 miles east of Carson Pass. The paved road ends in 6.7 miles and you reach the junction for the Tamarack Lake trailhead 3.4 miles farther—go straight. Reaching the Mokelumne Hydroelectric Project 0.9 mile later, the road becomes paved again; bear right and drive 1.7 miles toward Upper Blue Lake dam. The trailhead lot is on your left past Lower Blue Lake Campground (within eyeshot of Upper Blue Lake dam).

Description: From the parking lot (0.0/8140), the trail immediately passes along a seasonal creek beneath a thick cover of lodgepole pine and mountain hemlock. Corn lilies, alpine asters, and a variety of other seasonal wildflowers decorate the moist understory along this early section of trail. Veering west, the trail crosses a stream and diverges in three directions—go left (downstream), paralleling the stream briefly before angling away from it. As you gradually climb to Granite Lake, western white pines replace the lodgepole pines and you soon cross into Mokelumne Wilderness. Behind you, The Nipple (9342) is visible immediately northeast, the rocky turret of Jeff Davis Peak (8960) east-northeast, and the dark brown ridge of pyramidal Raymond Peak (10014) and more distant Reynolds Peak (9679) southeast. All these darker peaks are remnants of ancient volcanic flows that intermittently coursed over the rolling granite landscape of Mokelumne Wilderness during the past 30 million years. Today's rivers have eroded through most of these overlying volcanic rocks to reach the granite bedrock, but the higher peaks remain capped by these reddish-brown flows.

Ringed by broken hills of granite, pretty Granite Lake (1.8/8700) is a pleasant spot for a breather and offers good fly-fishing. Passing its western edge, the trail forks—head away from the lake. Cresting a small rise, you get the first views of the deep canyon of North Fork Mokelumne River. A few Sierra junipers can be identified as the now undulating trail slowly climbs to a distinct granite/volcanic interface near the ridgetop, passing several easy side trips to spectacular views south. Immediately prior to reaching the darker volcanics (4.0/9220), the trail passes below a striking illustration of the local geology. Along the interface above, granite boulders can be seen protruding from an eroding shell of loose volcanic rock, graphic evidence that the first lava flows pooled around and covered earlier existing features.

Traversing above meadow-filled Snow Canyon, the trail crosses several lush gullies, fed by springs emerging from the interface. Approaching the edge of the Snow Canyon watershed, the trail becomes indistinct; you encounter a triangular meadow bordered by several springs. Follow the farthest spring approximately 50 feet before crossing it near the edge of the exposed granite. The route is marked with small rock piles where it crests a slight ridge into the Grouse Creek drainage. Grouse Lake soon becomes visible over 600 feet below you. The trail descends quickly to meet it (5.5/8540), passing through a healthy forest of western white pine and mountain hemlock on its way down. Note your route as you descend; it looks considerably different on the ascent.

Go beyond the west shore of Grouse Lake for views southwest of Mokelumne Peak (9334) and the tantalizing upper cliffs of the Summit City Creek gorge. Return the way you came.

Nearest Visitor Center: The Forest Service runs an excellent joint visitor center with the local Chamber of Commerce in Markleeville, (530) 694-2911. Open from the end of April through mid-October daily 8 A.M.–4 P.M. A closer source of information is the Carson Pass Information Center, located at the pass itself. Open daily during the summer approximately 9 A.M.–5 P.M.

Backpacking Information: There are campsites at Grouse Lake. Wilderness permits are required and can be obtained at Carson Pass during open hours, and anytime at the register outside of the Markleeville visitor center.

Nearest Campground: There are 3 campgrounds around Upper and Lower Blue lakes ($10–15).

MUH-KULL-UH-MEE

Hike 80—The Forgotten Sierra

Location	Carson-Iceberg Wilderness
Agency	Stanislaus National Forest
Highlights	The summit of Hiram Peak. The heart of Carson-Iceberg Wilderness.
Distance	2.4 miles round trip
Total Elevation Gain/Loss	1250´/1250´
Hiking Time	2–3 hours
Difficulty	★★★
Best Times	mid-June through September
Optional Map	Forest Service *Carson-Iceberg Wilderness* topographic map

Forgotten Carson-Iceberg Wilderness is a little-visited landscape of volcanic peaks that straddles the central Sierra between Yosemite and Lake Tahoe. Set apart, Hiram Peak (9795) provides summit views extraordinaire of the high wilderness heartland.

The Hike is a short, steep, easy-to-follow cross-country route from Highland Lakes Campground to the top of Hiram Peak. The region receives light use with the majority of visitors fishing at Highland Lakes. Snow usually clears by late June; July and August are the best for wildflowers. Water is available at the trailhead.

To Reach the Trailhead, take Hwy. 4 toward Ebbetts Pass and bear south on Highland Lakes Rd.—the posted turnoff is 15.6 miles east of Bear Valley Road and 1.2 miles west of Ebbetts Pass. Approaching from the east, the turn is an easily missed hairpin on the left, so pay close attention. Unpaved Highland Lakes Rd. is passable for all vehicles and winds for 5.3 miles to its terminus at Highland Lakes Campground. Hiram Peak is plainly visible southeast of the campground on the opposite side of lower Highland Lake. Located behind site 31 in the eastern half of the campground, the trailhead is indicated by a small wooden TRAIL sign.

Description From the trailhead (0.0/8670), follow the obvious route upward through red fir and western white pine before breaking out onto an open hillside. Seasonal wildflowers here include Mariposa lilies, explorer's gentian, wild carrot, lupine, and mule's ears. Weaving along the forest edge, the trail begins to fan out and disappear as the summit of Hiram Peak comes into view south. Continue to the ridgetop above you (0.5/9130), and then traverse south to the base of the talus slopes. As you begin your ascent, use paths make clambering up the slopes somewhat easier. You soon reach the ridge that bends southeast and leads you to the summit (1.2/9795). You pass a few stumpy, twisted whitebark pines along the way to the top.

Beginning some 30 million years ago, intermittent volcanism covered the land of today's Carson-Iceberg Wilderness in layers of lava, mud flows, and volcanic debris. The region surrounding Hiram Peak is a complex composite of flows, which continued as recently as 4 million years ago (Schaffer 1997). Feast on the view and admire the headwaters of three major California rivers. Looking east, the closest mountain is Arnot Peak (10054), part of the Sierra Divide. Its northeastern slopes are the headwaters of Wolf Creek, whose glacially carved valley can be seen trailing off northeast to join the Carson River. Flowing to the Stanislaus River, Disaster Creek drains the western flanks of Arnot Peak and is visible in the tarn-dotted open basin below you to the northeast. Looking south, the towering massif of Airola Peak (9942) and mostly-hidden Iceberg Peak (9781) split the headwaters of Arnot Creek (east) and Highland Creek (west). Highland Creek flows into visible Spicer Meadows Reservoir before also joining the Stanislaus River. The two Highland lakes to the north actually mark a significant watershed between the Mokelumne River, fed by the upper lake, and the Stanislaus River, fed by the lower lake. On the horizon, the peaks of Mokelumne Wilderness (Hike 79) lie northwest and the mountains of Emigrant Wilderness (Hike 81) rise southeast. Return the way you came.

Nearest Visitor Center: Alpine Ranger Station, located 1.3 miles east of Bear Valley Rd. in a small hut by Hwy. 4. Open sporadically in season Thursday through Monday 8 A.M.–4:30 P.M. A more reliable information source is the Calaveras Ranger District Office, (209) 795-1381, located in Hathaway Pines on Hwy. 4. Open Monday through Friday 8 A.M.–5 P.M., Saturday 8 A.M.–3 P.M.

Backpacking Information: A wilderness permit is required, obtainable at the above ranger stations during business hours. While there are no campsites along this hike, options do exist east of Hiram Peak along the cross-country route toward Arnot Creek.

Nearest Campground: Highland Lakes Campground (40 sites, $8).
Additional Information:
www.r5.fs.fed.us/stanislaus/visitor/carson.htm

THE FORGOTTEN SIERRA

Hike 81—Blue Canyon

Location	Emigrant Wilderness
Agency	Stanislaus National Forest
Highlights	The volcanic High Sierra. Solitude among falls, creeks, lakes, peaks.
Distance	4.5 miles round trip
Total Elevation Gain/Loss	1700′/1700′
Hiking Time	3–5 hours
Difficulty	★★★
Best Times	July through September
Optional Map	USGS 7.5-min *Sonora Pass*

Emigrant Wilderness receives only the smallest fraction of the hordes that descend upon neighboring Yosemite National Park. Blue Canyon lies in a most remote corner of the wilderness. Solitude anyone?

Above 9,000 feet near the Sierra Divide, Blue Canyon exists in a landscape of volcanic rubble unusual in this land of naked granite. Roughly 10 million years ago, a period of volcanism centered east of today's Sonora Pass smothered the landscape beneath numerous flows of mud and molten rock. Today these looser volcanic sediments have largely been eroded away, but sections still remain north of Yosemite near the Sierra crest. The layered, multihued bands exposed in the rocks and cliffs of Blue Canyon are part of these geologic remnants.

The Hike winds upward through Blue Canyon along the headwaters of Blue Canyon creek, passing starkly beautiful waterfalls en route to a couple of vibrantly blue lakes—Blue Canyon Lake and Deadman Lake. The single-track trail is steep and rocky, the lakes are surrounded by loose talus slopes, and the final mile to Deadman Lake is cross-country. Due to the high elevation, snow lingers deep into June and can return as early as October. While no water is available at the trailhead, Blue Canyon creek is regularly accessible.

To Reach the Trailhead, take Hwy. 108 toward Sonora Pass. The unposted trailhead is accessed from a small pull-out on the south side of Hwy. 108. Approaching from the west, it is 1.9 miles past Chipmunk Flat primitive campground; your landmark is the distinctive waterfall where Blue Canyon creek joins Deadman Creek and the pull-out is immediately after the falls disappear from view. Approaching from the east, the trailhead is 2.6 miles past Sonora Pass (the pull-out is 0.1 mile after the road begins its steepest descent from Sonora Pass). A dozen small lodgepole pines line the edge of the pull-out, bare granite blocks sit across Hwy. 108 from it, and there is space for four cars.

Description: From the pull-out (0.0/8920), a discernible trail drops 40 feet to cross both Deadman Creek and the granite/volcanic geologic divide before quickly ascending the steep opposite slope to enter Blue Canyon. A few wilderness signs indicate you're on the right track as the trail winds through lodgepole pines and begins to offer views up-canyon. A use trail converges from the west side immediately before you cross a small feeder creek. Western white pines begin to appear, easily identified by the deep red of their plated bark. The trail then swings away from the creek and begins steeply climbing, soon crossing the most significant feeder creek yet (0.8/9520). Shortly thereafter, you come to a very sheer section of trail where the main path diverges in two directions—drop down to the creek and follow the obvious path alongside it. The trail next curves away from the creek and peters out immediately before reaching Blue Canyon Lake (1.5/10037). At the bottom of a rubble-filled glacial cirque, the sapphire lake offers a few, exposed campsites. Looking down-canyon, the peaks of Carson-Iceberg Wilderness (Hike 80) are visible on the skyline.

Begin your cross-country adventure to Deadman Lake from here by ascending east toward the col of the long ridge, which lies between the small shark's-fin peak seen from the early sections of trail and the thumblike peak that juts from the ridge. Having obtained the ridgetop (1.8/10300), traverse north around the thumb on its east side and then scramble down over the tinkling piles of loose rock to reach the lake (2.2/10484). Barren, brilliantly blue, and ringed by naught but snow, rock, and lichen, Deadman Lake has a desolate beauty. Looking east, the nearby ridge marks the Sierra Divide and the routing of the Pacific Crest Trail. Return the way you came.

Nearest Visitor Center: Summit Ranger District Office, (209) 965-3434, located in Pinecrest on Hwy. 108. Open daily 8 A.M.–5 P.M., but closed Sundays and holidays October through May. Seasonally operated Brightman Flat Visitor Center is sometimes open as well, located 7 miles west of Kennedy Meadows' turnoff on Hwy. 108.

Backpacking Information: A wilderness permit is required, obtainable at the above visitor centers. The few campsites along this hike are bare and exposed, with Blue Canyon Lake offering the best sites. No quota is in effect for this trailhead.

Nearest Campground: Chipmunk Flat primitive campground, 5 miles east of the turnoff for Kennedy Meadows on Hwy. 108 (free, river water only). Numerous other campgrounds line Hwy. 108.

Additional Information:
www.r5.fs.fed.us/stanislaus/visitor/ emigrant.htm

BLUE CANYON

Hike 82—Mono Tufa

Location	Mono Lake
Agency	Mono Lake Tufa State Reserve
Highlights	Magical tufascapes. Mono Lake.
Distance	1.5 miles
Total Elevation Gain/Loss	30´/30´
Hiking Time	1 hour
Difficulty	★
Best Times	May through October
Optional Map	USGS 7.5-min *Lee Vining*

Explore the wild wonderland of Mono Lake—its water, tufas, and wildlife.

Mono Lake sits in a natural basin where the sun evaporates 45 inches of fresh water annually, leaving large quantities of dissolved solids behind in the lake. Ongoing for over 700,000 years, this process has left Mono Lake exceptionally salty and alkaline—at present, with the lake being two times saltier than the ocean and 100 times more alkaline, 10% is dissolved solids. The water has a greasy, slippery feel and provides enough buoyancy to easily float a person.

Mono Lake currently has a surface area of approximately 60 square miles with an average depth of only 50 feet and a maximum depth of 150 feet. In 1941 the water-hungry city of Los Angeles began diverting four of the five streams that feed Mono Lake, which caused the lake level to drop more than 40 feet and upset the natural ecological balance. Concerned citizen groups took initiative in the 1980s to save the shrinking lake and, after 16 years of legal and political wrangling, the State Water Resources Control Board ordered in 1994 that Mono Lake be protected, and its level be raised 17 feet over the next 20 years. With the lake level recovering, current efforts now focus on how best to rehabilitate the lake environment.

Mono Lake's receded shoreline has exposed many of the spectacular tufa formations previously hidden beneath the lake's surface. Formed by a reaction between calcium-bearing freshwater springs that bubble up beneath the lake and the carbonate-rich lake water, the tufas are composed of solid calcium carbonate (limestone). A tufa tower grows upward from the lake bottom around the mouth of the spring until exposed above the surface of the lake. The towers of South Tufa Area were completely submerged prior to 1941 and will gradually return to the lake with rising water levels. Numerous active tufa towers continue to grow unseen beneath the lake today.

The lake's wildlife is as bizarre as the surrounding tufascapes. While the inhospitable water precludes survival of most aquatic life (there are no fish in Mono Lake), a few species thrive here in mind-boggling numbers. The lake's winter algae bloom provides sustenance for the brine shrimp, which begin to hatch in the spring. By midsummer, an estimated four *trillion* tiny brine shrimp are swimming in the lake; thousands of pounds are harvested annually for sale as tropical fish food. Brine fly pupae, the lake's other primary denizen, also depend on the algae for sustenance. During the summer, mature flies blanket the lakeshore and produce harmless knee-high swarms when disturbed. The *Kuzedika* (Fly-Pupae Eaters), a band of the Paiute Tribe that once lived by the lake, harvested the fly pupae for food and trade. The size and color of brown rice grains, the prepared pupae taste like bacon bits. By late summer the algae is gone and the lake is once again clear and blue. Millions of birds pass through Mono Lake annually as they migrate, or winter here, consuming shrimp and flies as they go. Osprey nest on top of a few exposed tufa towers. Safe from predators, the osprey hunt in the nearby creeks and lakes.

The Hike is an easy stroll on the lake's south shore through surreal tufa formations. The trail is open and accessible during the snow-free months of the year, with heavy visitation throughout the summer months. Due to the area's popularity, this is not a hike for solitude seekers. No water is available at the trailhead or anywhere along the route. A swim in Mono Lake can be an unforgettable experience. Nearby Navy Beach offers the best opportunity and can be accessed either by hiking along the lakeshore or driving from the South Tufa Area. Avoid getting water in your mouth or eyes and be prepared for a salty, crusty coating on your body—no showers are available.

To Reach the Trailhead, take Hwy. 395 south from Lee Vining for 6 miles to the Hwy. 120 junction. Follow Hwy. 120 east for 4.5 miles to the posted turnoff on your left for the South Tufa Area; a mile-long dirt road leads to the large trailhead parking lot. There is a $3 per person entrance fee (Golden Eagle Pass accepted).

Description: A 7'-wide asphalt path leads from the kiosk to the lakeshore, passing numerous tufa towers and soon providing your first opportunity to touch the lake water. The now single-track clay trail heads east from shore, winding through odd configurations of tufa and seasonal swarms of brine flies. While numerous paths wind through the brush, your route is clearly indicated. After turning away from the lake, the trail forks. Bearing left takes you on a longer return loop (an extra 0.5 mile) to the parking lot. Going straight brings you directly back.

Nearest Visitor Center: The outstanding Mono Basin Visitor Center, (760) 647-3044, is located on Hwy. 395 just south of Lee Vining and 1.3 miles north of the Hwy. 120 junction. Open daily from June through September 9 A.M.–5:30 P.M., from October through May Thursday–Monday 9 A.M.–4 P.M. Additionally, the Mono Lake Committee runs an information center in Lee Vining, (760) 647-6595, on the west side of Hwy. 395. Open daily from late June through Labor Day 9 A.M.–10 P.M., the rest of the year daily 9 A.M.–5 P.M.

Nearest Campground: While there are no campgrounds around Mono Lake itself, numerous options exist south of Mono Lake along Hwy. 120 and Hwy. 158 (the June Lake loop).

MONO TUFA

Hike 83—Foaming Violent Thunder

Location	Nevada & Vernal Falls
Agency	Yosemite National Park
Highlights	The raging river. The incredible waterfalls. The spectacle of Yosemite.
Distance	5.9 miles
Total Elevation Gain/Loss	1900´/1900´
Hiking Time	5–7 hours
Difficulty	★★★
Best Times	Mid-May through June
Optional Map	USGS 7.5-min *Half Dome*

Ah, Yosemite. Despite the crowds, despite the hassle, there is no other place on Earth like it. Go.

The Hike climbs from Yosemite Valley to the top of Nevada Fall, passing Vernal Fall along the way via the Mist Trail and returning on the John Muir Trail. The more water there is in the river, the more spectacular the hike—snowmelt increases its flow until the end of June, at which point it begins to decrease considerably. Exploding spray courses over the trail below Vernal Falls for much of the season, making good raingear and waterproof boots useful but not essential to have. Crowds are somewhat lighter in May; otherwise they are unavoidable and for some perhaps overwhelming. With winter routes available, much of the hike can be done year-round—check conditions at the visitor center (see below). Water is available at the trailhead.

To Reach the Trailhead, park in one of Yosemite Valley's day-use parking lots and take the free Yosemite Valley Shuttle Bus to Happy Isles Nature Center. There is a $20 entrance fee for Yosemite National Park, valid for 7 days.

Description: From the bus stop (0.0/4030), cross the Merced River bridge and head up-river on the 15´-wide superhighway of packed dirt to quickly reach the gigantic trailhead sign. Just beyond the sign, the trail winds up among huge granite boulders and closely parallels the now violent river. As you ascend, look for two of Yosemite's other landmark waterfalls—Upper Yosemite Fall is briefly visible behind you down-canyon before being cut off from view by Glacier Point, and the wispy fall of Illilouette Creek to the Merced River can be momentarily seen cross-canyon.

Vernal Fall Bridge (0.8/4400) provides your first views of the waterfall. Its smooth foaming curtain of water drops 317´ and is dominated by two towering granite peaks—Mt. Broderick (6706) left and Liberty Cap (7076) just beyond it. Restrooms and a drinking fountain are available. Postings around the bridge indicate that, yes, THE STRONG CURRENT CAN BATTER YOU TO DEATH AGAINST THE ROCKS. Here, as everywhere along this hike, **do not go in the water!**

Climbing from the bridge, the trail quickly reaches a junction for the John Muir Trail (1.0/4440)—continue straight up the Mist Trail. Billowing clouds of spray soon wash over the trail as it climbs through a lush garden of dripping greenery. You *will* get wet, so protect your camera! Just where the mist tapers out, you can peer into the heart of the fall over the top of a glistening rainbow, an unforgettable sight. Climbing to the top of the fall, the trail becomes steep and narrow; it traverses the face of a granite cliff, where hikers are protected by a metal guardrail. Surmounting this section, you reach a wide, open space above the fall where hikers dry out or sunbathe (1.5/5050). Look over the lip of the fall at the Mist Trail below you. Do not be tempted to go in the river—almost every year some foolish person is swept over the fall and killed.

Continuing to Nevada Fall, parallel the river on any one of the many use paths to regain the main trail. Passing another short connector to the John Muir Trail, the trail crosses the river and climbs gradually to near the base of Nevada Fall. Here the mist is blown

down-canyon rather than over the trail and forms a towering wall of spray visible through the trees. A short scramble would take you into the mist, but the fall itself would be obscured if the river level is high.

With the sheer cliffs of Liberty Cap looming overhead, the trail then climbs 600 feet via nearly two dozen ever-tightening switchbacks to reach another junction with restroom facilities (2.3/6000). Those continuing on to **Half Dome** should bear left here and turn to Hike 84 for the continuing description. Those returning to the Valley should go right on the John Muir Trail. In 0.2 mile you reach the top of Nevada Fall; you can access the protected lip via a short spur trail before the river crossing. Nevada Fall explodes, its water blown into swirling clouds that flow like an air-

FOAMING VIOLENT THUNDER & THE BURN

borne river. Peering over the edge, buffeted by its winds, marvel at the torrent plummeting 571' to the rocks below.

The trail continues across the river and soon reaches a fork—go right. Traversing below the escarpment of Panoramic Cliffs, the John Muir Trail provides outstanding views of Liberty Cap and Nevada Fall, before descending along seemingly endless switchbacks to rejoin your earlier trail just above Vernal Fall Bridge (5.1/4440). Halfway down, you have the option of retracing your steps on the Mist Trail by taking the posted connection to the top of Vernal Fall. Return to Happy Isles to end your day on the trail.

Nearest Visitor Center: Valley Visitor Center, located in Yosemite Village (shuttle bus stops 6 and 9). Open 365 days a year. In summer open daily 9 A.M.–7 P.M., with reduced hours the rest of the year. For general recorded information call (209) 372-0200.

Backpacking Information: The closest backcountry camping is in Little Yosemite Valley, 0.5 mile past the top of Nevada Fall. See Hike 84 for more information.

Nearest Campground: Reservations are required year-round for the 3 car-accessible campgrounds in Yosemite Valley. Reservations are available 7 A.M.–7 P.M. up to five months in advance, in blocks of one month at a time, with the next block becoming available on the 15th of each month. To make reservations, call 1-800-436-7275 or go online at *reservations.nps.gov*—it is recommended that you call early on the 15th. Arriving without reservations, you will have to camp outside the Valley—try Tuolumne Meadows Campground in the morning and the Forest Service campgrounds just west of the park in the afternoon and evening.

Additional Information: *www.nps.gov/yose*

Hike 84—The Burn

Location	Half Dome
Agency	Yosemite National Park
Highlights	Scaling Half Dome by cable. Dizzying vertigo.
Distance	16.4 miles round trip
Total Elevation Gain/Loss	4800´/4800´
Hiking Time	10–12 hours
Difficulty	★★★★★
Best Times	mid-June through September
Optional Map	USGS 7.5-min *Half Dome*

There is no other hike in the world like this one.

The Hike is an extremely strenuous all-day affair that climbs to the summit of Half Dome from Yosemite Valley. The final stretch to the top is by a cable route so steep that both arms are needed to pull yourself up. Hikers should be in good shape and not suffer from acrophobia. Installed by the park once conditions allow, the cable route is usually up by mid-June and removed in mid-October. It is closed during winter months. Sunscreen is essential for this hike as the bare rock of Half Dome provides no protection against the sun's burning rays. Crowds are constant all season long, although they're somewhat lighter after Labor Day. The trail gets congested by late morning, and the single-track cable

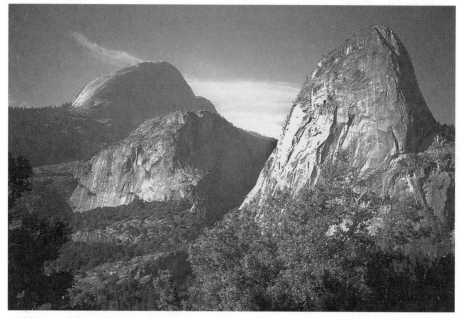

Half Dome (left) and Liberty Cap

route on top backs up by lunchtime. The earlier you start, the better. The route up to the junction above Nevada Fall is described in Hike 83.

To Reach the Trailhead, please see Hike 83.

Description: From the junction above Nevada Fall (2.3/6000) head left, immediately passing the restroom on your way toward Little Yosemite Valley. Now gently climbing, the trail crests a small rise; it loses elevation for the first time where the top of Half Dome becomes visible northwest. Wide and sandy, the path rejoins the much calmer river before arcing away from it and passing the designated campground and seasonal ranger station on the right. Bear left at all junctions. Little Yosemite Valley is your last opportunity to get water for the next 1,500 feet of elevation gain.

Turning north, your trail ascends upward through a dense red fir forest to reach the junction with the Half Dome Trail (4.8/7000). While the John Muir Trail bears east here on its long journey to Mt. Whitney, you continue north to begin the ultimate ascent. You soon encounter a spring on the left where a small pipe conveniently diverts water for easy fill-up. Note that this non-potable water must be purified; it is the last source on this hike. Views across Tenaya Canyon open up through the trees where the trail heads west to the base of the open slopes on the ridgetop (6.3/7900).

Signs in many languages warn of the danger of lightning strikes. Take them seriously and **do not proceed if thunderstorms are threatening**. With your horizon clear, continue upward on the zigzagging stairway of granite blocks. As you pass twisted trees clinging to life in the nooks and crannies of bare rock, the trail gets progressively steeper. It soon crests a small rise and then drops to the bottom of the cable route (7.3/8410).

Unless you arrive early, this final section will be a thin line of humanity creeping to the top. Blubbering acro-phobes and exhausted hikers contribute to the line's slow pace; it can take upwards of 30 minutes to reach the top. Be patient and savor this unforgettable experience while you wait. With both arms needed to pull yourself along, hand protection is important for preventing cable burn—a huge pile of mangled gloves found at the base of the cable route are free to use. The climb steepens on the upper section before finally reaching the end of the line (7.5/8810). The actual summit (8838) is at the north end.

Experience the dizzying vertigo of Half Dome as you creep toward the edge, staring almost 5,000 feet down to the valley floor. Half Dome's northwest face is a vertical, 2,000-foot sheer wall of granite, on which climbers can often be spotted. With unparalleled views from here, most of the southern half of the park is visible. Almost due north is Mt. Hoffman (10850), below which runs Tioga Road. Looking east beyond Little Yosemite Valley, the peaks of the Cathedral Range line the horizon. Southeast are the spires of the Clark Range, all of which exceed 11,000 feet. Closer by, Clouds Rest (Hike 85) is immediately northeast along the ridge, with the bulges of Quarter Domes between it and Half Dome. If you look west down Yosemite Valley, many of the Valley's most prominent landmarks can be identified—Glacier Point is across the Merced River canyon and Cathedral Spires, El Capitan, and Yosemite Village are all visible.

Done reveling in this awe-inspiring place? Go back the way you came, rejoining Hike 83 above Nevada Fall to return via the John Muir Trail for the easiest descent.

Nearest Visitor Center: See Hike 83.

Backpacking Information: Turning the marathon ascent of Half Dome into an overnight trip allows you to beat the morning rush on the cable route. Wilderness permits are required and there is a quota for this trailhead that always fills up. Half of the permits are subject to reservation, the other half are available on a first-come, first-served basis the day before or day of travel. To get a permit, arrive at a permit window the moment it opens (usually 7–8 A.M.), or make a reservation in advance by calling (209) 372-0740 ($5/person reservation fee). Permits can be obtained at the Valley Visitor Center and from permit stations at Tuolumne Meadows, Wawona, Big Oak Flat (just past the west entrance station on Hwy. 120), and Hetch Hetchy. Bear canisters are absolutely essential and can be rented for a nominal fee when you pick up your permit. The wily bears *will* get your food otherwise, no matter how well you hang it. In Little Yosemite Valley, camping is allowed only at designated sites. Sleeping above 7,600 feet on Half Dome is prohibited.

Nearest Campground: See Hike 83.
Additional Information:
www.nps.gov/yose.

Half Dome above Yosemite Valley

Hike 85—Sky Walker

Location	Clouds Rest
Agency	Yosemite National Park
Highlights	Half Dome minus the madness.
Distance	14.0 miles round trip
Total Elevation Gain/Loss	2500´/2500´
Hiking Time	8–10 hours
Difficulty	★★★★
Best Times	Mid-June through September
Optional Map	USGS 7.5-min *Tenaya Lake*

Let's face it, Yosemite Valley is crazy. If the congestion there is too much for you, then you should be on the Tioga Road. And if you're on the Tioga Road, you should be climbing Clouds Rest.

The Hike ascends Clouds Rest (9926) from Tenaya Lake, a steady climb with rewarding summit views of Half Dome and much of the national park. As throughout Yosemite, there will be people on the trail with you. However, there will be far fewer people than you would encounter on trails emanating from the Valley. Snow generally clears by mid-June, although it can linger into early July in years of deep snowpack. No water is available at the trailhead and sources beyond Tenaya Creek can be non-existent late in the season.

To Reach the Trailhead, go east on Tioga Rd. (Hwy. 120) to just west of Tenaya Lake in central Yosemite National Park, and park in the Sunrise trailhead lot, located 30 miles east of Crane Flat and 8 miles west of Tuolumne Meadows Campground. There is a $20 entrance fee for Yosemite National Park, valid for seven days.

Description: At the trailhead by the food storage lockers, the trail immediately splits—go left toward Sunrise High Sierra Camp. Passing among lodgepole pines, the wide concrete path soon becomes dirt. Skirting a pleasant meadow before crossing Tenaya Creek, the trail quickly reaches a junction for Tuolumne High Sierra Camp—bear right toward Sunrise. After briefly paralleling the creek, the trail curves south and passes on a long level stretch, weaving through boulders, lodgepole pines, and clearings seasonally flush with tiger lilies and other wildflowers. Red fir and western white pine appear as the trail climbs again; you soon find yourself switch-backing steeply to the top of a forested saddle. There is a four-way junction here—continue straight ahead. The unmarked trail that comes in from the right leads to surprise viewpoints of upper Tenaya Canyon. Left leads to the nearby Sunrise Lakes.

Descending south, the trail passes a shallow pond before crossing a small tributary of Tenaya Creek, which can run dry late in the season. This is your last source for water. Your route is a gentle rise from here to the next junction, where you continue straight ahead. The trail drops briefly before making a quick ascent to a broad saddle where views south are obscured by the trees…but not for long.

Continue along the ridgeline. Suddenly nothing impairs your view of the naked flanks of Clouds Rest shearing

4,000 feet into Tenaya Canyon below. Sheets of exfoliating granite peel away from the slopes. The trail becomes indistinct the final 200 feet to the summit; take the broad granite runway directly along the ridgeline to the top (9926).

Visible for the first time, Half Dome immediately draws your attention southwest. Those with binoculars can pick out the cable route's ant line on the northeast shoulder (Hike 84). Yosemite Valley winds away west below it all. Southeast beyond Little Yosemite Valley, the peaks of the Clark Range can be seen. Northeast on the skyline are the jagged pinnacles of the Cathedral Range. North is Mt. Hoffman (10850), below which the Tioga Road winds around Tenaya Lake. Return the way you came.

Nearest Visitor Center: Tuolumne Meadows Visitor Center, (209) 372-0263. Open mid-June through mid-October daily 9 A.M.–7 P.M. For general Yosemite information call the information center at (209) 372-0200.

Backpacking Information: Numerous campsites exist along or near this hike, although few have convenient access to water. Try Sunrise Lakes. There are no legal options on the summit. Wilderness permits are required and are most readily obtained from the permit station east of Tuolumne Meadows (open daily 7 A.M.–7 P.M.). There is a quota of 20 people for this trailhead and it always fills up. Half of the permits are subject to reservation, the other half are available on a first-come, first-served basis on the day before or day of travel. To get a permit arrive at the permit window

the moment it opens, or make a reservation in advance by calling (209) 372-0740 ($5/person reservation fee).

Nearest Campground: Tuolumne Meadows Campground (318 sites, $15). Half the sites are first-come, first-served and the other half can be reserved. Reservations are available up to 5 months in advance, in blocks of one month at a time, with the next block becoming available on the 15th of each month. To make reservations, call 1-800-436-7275 or go online at *reservations.nps.gov.*

Additional Information: *www.nps.gov/yose.*

SKY WALKER

Hike 86—Grizzly Giants

Location	Mariposa Grove
Agency	Yosemite National Park
Highlights	The largest living things on Earth.
Distance	5.8 miles
Total Elevation Gain/Loss	1100´/1100´
Hiking Time	3–4 hours
Difficulty	★★
Best Times	May through October
Optional Map	USGS 7.5-min *Mariposa Grove*

Incomparable, indescribable, unbeliev-able, the giant sequoias must be experi-enced firsthand. Visit the Valley only and you have seen but half the wonders of Yosemite.

The Mariposa Grove is one of the most northerly of 75 recognized giant sequoia groves that dot the western slopes of the Sierra Nevada. It is also the best known and most heavily visited. Not a spot for solitude, the grove receives hundreds to thousands of visi-tors daily. But most either select the nar-rated open-air tram tour, which putts along the paved roads of the grove, or walk but a short distance from the park-ing lot to the Grizzly Giant before return-ing to their vehicles, leaving the trails to far fewer people.

The Hike explores the entire grove by trail, and allows you to briefly escape the Yosemite bustle and peacefully com-mune with these giant trees. Mariposa Grove is open daily from approximately late April until snow once again closes the road in the fall. Crowds are lightest in the evenings and early mornings. Water is available at the trailhead.

To Reach the Trailhead, take the turnoff for the Mariposa Grove, located immediately inside the park just past the South Entrance Station on Hwy. 41, 35 miles (75 minutes) south of Yosemite

Valley. Trailers are prohibited on the narrow 2-mile road to the parking lot, and RVs are not allowed between 9 A.M. and 4 P.M. Despite its massive size, the parking lot is usually full by 10 A.M. dur-ing summer months. Additional parking is provided near the entrance station and a free shuttle bus runs to the lot every 20 minutes during the busy season. There is a $20 entrance fee for Yosemite National Park, good for seven days.

Description: To preserve the grove for future generations of trees (and visi-tors), **do not take cones as souvenirs!** From the parking lot, pass the gift shop and Tour Center on your way to the upper parking lot. The trail begins beside a kiosk where free brochures printed in five languages can be obtained (0.0/5600). First head nearby to The Fallen Monarch, which is believed to have toppled more than 300 years ago. Crossing the road, you ascend numerous oversized steps before recrossing the road by the Bachelor and Three Graces (0.5/5760). Swelling in size near its base, the Bachelor provides a good example of what is known as a *buttressed trunk*.

The Grizzly Giant, fifth largest living thing on Earth, is next. Blackened and scarred, huge and grizzly indeed, its esti-mated age of 2,700 years makes it one of the oldest living sequoias known. Just beyond it is the California Tunnel Tree, one of two trees in the grove tunneled by man, which poses a challenging physics problem of torque and balance. Walk through the tree, cross the road, and bear left at both trail junctions. The trail follows the road and soon reaches the Faithful Couple (1.5/6140), a pair of enormous trees sutured together for more than 50 feet. The posted trail continues across the road to the Clothespin Tree, so named because of the enormous symmetrical gash that runs through it. Climbing into the Upper Grove, the trail reaches the road again near four magnificent specimens. Paths split off in all directions—continue right on the posted Outer Loop Trail, following the road's upper loop. The Mariposa Grove Museum (open daily 9 A.M.–4:30 P.M.) is visible beyond the restrooms and has informative displays, books, and a welcome drinking fountain (2.2/6460).

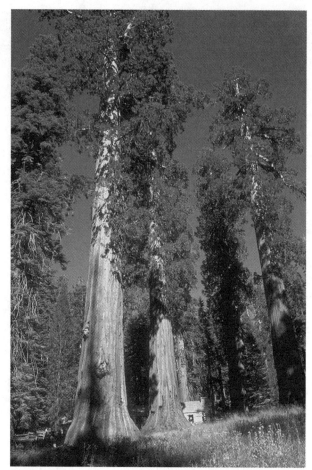

Upper Mariposa Grove and the Mariposa Grove Museum

Continuing on the Outer Loop Trail, take time for a quick side trip inside the Telescope Tree. Without blemish on the outside, inside it's hollow and blue sky can be seen through the opening on top. The trail next loops to the famous Wawona Tunnel Tree (2.8/6600), lying on its side below the trail. The final landmark tree on this hike is the Galen Clark Tree, named for the man who tirelessly promoted the grove and urged its protection in the late 1850s and 1860s.

Immediately past the Galen Clark Tree is the junction for Wawona Point Vista, which offers views across the South Fork Merced River to Wawona Dome. The return to the parking lot on Outer Loop Trail leaves the sequoias behind and passes instead through a quiet forest of sugar pine, incense cedar, white fir, and Jeffrey pine. Those wishing to return through the sequoias should backtrack to the museum and descend from there. Otherwise, continue straight at all junctions in the upper grove. Halfway down to the parking lot (4.5/6120) the trail to Wawona splits off west, but you continue straight and bear right at the remaining junctions to reach the lot.

Nearest Visitor Center: Wawona Information Station, (209) 375-9501. From Hwy. 41 in Wawona take Chilnualna Falls Rd. to the first right-hand turn past the stables. Open in summer daily 8:30 A.M.–4:30 P.M. (closed for lunch). For general recorded park information call (209) 372-0200.

Nearest Campground: Wawona Campground, located near Wawona (93 sites, $15). Open year-round. Reservations required May through September. Reservations are available up to 5 months in advance, in blocks of one month at a time, with the next block becoming available on the 15th of each month. To make reservations, call 1-800-436-7275 or go online at *reservations.nps.gov*. Also try Summerdale Campground in Sierra National Forest, located immediately south of the park on Hwy. 41 (30 sites). For the adventurous with a map of Sierra National Forest, secret Nelder Grove Campground is not too far away (free).

Additional Information:
www.nps.gov/yose

GRIZZLY GIANTS

Hike 87—The Upper Crest

Location	Mammoth Crest
Agency	Inyo National Forest
Highlights	Mammoth Lakes Basin. The Sierra Divide.
Distance	4.5 miles round trip
Total Elevation Gain/Loss	1700´/1700´
Hiking Time	4–6 hours
Difficulty	★★★
Best Times	June through October
Optional Map	USGS 7.5-min *Crystal Crag*

In the town of Mammoth Lakes you can buy fresh arugula at the grocery store. You can also hike to the top of Mammoth Crest, view the entire crystalline basin, and then stare west into the heart of the Sierra Nevada.

Mammoth Lakes occupies the western end of the Long Valley caldera, an enormous depression formed 760,000 years ago in a massive volcanic eruption that blew ash as far away as Missouri. After the eruption, the top of the volcano collapsed to create this 10 by 20-mile-wide elliptical basin. Volcanic activity continued here over the next 560,000 years, producing lava flows and the bulging dome of Mammoth Mountain. While the past 100,000 years have been quiet, a large body of magma is believed to still exist as close as 3 miles below the caldera surface. Between 1980 and 1986 swarms of earthquakes struck the area and were accompanied by ground uplift, an indicator of magma movement below and a warning of a potential eruption. Although the region quieted down after 1986, activity and uplift in portions of the caldera continue today, making this region California's greatest volcanic hazard.

The Hike climbs from Lake George to the top of the Sierra Divide, which separates the Mammoth Lakes Basin from the drainage of the San Joaquin River. Crystal Lake makes a nice stopover halfway up, and is the end destination for many hikers. Above it people are fewer, a pleasant contrast to the crowds that frequent Mammoth Lakes virtually year-round. September is your best bet for tranquility. Fishing is possible in Crystal Lake. Water and all the amenities are available at the trailhead.

To Reach the Trailhead, take Hwy. 203 west to the town of Mammoth Lakes—the turnoff is on Hwy. 395 roughly midway between Lee Vining and Bishop. At the first stoplight, continue straight on Main St. At the second stoplight, bear left onto Lake Mary Rd. and proceed 3.4 miles to a junction near Lake Mary—continue straight toward Mamie Lake. By the Pokonobe Marina 0.4 mile farther turn left; drive 0.3 mile—immediately passing Lake Mary Campground—to a posted junction for Lake George. Turn right and go 0.3 mile to the large but often full lot by Lake George Marina and Campground.

Description: Begin by the entrance to the parking lot (0.0/9030) in a forest of lodgepole pine, western white pine, and mountain hemlock. The jagged granite thumb of Crystal Crag (10377)—visible from the lot—juts above Lake George; watch perspective on this landmark change dramatically over the course of the hike. Switchbacking west along the ridge above Lake George, the trail soon reaches the junction for Crystal Lake (0.9/9650). A short spur leads down to this exquisite body of water, flanked by Crystal Crag on the east and Mammoth Crest on the west. A maze of use paths surround the lake.

After you've resumed climbing on the main trail, mountain hemlock soon disappear in a predominantly lodgepole pine forest, and views of the basin below open up. Just beyond Lake George, a small flotilla of boats plies Lake Mary, the largest of the lakes. Mammoth Creek drains Lake Mary, passing through Lake Mamie and Twin Lakes on its way to Owens Valley. To the north, Horseshoe Lake lies between you and Mammoth Mountain (11053) and McLeod Lake is farther west, just below Mammoth Pass (9360). Traversing southeast near the ridgetop, you enter John Muir Wilderness (1.5/10080), where the rock changes from pale granite to red volcanics. You can see in the rocks behind the sign the turbulent flow currents and air bubbles preserved as they solidified. As you round the flank of a false crest, the true ridgetop becomes visible across a barren landscape dotted with krummholz trees. Once you've attained it, an off-trail stroll will bring you to the western edge of the ridge and views into the San Joaquin drainage.

Raking the northern sky are the dark Minarets of the Ritter Range, remnants of volcanoes that erupted some 100 million years ago. Magma that fed those volcanoes is today's granite beneath your feet; it crystallized miles below the surface but later was exposed by erosion. The tallest mountains of the Ritter Range are Banner Peak (12945), seen farthest east, and adjacent Mt. Ritter (13140). The trail continues southeast along Mammoth Crest and offers ever-changing panoramic vistas, but this hike ends here having conquered the Sierra Divide.

Nearest Visitor Center: Mammoth Lakes Visitor Center, (760) 924-5500, located immediately east of town on Hwy. 203. Open daily 8 A.M.–5 P.M.

Nearest Campground: There are nearly a dozen campgrounds around Mammoth Lakes, including one by the trailhead at Lake George (16 sites, $13).

THE UPPER CREST

Hike 88—The Land of Balloon Dome

Location	Ansel Adams Wilderness
Agency	Sierra National Forest
Highlights	Monolithic Balloon Dome. The Mighty San Joaquin.
Distance	9.5 miles round trip
Total Elevation Gain/Loss	2150´/2150´
Hiking Time	8–10 hours
Difficulty	★★★★
Best Times	May through October
Optional Map	USGS 7.5-min *Balloon Dome*

A naked bubble of granite rising nearly 3,000 feet from canyon bottom, Balloon Dome stands—a monolith, an inspiration, a companion on your descent to the sandy banks of the mighty San Joaquin River. Carving the Sierra Nevada between well-trod Yosemite and Kings Canyon national parks, the river pours through a delightful, less-visited landscape of abundant wildlife.

To Reach the Trailhead, go 4.1 miles north on Hwy. 41 from the Hwy. 49 junction in Oakhurst and turn east on Bass Lake Rd. In 5.5 miles, turn left on Beasore Rd. (FS Rd. 7). Follow it northeast for nearly 30 miles. Cold Springs Summit is reached in 11.0 miles, where the road becomes a Forest Service Scenic Byway. Paved FS Rd. 6S01 branches right 2.5 miles later—continue straight. The pave-

Your landmark—Balloon Dome

ment ends 4.7 miles later just past a posted junction for Mugler Creek and Grizzly Road. Continuing for another 10.1 miles on increasingly rough road (the last 2 miles are the worst), you reach a stop sign and the end of FS Rd. 7. Go straight on FS Rd. 5S30 for 1.1 miles, and turn right at the posted turnoff for Cassidy Trail. The first 1.7 mile is very rough but passable for all vehicles; then the access road drops steeply down a granite ramp. Park here if you can't go farther. The final 1.3 miles requires a high-clearance vehicle, and terminates in an open parking area just before Granite Creek.

The Hike begins at the western border of Ansel Adams Wilderness and follows Cassidy Trail as it descends steadily to the San Joaquin River. A lower elevation hike, it makes an exciting option in spring and late fall when snow has closed the higher regions. Fishing and swimming are possible in the San Joaquin. Bring sun protection. Water is available at the trailhead from Granite Creek.

Description From the parking area (0.0/6390), descend 50 feet on a grit-coated granite slab to Granite Creek, your only opportunity to obtain water prior to reaching the San Joaquin River. From here, Cassidy Trail follows Granite Creek on the opposite side more than 100 feet above it; no designated trail leads from this trailhead up to it. To reach it, cross the creek (the unmarked border of Ansel Adams Wilderness) and climb the steep slope, bearing slightly south until you spot a deep and difficult-to-cross gully. Follow this upslope until you encounter the obvious trail, which crosses the gully 130 feet above the creek. Remember this routing for your return!

Initially heading southwest, the trail passes through a dense forest of large Jeffrey pine, sugar pine, white fir, and incense cedar. The bald hump of Squaw Dome (7818) appears directly ahead before the trail begins to descend slowly

and bend southeast. Suddenly you see Balloon Dome between the trees!

A granite dome occurs when a huge block of fracture-free granite is exposed at the surface after overlying layers have eroded away. Freed from the pressure of overlying rock, the dome begins slowly shedding giant curved layers of rock in a process known as *exfoliation*. Such an unusually solid mass of rock takes a long time to wear away and will stand sentinel over the landscape for eons. Half Dome (Hike 84) is the most famous example.

Changing views of Balloon Dome finally disappear as the trail begins a long arcing traverse to the east. Look for Sitting Hen Rock on the left, posted with the only sign you will encounter on this hike. At the upper elevation of their range, black oak appear along this section. At the end of the traverse (2.5/5950), the trail begins its 1,500-foot descent to the river. Looking northeast, the Middle Fork San Joaquin can be seen curving west from Mammoth Crest (Hike 87) on the horizon. The South Fork flows just south of Balloon Dome and although you can't see it, the northern headwaters drain the peaks of the Silver Divide on the east skyline.

The descent to the river is rocky, often exposed to the sun, and comprises more than 40 switchbacks. Poison oak appears near the bottom. Finally a metal bridge comes into view and river sounds fill your ears (4.7/4410). Helicoptered to this site in 1956, the bridge has sustained recent flood damage: its bent central girders testify to the river's mind-boggling height that day. Exploration up- and down-river is easy and fishing holes are aplenty. While Cassidy Trail continues across the bridge toward Rattlesnake Lake, to keep this a dayhike you must return the way you came.

Nearest Visitor Center: Tiny Clover Meadow Ranger Station, (559) 877-2218 ext. 3136, located 0.6 mile past the turnoff for Cassidy Trail on FS Rd. 5S30.

Open mid-June through mid-September daily 8 A.M.–noon and 1–5 P.M.

Backpacking Information: Wilderness permits are required and are available at Clover Meadow. There is no quota for Cassidy Trail.

Nearest Campground: Clover Meadow (7 sites, free). There is almost always space.

Additional Information: *www.r5.fs.fed.us/sierra*

THE LAND OF BALLOON DOME

Hike 89—The Riser to Kaiser

Location	Kaiser Wilderness
Agency	Sierra National Forest
Highlights	A panoramic view of the central Sierra Nevada.
Distance	10.0 miles round trip.
Total Elevation Gain/Loss	3200´/3200´
Hiking Time	6–8 hours
Difficulty	★★★★
Best Times	Mid-June through September
Optional Map	Forest Service *Kaiser Wilderness* topographic map

Kaiser Peak stands alone—a western spur of the towering Sierra ridge that bounds the San Joaquin River. Ascend this peak and stand upon the lip of a great divide.

The Hike climbs steadily up the southern slope of Mt. Kaiser (10310) and offers increasingly expansive views of the Huntington Lake basin, before reaching the summit crest and superlative vistas north. Despite its immediate proximity to popular Huntington Lake, Kaiser Wilderness attracts few hikers. A visit in late June or September will provide an unusual degree of solitude. Potable water is available at the pack station near the trailhead, and there are two sources along the trail—Deer Creek near the beginning and Bear Creek near the goal.

To Reach the Trailhead, take Hwy. 168 east from Clovis to its end along the east shore of Huntington Lake; turn left at the T-junction. In 0.9 mile turn right at the posted turnoff for the D&F Pack Station (just before the entrance to Deer Creek Campground). Bear right on Upper Deer Creek Lane after 0.1 mile and right again onto Deer Lane after another 0.5 mile. While the dirt road horseshoes over a creek and into the pack station, you should park in the small lot before the creek. The trailhead is at the north end of the pack station customer parking lot.

Description: At the trailhead (0.0/7200) two trails split off—bear left toward Kaiser Peak. Ascending among large Jeffrey pines, you reach another junction 100 yards along—continue straight ahead. The trail narrows to single-track and slowly climbs to meet Deer Creek on the right (0.5/7600). Briefly paralleling the creek, the trail then begins a long switchbacking ascent to College Rock among enormous, fantastically shaped granite boulders. Flowers abound in season, including lupine, paintbrush, and Western hound's-tongue. The red cones of snow plants protrude from the litter of the forest floor.

An ideal picnic spot, College Rock (2.5/9055) can be surmounted with a bit of scrambling for some exciting views. Ringed by mountains, all of Huntington Lake is spread out below. If you look southwest into the Great Central Valley, the Coast Range outline often appears above the haze—a distance of more than 100 miles!

From here, several tight switchbacks lead up 200 feet before the trail slowly traverses to Bear Creek, joining it at a large flat meadow (3.0/9340) among lodgepole and western white pines.

Weaving to and from creekside, the trail passes below a massive fortress of granite as it ascends to a crest (4.0/9800). Suddenly, the strange moonscape of upper Kaiser Ridge comes into view, devoid of all trees and only occasionally matted with plant life. Traversing around a false summit, you reach a small cleft below now visible Kaiser Peak, with Jewel Lake (closer) and Campfire Lake (farther) several hundred feet below. The summit (5.0/10310) is finally obtained via a very short, posted spur trail.

The view! Before you drains the mighty San Joaquin. The prominent granite knob north poking out of the river valley is Balloon Dome (Hike 88). Farther north, the saw-toothed Minarets of the Ritter Range are easily identified, with the North Fork San Joaquin draining west below them. The Middle Fork wraps east around them, curving north below Mammoth Crest (Hike 87). The high peaks west of the Minarets form the southern border of Yosemite National Park. East-southeast, the South Fork San Joaquin drains the distant mountains of northern Kings Canyon National Park, visible along the skyline. Just below to the northwest is Bonnie Lake. The small twins of Bobby Lake lie nearly 1,000 feet beneath you. Don't be so distracted by the view that you leave your food unattended. Several marmots that make the summit rocks their home love to pilfer! Return the way you came.

Nearest Visitor Center: Pine Ridge Ranger District Office, (559) 855-5355, located in Prather on the way up Hwy. 168. Open daily 8 A.M.–4:30 P.M.

Backpacking Information: A wilderness permit is required, obtainable in Prather during business hours. Due to a lack of good campsites on this hike, there is a quota of 6 people in effect for this trailhead from the last Friday in June through mid-September.

Nearest Campground: 11 campgrounds line the shores of Huntington Lake ($14–16).

Additional Information: *www.r5.fs.fed.us/sierra*

The Riser to Kaiser

Hike 90—Mighty Dinkey

Location	Dinkey Lakes Wilderness
Agency	Sierra National Forest
Highlights	Remote meadows. 4 lakes. Adventure road access.
Distance	6.7 miles
Total Elevation Gain/Loss	850´/850´
Hiking Time	3–5 hours
Difficulty	★★
Best Times	May through September
Optional Map	Forest Service *Dinkey Lakes Wilderness* topographic map

The bear charged. Dinkey attacked. Biting the hind leg of the massive brute, Dinkey was exterminated seconds later. Yet the bravery of this tiny dog saved its owner, giving him enough time to grab his gun and kill the bear. Although he was "no bigger than a rabbit," local legend and appellation honor mighty Dinkey to this day (Kings River Ranger District 1997).

The Hike gently climbs along sweetly flowing Dinkey Creek before weaving among four pleasant lakes. Wildflowers are abundant in the early summer— shooting stars can ring First Dinkey Lake with a pink halo, while mountain pride penstemons and crimson columbines lend color to quiet forest glades. Due to the boggy nature of the lake plateau, mosquitoes swarm in uncommon numbers throughout June and July, and are present to some degree all summer long. While there is no water available at the trailhead, Dinkey Creek is accessible over the first 1.2 miles.

To Reach the Trailhead, a high-clearance vehicle is all but essential. Although 4WD is not necessary, passenger cars with low clearance risk a bottom-scraping experience on the roughest access roads covered in this book. Take Hwy. 168 east from Clovis to the town of Shaver Lake and turn east onto Dinkey

Creek Road. In 8.7 miles, turn left onto posted Rock Creek Road (FS Rd. 9S09)— mostly paved but dotted with treacherous potholes. In 5.8 miles, you reach a T-junction. Go right on marginally paved FS Rd. 9S10 for 4.5 miles, until you reach a posted junction for FS Rd. 9S62. Make the hard right, and jounce along for 2.2 miles (bearing left at all forks the final 1.3 miles) through a hellish section of roots and ruts to the substantial trailhead lot.

Description: From the information sign (0.0/8640), the trail immediately drops down to Dinkey Creek and a small waterfall. The taffylike exposures of metamorphic rock here are part of the Dinkey Creek Roof Pendant, a remnant of the landscape that existed prior to the granite intrusion of the Sierra Nevada. A distinct interface between the layered metavolcanics and a marble outcrop's gray smoothness can be seen on the opposite shore. This roof pendant is the likely metamorphosed remains of an ancient offshore volcanic island, similar to the one exposed near Boulder Creek in Kings Canyon National Park (Hike 94).

Recrossing the creek by another fountainlike waterfall, the level trail soon reaches the more typical granite of the Sierra. Here the trail climbs over a bouldery terminal moraine formed by the glacier that once filled this valley. Glacial polish can be identified intermittently from this point onward. Winding through lodgepole pines, the trail reaches the posted junction for Mystery Lake (1.2/8840) and the start of the four-lake loop. While the hike can be completed in either direction, this description heads first to Mystery Lake, allowing you to reach the lakes in rough order of their increasing scenic beauty.

Bear right, cross Dinkey Creek, and make a gradual ascent to reach Mystery Lake near its outlet (1.5/8960). Numerous use paths lead to the shores of this shallow, rather unexciting lake. The trail skirts the lake, passes through its boggy east end, and then crosses the outflow stream from Swede Lake. Climbing a dozen switchbacks, the trail regains the stream just prior to reaching Swede Lake itself (2.4/9220). Backed by bare granite faces on its southeast shore, round Swede Lake presents better swimming and angling opportunities at its deeper north end. Past its north end, you quickly gain 150 feet before a mellow traverse and a slight drop bring you to South Lake (3.1/9300). Bigger, deeper, and prettier, South Lake is fed by a waterfall

rushing over an exposed granite ledge on its south side.

Beyond South Lake the trail becomes difficult to identify as use paths diverge in all directions. Most head down to the bogs around First Dinkey Lake's east shore, a very wet and soggy option. The actual trail crosses the lake's outflow creek and gradually traverses above the bogs to rejoin Dinkey Creek. Trees are blazed along the correct route but if you find yourself off-track, continue traversing on the level until you reach Dinkey Creek and the very obvious trail alongside it. Upstream leads to further adventure and three more lakes (Second Dinkey, Rock, and Island lakes) less than a mile away. This hike heads downstream to the north shore of First Dinkey Lake (3.7/9240). The lake is meadow-fringed and deep, with the studded granite ridge of the Three Sisters visible beyond its southern shore. Depending on the mosquito swarms, this is the nicest, most scenic picnic spot on the hike. From here, the trail arcs around the lake's north shore, reaching a junction just past the large boulders by the lake's outlet. Bear left and begin a gradual descent along or near Dinkey Creek.

Mighty Dinkey

Look for the small but plentiful brook trout in the many limpid pools, as you return to the earlier junction for Mystery Lake and continue back to the trailhead.

Nearest Visitor Center: Dinkey Creek Ranger Station, located on Dinkey Creek Rd. 2.8 miles past the turnoff for Rock Creek Rd. Open sporadically mid-May through September, Thursday through Monday 8 A.M.–4:30 P.M. A more reliable source of information is the Pine Ridge Ranger District Office, (559) 855-5355, in Prather on Hwy. 168. Open daily 8 A.M.–4:30 P.M.

Backpacking Information: A wilderness permit is required, obtainable from either ranger station during business hours. The best campsites are found at Swede and South lakes. There is no quota in effect for this trailhead.

Nearest Campground: Dinkey Creek Campground, located adjacent to Dinkey Creek Ranger Station (128 sites, $14).

Additional Information: *www.r5.fs.fed.us/sierra*

First Dinkey Lake

Hike 91—Methuselah

Location	Ancient Bristlecone Pine Forest
Agency	Inyo National Forest
Highlights	Phantasmagoria. The oldest living things on Earth.
Distance	4.2 miles
Total Elevation Gain/Loss	1000´/1000´
Hiking Time	2–3 hours
Difficulty	★★★
Best Times	Mid-June through September
Optional Map	USGS 7.5-min *Westgard Pass*

Gnarled and twisted, sculpted and sublime, the bristlecone pines endure. Commune with trees more than 4,000 years old.

The rocks of the White Mountains were deposited as sea-floor sediment approximately 600 million years ago, making them the oldest rocks described by this guidebook. Thrust into mountains about 350 million years ago, the rocks today contain numerous exposed pockets of dolomite, a form of metamorphic limestone that is highly alkaline and inhospitable to most plants. In this soil, at elevations from 9,000 to 11,000 feet, the hardy bristlecone pine sets its roots.

Pinus longaeva (long-lived pine) is readily identified by its curved branchlets resembling long foxtails; its dark green, short needles growing in clusters of five; and its gooey sap-laden purple cones. The small bristle that appears at the end of mature cones gives the tree its name. Precipitation is minimal in the White Mountains. Between 12 and 15 inches fall annually, limiting the trees to only six to eight weeks of growth each year. The short growth cycle, coupled with the nutrient-poor dolomitic soil, allows the trees to produce only very small amounts of wood each year. Extremely dense and resinous, the wood is highly resistant to rot, pests, and fire.

Ironically, the oldest trees grow in the most inhospitable sites: steep slopes of poor soil that retain little water. These restricted conditions cause slower than normal growth, producing denser (up to 150 rings per inch) and more durable wood than trees growing in better spots. During times of adversity, a bristlecone can also let entire limbs die, often maintaining adequate nutrient flow to only a single branch. Dead branches take thousands more years to decay, becoming sculpted into fantastical shapes by wind-blown sand and ice crystals. Tree roots are seldom deeper than 2 feet, and despite the slow rate of slope erosion (less than one foot per 1,000 years), death by toppling over is a common end for the most ancient trees. Fallen trees can remain on the ground for up to 7,000 years! A dendrochronologist's delight, bristlecone pines provide a nearly complete chronology of the past 10,000 years through living and dead wood samples.

The Hike winds down to Methuselah Grove, location of more than 20 trees older than 4,000 years and home of Methuselah, at 4,700 years the world's oldest living thing. In order to protect Methuselah, its exact location is kept secret. Throughout this hike, it is critical that you stay on the trail—off-route hiking greatly increases the rate of erosion and can damage the root system of the trees. Additionally, the removal of any wood, living or dead, is strictly prohibited. Because trail elevation hovers around 10,000 feet, altitude sickness is a real concern, especially for those driving straight up from Owens Valley 6,000 feet below. A morning start is best for solitude on the trail, as many day-trippers arrive in the early afternoon from Owens Valley. Weather can range unpredictably from cold to sudden thunderstorms to scorching sun. It can snow year-round.

To Reach the Trailhead, take Hwy. 168 east from Hwy. 395 in Big Pine—the turnoff is 0.5 mile north of the Texaco station. After 12.3 miles, turn left onto White Mountain Road. You reach an entrance station 0.4 mile later, where a fee of $2 per person is collected (maximum $5/car, Golden Eagle Pass accepted). With the exception of small bottles available for purchase at the visitor center; **water and supplies are not available past this point!** Be prepared! The trailhead is at the Schulman Grove Visitor Center parking lot, a steep 9.7 miles past the entrance station.

Description: The trail begins left of the picnic tables, where a self-guiding trail brochure can be picked up for $1 (0.0/10100). After a short 0.2 mile, bear right at the fork. (You'll return from the left.) Curving along south slopes of a deep creek gully, the trail climbs to the first rest bench (0.5/10220), which provides views east far into Nevada. The trail brochure's stop 7, past the second bench, overlooks Methuselah Grove, occupying a small, distinctly white ridgelet in the valley below. As you hike there, you cross a vegetation zone where sage

and mountain mahogany dominate, due to more hospitable sandstone soils.

Descending from the ridge, you soon begin passing through the ancient Methuselah Grove. With many of these trees predating the Pyramids of Egypt, there is an impalpable feeling of time. Are you walking softly? Departing the grove at the trail's lowest point (2.3/9730), the trail bends west and gradually switchbacks up the creek canyon to return to the parking lot.

Nearest Visitor Center: Schulman Grove Visitor Center, (707) 873-2514, located at the trailhead. Open Memorial Day through mid-November daily 9 A.M.–6 P.M., with reduced hours in spring and fall.

The ancient bristlecone pine

Camping Information: There is no backpacking or backcountry camping allowed in the Methuselah Grove or anywhere within the designated Ancient Bristlecone Pine Forest, a 44-square-mile area straddling most of the White Mountains above 9,000 feet. Backcountry camping is allowed with a valid campfire permit in the surrounding Inyo National Forest, however. The closest organized camping is at Grandview Campground (no water), a free option 5.1 miles beyond the entrance station on White Mountain Rd., which doesn't quite live up to its name.

Additional Information:
www.r5.fs.fed.us/inyo/vvc/bcp

METHUSELAH

Hike 92—Emerald Lakes

Location	John Muir Wilderness
Agency	Inyo National Forest
Highlights	Lakes of glacial green in the eastern Sierra.
Distance	12.0 miles
Total Elevation Gain/Loss	2800´/2800´
Hiking Time	8–12 hours
Difficulty	★★★★
Best Times	Mid-June through September
Optional Map	USGS 7.5-min *Split Mountain, North Palisade, Mount Thompson, Coyote Flat*

Stride the east side. Less than five miles from the trailhead, above an idyllic basin studded with emerald lakes and naked granite, the Sierra Divide splits the sky.

The Hike follows North Fork Big Pine Creek into a substantial basin and then completes a semi-loop among five spectacular lakes. Due to the high elevation, snow can linger well into July and usually returns by mid-October. The limited trailheads of the Sierra's eastern slopes tend to funnel crowds into small geographic areas, and this hike is no exception. Obtaining a wilderness permit for overnight trips can be challenging (see below), and the best time to visit is September when summer crowds begin to dwindle. Even then, don't expect solitude. Fishing is possible at all the lakes. No water is available at the trailhead but the river is regularly accessible after the first mile.

To Reach the Trailhead, take Crocker St. west from Hwy. 395 in Big Pine—the turnoff is between the Texaco and Mobil stations. Crocker St. becomes Glacier Lodge Rd., snaking upward 9 miles to the trailhead lot on the right, immediately past Upper Sage Flat and Sage Flat campgrounds. The road continues another 0.3 mile to Big Pine Creek Camp-

ground, but all hikers must leave their vehicles in the designated trailhead lot.

Description: Beginning by the octagonal outhouse (0.0/7750), the single-track trail strikes west through open sage; it passes above the Glacier Pack Station before gently climbing to First Falls Walk-in Campground (0.9/8250). A short drop below the trail, the free campground has five sites with picnic tables and fire rings (although firewood is non-existent). Unseen and inaccessible because of the brush, First Falls can only be heard.

On the next section from First Falls to the base of Second Falls, you have two options. The more scenic route traverses the creek's partly exposed northeast slopes, offering good views up-canyon. The alternative—along the valley floor from First Falls Campground—provides easy walking on a wide path, before it climbs steeply to rejoin the main trail. It is shadier and has regular access to water. The trails join at a junction for Baker Lake (1.7/8580)—continue straight ahead toward impressive Second Falls. The trail switchbacks tightly near the top of the falls, where numerous overlooks let you view the tumbling river.

Now almost level, the trail meanders a dense riparian corridor of lodgepole pine, cottonwood, and alder, with a few Jeffrey pines. Big Pine Wilderness Ranger Camp (2.6/9160), an impressive granite building soon encountered on the left, once belonged to actor Lon Chaney. The fluted massif of Temple Crag comes into full view south as the trail enters more open terrain. You soon reach the posted junction beginning your loop (4.2/10000)—continue straight toward First Lake.

The surreal color of First Lake (4.4/ 9960) can be spotted through the trees

and numerous use paths lead to the rocky shore. Like Second and Third lakes, First Lake is fed by meltwater from Palisade Glacier. Extremely fine sediment ground by the glacier (glacial flour) is suspended in the water, causing the startling green hue of the three lakes. From shore the rounded summits of Mt. Gayley (13510) and—farther—Mt. Sill (14153), just west behind landmark Temple Crag, can be identified . The serrated ridge visible on the southwest skyline includes (from south to north) North Pal-

Emerald Lakes & Palisade Glacier

isade (14242), Mt. Winchell (13775), and Mt. Agassiz (13893).

The trail traverses some 100 feet above Second Lake (10059), the largest, before passing near Third Lake (10249). While both are readily accessed via a number of use paths, Second Lake provides the more impressive lakeshore. Paralleling much-diminished Big Pine Creek above Third Lake, the trail climbs quickly to a large meadow, where the posted Glacier Trail splits off (6.0/ 10640). Leading to the edge of Palisade

Glacier, this trail's epic adventure is described in Hike 93.

By continuing straight, a final ascent brings you to Fourth Lake (6.3/10760). Fed by snow rather than glacial ice, its water contrasts sharply with the Technicolor of the first three. The long descent home begins here. After dark Black Lake (6.8/10680), the trail then descends 500 feet via nine switchbacks to join the earlier trail. Return the way you came.

Nearest Visitor Center: White Mountain Visitor Center, (760) 873-2500, located on Hwy. 395 in downtown Bishop (across the road from Burger King). Open mid-June through mid-September daily 8 A.M.–5 P.M.; the rest of the year Monday–Friday 8 A.M.–noon and 1–4:30 P.M.

Backpacking Information: Wilderness permits are required and there is a quota of 24 people per day for this trailhead, effective from the last Friday in June through mid-September. Due to its deserved popularity, the quota always fills. 60% of the permits are reservable, with the remaining 40% available on a walk-in (first-come, first-served) basis on the day before or day of your trip. Reservations must be made at least 10 days in advance of your trip, after which it is walk-in only. The fee for reserved permits is $5/person and reservations for the quota season can be made beginning March 1 by calling 1-888-374-3773 or (760) 938-1136. Permits, whether walk-in or reserved, may be picked up at the White Mountain Visitor Center (see above), Mono Basin Scenic Area Visitor Center (see Hike 82), Mammoth Lakes Visitor Center (see Hike 87), or Mt. Whitney Ranger Station.

Nearest Campground: Big Pine Creek Campground, located at the road's end ($11). Also try Upper Sage Flat and Sage Flat campgrounds near the trailhead.

Additional Information:
www.r5.fs.fed.us/inyo

Hike 93—Palisade Glacier

Location	John Muir Wilderness
Agency	Inyo National Forest
Highlights	The Sierra Nevada's largest glacier.
Distance	17.0 miles round trip
Total Elevation Gain/Loss	5200′/5200′
Hiking Time	12–16 hours
Difficulty	★★★★★
Best Times	Mid-July through September
Optional Map	USGS 7.5-min *North Palisade*

Attaining the edge of the Palisade Glacier as a dayhike is the greatest challenge this book offers. It is a mile of vertical gain to an active glacier below a serrated ridge of 14,000-foot peaks. In this highest mountain zone life is left behind for a land of rock and ice.

The Hike, an extended variation of Hike 92, climbs an additional 1,800 feet along an increasingly thin trail to reach the glacier. The final 700 feet of ascent are cross-country, and the hike tops out at over 12,000 feet. Due to its high elevation, altitude sickness can be a problem and snow can linger deep into the summer, sometimes well beyond mid-July. Wear the sturdiest and stiffest hiking boots for this hike, as loose rock and constant boulder-hopping can wreak havoc on your feet.

To Reach the Trailhead, see Hike 92.

Description: After following Hike 92 to the Glacier Trail junction (6.0/10640), cross the creek and follow Glacier Trail upward on numerous tight switchbacks. Paralleling an oft-hidden stream coursing beneath granite rubble, the trail eventually crests into Sam Mack Meadow (6.8/11050). Waving with shooting stars and paintbrush, the meadow contains a shallow creek whose blue-gray tint indicates its glacial origin. While an obvious trail continues through the

meadow to a few high-elevation campsites, you should rockhop across the creek near the foot of the meadow. Continue climbing on the opposite slope, where the trail is marked.

Increasingly rough and rocky, the trail passes krummholz whitebark pine, marking the upper limit of tree growth. As you attain the top of a small ridge and continue traversing upward on the far side, incredible views down-canyon of First, Second, and Third lakes open up. The distinctive linear heap of small stones and loose scree now visible above you is a lateral moraine left behind by receding Palisade Glacier. Wrapping around the base of the moraine (8.0/11780), the trail fades completely after crossing the loosest (and most maddening) rock of this trip. Indicated by numerous small cairns, the now completely cross-country route ascends the former glacier path, an undulating polished granite ramp. Sucking enough oxygen from the thin air is now the hardest part. When you finally crest the rubble of the terminal moraine (8.5/12300), you behold the great amphitheater of Palisade Glacier.

The glacier's snout terminates in an ice-choked pond 150 feet below you; the towering peaks scrape the sky 2,000 feet above. Hidden from all angles but this one, Palisade Glacier gouges a barren alpine landscape. Time and energy permitting, scramble down the loose moraine slopes to walk on the glacier itself. Unlike its larger relatives, Palisade Glacier generally lacks crevasses or cracks that would pose serious risk— especially on its lower, boulder-strewn surface—but always exercise caution. The notable features from south to north above the glacier are: Mt. Sill (14153), the prominent dome-shaped summit; V-notch and U-notch, two neighboring gaps in the ridge clearly resembling these letters; North Palisade (14242), though small and rounded immediately north of U-notch, the highest point; and Thunderbolt Peak (14003), the incisor-sharp spires above the glacier's far northwest corner. North beyond the glacier basin are the summits of Mt. Winchell (13775) and Mt. Agassiz (13893). Dozens of climbing routes lead to the various summits, but none are dayhikes (Secor 1999). Return the way you came. Feel the air thicken as you descend.

Nearest Visitor Center: See Hike 92.

Backpacking Information: Unless you bivouac on the loose and uneven rock near the glacier, the only place to camp on this hike is at Sam Mack Meadow, a very fragile life zone at high elevation. Walk carefully here. Wilderness permits are required. See Hike 92 for more information.

Additional Information: *www.r5.fs.fed.us/inyo*

PALISADE GLACIER

Hike 94—Leaves of Three

Location	Boulder Creek
Agency	Sequoia National Forest
Highlights	Mountains of marble. Secluded swim spots.
Distance	2.0 miles round trip
Total Elevation Gain/Loss	300´/300´
Hiking Time	1–3 hours
Difficulty	★★★
Best Times	May through September
Optional Map	USGS 7.5-min *Wren Peak*

Here, ancient coral reefs have been compressed and sutured, metamorphosed and thrust into the sky as mountains of marble. While a perilous sea of poison oak is an unfortunate obstacle, mellifluous Boulder Creek is a compelling attraction.

In a land of granite, the Windy Cliffs and surrounding peaks are a geologic island. Made of marble, this anomaly was once a coral reef ringing a volcanic island far off the coast of ancient North America. Heavily deformed fossils within the rock indicate that the reef formed between 190 and 220 million years ago. Through the action of plate tectonics, the volcanic island and its reef were mashed against and accreted to the North American continent approximately 160 million years ago. Subjected to intense pressures and temperature, the reef was transformed into marble, and the layered volcanic rocks folded like warm taffy into the metavolcanics of Boulder Creek. Sometime during the next 80 million years, rising magma solidified to granite, surrounding but not otherwise altering the marble. An isolated remnant of the pre-Sierra landscape such as this is referred to as a *roof pendant*. As land above was wasted away by erosion, the marble was exposed at the surface, forming the blank gray cliff faces of the

Windy Cliffs region (Nokleburg and Sisson 1994).

The Hike is short and moderate, following a gentle traverse above the Kings River and Boulder Creek to reach a great swimming hole. You can't avoid the poison oak, however, growing over, next to, and actually in the trail at times. Long pants and long sleeves are highly recommended, as well as some anti-poison-oak treatment for after the hike. The trail's poison oak, brushiness, and (a few) exposed slopes bump up the overall difficulty rating. While no potable water is available at the trailhead, snacks and bottled water can be purchased at the Boyden Cave souvenir shop and the Kings River rushes adjacent to the parking lot.

To Reach the Trailhead, take Hwy. 180 east from Grant Grove Visitor Center in northern Kings Canyon National Park to the large parking lot for Boyden Cavern, located where the highway crosses the Kings River on its south bank. Although this hike is in Sequoia National Forest, access requires passage through Kings Canyon National Park where a $10 use fee is collected at Big Stump Entrance Station.

Description: Begin by the souvenir shop, following the paved trail that leads to Boyden Cavern. After climbing 80 feet above the Kings River, the paved trail switchbacks by a metal gate—the unposted junction for this hike. Go through the gate and continue up the narrow trail over a mildly precarious rocky slope. A few railings provide intermittent security on the steep slopes above the Kings River. Poison oak soon appears in the shade of California bay and canyon live oak, growing ever thicker as you continue.

The brushy, overgrown trail curves slowly south above the Boulder Creek drainage, providing exceptional views of the crenelated marble peaks soaring above you. Though the trail gets narrow and spotty, you finally reach the water at a prime swimming hole and picnic spot, accessed via a quick jog where the trail swings closest to the creek. Exploratory journeys await both up- and downstream, and native rainbow trout populate the many holes. Return the way you came and wash off that poison oak!

Nearest Visitor Center: Grant Grove Visitor Center, (559) 565-4307, located 2.4 miles past the park entrance station along Hwy. 180. Open May through June daily 9 A.M.–5 P.M., July through September daily 8 A.M.–6 P.M., with reduced hours in winter. The nearest visitor center for Sequoia National Forest is Hume Lake District Office, (559) 338-2251, 19 miles west of the Big Stump Entrance Station on Hwy. 180. Open Monday through Friday 8 A.M.–4:30 P.M.

Backpacking Information: While backpacking is permitted, the poison oak and lack of campsites make it an unappealing option. A campfire permit is required.

Nearest Campground: There are more than a dozen campgrounds in Kings Canyon National Park and adjacent Sequoia National Forest. Check at the visitor center for current availability.

Additional Information: *www.r5.fs.fed.us/sequoia*

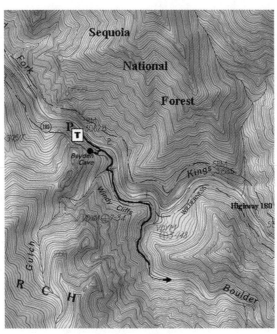

LEAVES OF THREE

Hike 95—King of Kings

Location	Yucca Point
Agency	Sequoia National Forest
Highlights	The deepest canyon in North America.
Distance	3.4 miles round trip
Total Elevation Gain/Loss	1150´/1150´
Hiking Time	2–3 hours
Difficulty	★★★
Best Times	Spring and Fall
Optional Map	USGS 7.5-min *Hume* and *Wren Peak*

Though Highway 180 winds a stunning course above the Kings River, gaining perspective from your car on the immense depth of Kings Canyon is difficult. Luckily, your descent to the river below Yucca Point will remedy this.

The Hike descends quickly to the confluence of the Middle and South Forks of the Kings River, and provides spectacular views up both river canyons. Due to the lower elevation here, spring and fall provide the most agreeable temperatures and May offers the best wildflowers. Summer months can be sweltering. The trail is also a popular access point for anglers, although there are strict regulations governing this stretch of river. In order to protect its population of large wild trout, catch-and-release fishing applies and only artificial lures with barbless hooks may be used. Current regulations should be posted by the trailhead. The river is usually not fishable until July, when the raging waters of melting snowpack subside. No water is available at the trailhead.

To Reach the Trailhead, take Hwy. 180 east from Grant Grove Visitor Center for 13.5 miles. On the left, a Forest Service sign for Yucca Point and a dirt lot with space for four vehicles mark your trailhead. This hike is in Sequoia National Forest but access requires passage through Kings Canyon National Park, where a $10 entrance fee is collected, valid for seven days.

Description: From the trailhead (0.0/3380), descend among manzanita, canyon live oak, cottonwood, California buckeye, and California bay until you reach the first switchback (0.5/2900). From here views of the South Fork canyon open up; the Windy Cliffs (Hike 94) are visible where the river bends out of sight. Look for wildflowers as you descend west to the second switchback. Along with the ubiquitous flowering yucca you can find western wallflower and farewell-to-spring—two wildflowers rarely seen at higher elevations.

Views along the upper section of trail are more expansive than from canyon bottom. Spanish Mtn. (10051), rising nearly 8,000 feet from the opposite bank, offers a neck-craning exercise in topographic relief. The Middle Fork tumbles southwest through nearly 10 miles of inaccessible gorge and is overshadowed south by Monarch Divide, a steep ridge ushering the two forks together.

At the third switchback (0.9/2600) a cottonwood tree can be readily identified by its heart-shaped leaves. Below the fourth switchback (1.3/2430), an unexpected and beautiful stream races over seven visible cascades—each one becoming progressively larger. Finally the water pours over a smooth granite face into a deep pool full of brook trout. This is Tenmile Creek, which drains the Hume Lake Reservoir 4 miles upstream. While pleasant in May and June, the water here gets funky as the flow decreases and Hume Lake receives its thousands of summer-camp visitors in July and August. Ten yards beyond where the falls first become visible, an unmarked spur trail leads down to a vantage point and a short scramble to the flat rocks at the base of the waterfall.

As you continue to Kings River, poison oak appears everywhere. The trail ends among the granite jumble of the riverbank (1.7/2250). Many boulders include excellent examples of *inclusions* (overlying rocks absorbed and partially melted by rising molten bubbles of granite) some 100 million years old. Sparrows dart above the river in search of insects. Return the way you came.

Nearest Visitor Center: Grant Grove Visitor Center. See Hike 94.

Backpacking Information: Backpacking is permitted but the lack of campsites make it an unappealing option. A campfire permit is required.

Nearest Campground: There are more than a dozen campgrounds in Kings Canyon National Park and adjacent Sequoia National Forest. Check at the visitor center for current availability.

Additional Information:
www.r5.fs.fed.us/sequoia

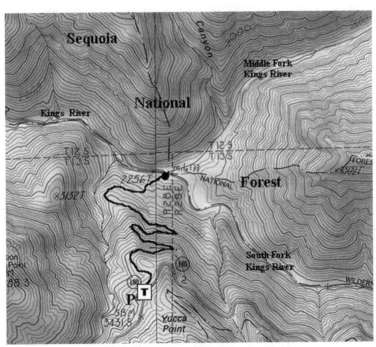

KING OF KINGS

Hike 96—Sequoia

Location	Redwood Canyon
Agency	Kings Canyon National Park
Highlights	Enchanted groves whose patriarchs dwarf your mind.
Distance	10.0 miles
Total Elevation Gain/Loss	1900´/1900´
Hiking Time	5–7 hours
Difficulty	★★★
Best Times	June through September
Optional Map	USGS 7.5-min *General Grant Grove*

Off the beaten track from the crowds found south in Sequoia National Park, Redwood Canyon provides the opportunity to peacefully commune with giant sequoias in the largest grove found anywhere on earth. One-on-one with these magnificent trees, while your mind gropes at scales of time and size, you feel the insignificance of humankind.

The Hike loops around the canyon slopes and ridges, dropping briefly to Redwood Creek and passing through numerous stands of giant sequoia. While it can readily be completed in either direction, this description covers the route clockwise. Late June offers abundant flowering lupines and dogwood as well as fewer people; it is the ideal time to visit. While no water is available at the trailhead, an ample number of streams are encountered along the way.

To Reach the Trailhead, take Hwy. 180 east from Fresno to Kings Canyon National Park. Continue 1 mile past the entrance station to a Y-junction—bear right onto Generals Highway heading south toward Sequoia National Park. In 3.5 miles you reach the posted turnoff for Hume Lake on the left. Instead, make a right here onto what appears to be a small dirt cul-de-sac. The bumpy dirt road to Redwood Canyon begins at this dirt lot and is easily navigable for all

cars, although trailers and RVs are definitely not recommended. Immediately beyond an ENTERING KINGS CANYON NATIONAL PARK sign, the road gradually descends 1.7 miles to the posted turnoff for the trailhead. There is a $10 entrance fee for Kings Canyon and Sequoia national parks, valid for seven days.

Description: The trail begins at the information sign by the far end of the parking lot (0.0/6250). Your return path winds in from the right but you head left down a 3-foot-wide loamy trail, immediately passing a fire hydrant and sign RED-WOOD CANYON-HART TREE TRAIL. You soon find yourself enveloped in the primeval giant sequoia forest, whose numerous large specimens dwarf the white fir, sugar pine, Jeffrey pine, and dogwood also found here. The trail descends steadily via several lazy switchbacks and comes to a posted junction (0.4/6070)—bear left towards the Hart Tree. (Right takes you directly down-canyon and is described in Hike 97.) From here the trail traverses the eastern slopes of the canyon, crossing three small tributaries of Redwood Creek before reaching a *log cabin* (1.1/6100).

Nothing more than a single fallen sequoia log, the cabin was originally owned by woodcutter John Crose. Utilized in the 1890s for equipment storage, the log was modified in the early part of the century by Crose's son Jack and nephew Willis. Upon scraping out the log's insides, the pair enclosed it with shakes, a door, and a fireplace and chimney. The Barlow family purchased Crose's holdings in the late 1920s and both families lived in the area well into the 1930s, inhabiting both Crose's log and a tiny cabin, now long gone, built atop a large sequoia stump. The federal government acquired the property in the late 1930s, bringing an end to this unique log lifestyle.

From here you briefly leave the sequoias and ascend 400 feet among black oak, incense cedars, and alders. The trail tops out at a large open space of bare granite, offering the only vista from the canyon's eastern slopes. Another undulating trail mile takes you past boggy Hart Meadow (and through another hollow sequoia log) to the East Fork Redwood Creek. Although it's too small to be fishable, keep an eye out for the small, native brook trout that populate its crystalline waters. A brief climb out of the creek gully brings you to a posted 100-yard spur trail to the Hart Tree (3.4/6200).

Once thought to be the world's 4th largest tree, the Hart Tree is now recognized as only the 16th largest on Earth. As of 1990 it was 278' tall, had a ground perimeter of 75.3', a diameter of 21', and was estimated to contain 34,407 cubic feet of wood. Back on the main trail, a gradual descent brings you to the Fallen Goliath (4.8/5700), just beyond view from the trail. Moist, covered in moss, nurse log to young sequoias sprouting from its crest, the Fallen Goliath probably sprouted more than 3,000 years ago; it provides an excellent example of the incredible decay resistance of sequoia wood.

The trail now descends to Redwood Creek (5.3/5400). Clear as glass, the creek flows through level surroundings studded with impressive sequoias, making this a great picnic spot. From mid-June through July, a sea of purple lupines washes the area, lapping at the cinnamon sequoia trunks. Just across the creek a signed junction indicates the route up-canyon to the right. (A left at this point leads down-canyon to Big Spring, described in Hike 97.)

A short 0.1 mile upstream, the trail reaches another junction—head west up the canyon slope toward Sugar Bowl Grove. (Those tired or short of time can take the shorter, more direct route up-canyon to reach the parking lot.) Climbing gradually to the ridgetop, the trail quickly breaks out of the dense forest after two quick switchbacks. The result of a recent fire, the clearing lets you see the proliferation of young sequoias whenever openings occur in the forest canopy. Extending spiny branches into the air, the young trees outgrow their neighbors to maximize sunlight. Extremely shade-intolerant, the trees shed any sickly yellow-green branches and will rapidly perish if overtopped by another tree. Beyond this clearing thimbleberry, bear clover, paintbrush, and green-leaf manzanita are abundant, as the trail steadily climbs to the ridgetop.

Before attaining the ridgetop you enter Sugar Bowl Grove (7.5/6600), a thick stand of mature sequoias interspersed with several gnarled, ancient specimens of stupendous size. A cluster of more than 20 stand sentinel within a 75-yard radius at the heart of this enchanted grove.

From here the trail follows the ridgetop, soon reaching its highest elevation of 1,500' above the canyon floor. Now slowly descending, you begin passing through Burnt Grove. Another thick stand of sequoias, Burnt Grove parallels the trail to the parking lot for the final mile.

Nearest Visitor Center: Grant Grove Visitor Center, (559) 565-4307, located 2.4 miles past the park entrance station along Hwy. 180. Open May through June daily 9 A.M.–5 P.M., July through September daily 8 A.M.–6 P.M., with reduced hours in winter.

Backpacking Information: A wilderness permit is required and can be obtained at Grant Grove Visitor Center. Due to the limited availability of campsites, there is a quota for this trailhead.

Nearest Campground: There are more than a dozen campgrounds in Kings Canyon National Park and adjacent Sequoia National Forest. Check at the visitor center for current availability.

Additional Information: *www.nps.gov/seki*

SEQUOIA & *GIGANTEUM*

Hike 97—*Giganteum*

Location	Redwood Canyon
Agency	Kings Canyon National Park
Highlights	Quiet humility before giant sequoias. Dry streambed wilderness adventuring.
Distance	12.4 miles round trip
Total Elevation Gain/Loss	2750´/2750´
Hiking Time	8–12 hours
Difficulty	★★★★
Best Times	June through September
Optional Map	USGS 7.5-min *General Grant Grove*

The first half of this journey quickly and easily accesses the heart of Redwood Canyon. The second half is a challenging wilderness adventure.

The Hike drops directly down Redwood Canyon, passing through a thick, continuous belt of superb giant sequoia to reach a beautiful lunch spot by Redwood Creek (and the junction with Hike 96). Those seeking a shorter Redwood Canyon experience can return to the parking lot from here, an easy 3-mile round-trip hike. Redwood Creek continues beyond the sequoia grove, however, and is joined some distance downstream by water gushing out of the hillside. This is little-visited Big Spring. An optional off-trail section along the way provides an ever deeper wilderness experience on Redwood Creek. No water is available at the trailhead, and none is accessible for the first 1.5 miles.

To Reach the Trailhead see Hike 96.

Description: At the information sign at the far end of the parking lot (0.0/6250), take the left trail that immediately passes a sign REDWOOD CANYON-HART TREE TRAIL. Sequoia are thick from the outset, and healthy white fir, sugar pine, Jeffrey pine, and dogwood are dwarfed by these cinnamon giants. Descending steadily, the trail soon reach-

es a junction (0.4/6070)—bear right. (Hike 96 continues to the left.)

In its descent the trail winds around the roots of the first of several toppled sequoias. The trail then cuts through a second fallen sequoia marked by huge fracture lines. Notice how the wood shattered upon striking the ground (a cataclysm barely imaginable)—a vivid illustration of the brittleness of sequoia wood. The trail gradient decreases gradually as you descend, leveling at the two junctions for Hike 96. The first splits right to Sugar Bowl Grove, while the second initially crosses the creek to an open area ideal for resting and relaxing (1.5/5400). For the easy, abbreviated sequoia experience, turn around here.

To see Big Spring continue downstream on the unposted trail, which soon reaches a sandy bench by the creek. The trail becomes spotty here—look for the sign indicating where the trail crosses the creek. Now winding away from the creek, you pass a few final sequoia before leaving the grove. The creek is now unseen from the trail, except where the route briefly skirts the bouldery creekbed (3.2/5300) and provides easy access. On the return trip, you could follow the creekbed upstream from here to the earlier crossing. This off-trail route follows an often-dry watercourse, where isolated pools full of trout and marble outcrops are highlights. Because this trail-access point is easily missed from the streambed, don't try to head down-stream to Big Spring and then retrace your route.

Continuing down-canyon, you soon reach an off-limits cabin in the woods (4.5/5180). The trail becomes darker—even mysterious—beyond this dwelling, passing a decrepit sign reading CHERRY FLAT TRAIL as it wends through a thick forest of many black oak. Initially level, the final stretch of trail drops 200 feet to

the creek through thick, young white fir, black oak, and cedar. A long-sleeved garment is recommended. Big Spring can be found a short distance down-stream from the bottom (6.2/4760), gushing more water than is in the creek. If the gaging station is a blemish, in July thousands of red-scaled ladybugs, hud-dled for warmth, can be found imparting their memorable blaze to the landscape. Carefully retrace your route to the trail-head.

Nearest Visitor Center, Backpacking Information, and Campgrounds: See Hike 96.

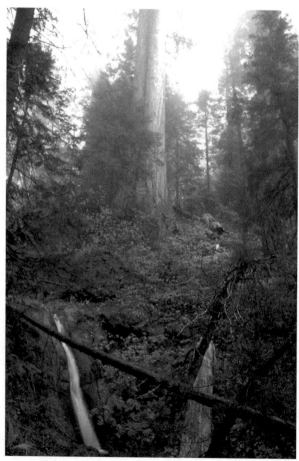

Redwood Canyon

Hike 98—Sequoia High Sierra

Location	Pear Lake
Agency	Sequoia National Park
Highlights	Shattered granite basins. The Watchtower.
Distance	12.4 miles round trip
Total Elevation Gain/Loss	2750´/2750´
Hiking Time	8–12 hours
Difficulty	★★★★
Best Times	July through September
Optional Map	USGS 7.5-min *Lodgepole*

Pear Lake's frigid green waters fill a granite bowl ringed by crenelated cliffs of fractured stone. En route are three choice Sierra lakes and The Watchtower, a titanic granite tower rising 2,000 feet above Tokopah Valley.

The Hike climbs steeply to The Watchtower before making a gradual traverse above impressive Tokopah Valley to reach the lakes. For those seeking a shorter hike, the round trip to The Watchtower is 7 miles, gains 1,700 feet of elevation, and can be completed in 4–6 hours. Snow usually clears from the trail by late June and returns in November. July provides spectacular wildflowers. Water is available at the trailhead in the nearby restrooms.

To Reach the Trailhead from Generals Highway in Sequoia National Park, take the road to Wolverton east to the parking lot at the road's end—your turnoff is 1.6 miles south of the one for Lodgepole Visitor Center and 0.6 mile north of the General Sherman Tree parking lot. The trail begins midway along its northern edge. Lockers provide the only safe storage of your foodstuffs while you're on the trail, because bears break into vehicles here all the time.

Description: Striking first through a forest dominated by white fir, the trail is quickly joined left by a small feeder trail from the Lodgepole complex (0.1/7400), and then right by a short spur from the Wolverton area. The trail now slowly gains elevation traversing a forest whose lush understory includes numerous wildflowers: lupines, phlox, tiger lilies, shooting stars, and paintbrush. Beyond a junction for Alta Peak Trail (1.8/8060), the path recrosses a small spring-fed creek before reaching the junction for The Hump (2.1/8160). A right turn, taking you over The Hump, provides a slightly shorter, more direct, route to Heather Lake. But this shortcut is steeper, more strenuous, and lacks the exceptional views of the main trail. If you bear left instead, a gradually rising traverse leads you to The Watchtower (3.5/8973).

Take a memorable break on The Watchtower by scrambling to the top of this towering granite pillar, skirting its precipitous chasm. With Tokopah Valley visible in its entirety, even Lodgepole Visitor Center can be spotted down-canyon. Below where the Marble Fork Kaweah River tumbles down 1,000 feet of granite chutes and faces are Tokopah Falls. Up-canyon, the high peaks on the southern rim overshadow your unseen destinations—Emerald and Pear lakes.

Views lost as the trail continues east become sweeping vistas as it heads southeast, now offering views of the

Heather Lake basin. The lake remains hidden until you pass the junction where The Hump shortcut rejoins the main trail (4.1/9260). Lodgepole and western white pine are scattered about this day-use-only lake, whose facilities include California's most rudimentary outdoor toilet. Like the others on this hike, Heather Lake brims with brook trout up to 8" in length.

Continuing to even prettier lakes, the trail briefly climbs before descending into the granite amphitheater of the Emerald Lake basin. Aster Lake can be seen north of the trail but there is no established access trail. Approaching Emerald Lake, you reach the organized campsites near its north shore (5.1/9030). Both food lockers and a downright luxurious restroom are provided. Glacial polish and striations on the rock are evidence of the glacier that once carved this cirque. The summit visible southeast across the lake is Alta Peak (11204).

Striking north, the trail winds among granite slabs and vibrant patches of seasonal wildflowers such as mountain pride, paintbrush, and meadow penstemon. Look here for Coville's columbine, a large cream-colored flower with five petals, extending into backward-projecting spurs up to 1" long. Found only at rocky, high elevations in the southern Sierra Nevada, it is closely related to, and can hybridize with, the crimson columbine (Spellenberg 1998). Magnificent examples of the rosy palette created by this cross-pollination can be found here soon after snowmelt—usually in late June and the first half of July. **Do not pick the wildflowers.**

Wrapping east, the trail passes a spur to seasonally staffed Pear Lake Ranger Station before turning southeast to reach the appropriately shaped Pear Lake (6.2/9550). A few lodgepole pine are sprinkled about the sloping granite shoreline; soaring ramparts of the basin heighten your sense of grandeur. The trail ends among the designated campsites near the lake's north shore (the "stem"), where food lockers and another plush outhouse can be found. Return the way you came.

Nearest Visitor Center: Lodgepole Visitor Center, (559) 565-3782, located on the road to Wolverton 1.6 miles east of Generals Highway. Open mid-June to mid-September daily 8 A.M.–6 P.M., with reduced hours in early June and late September.

SEQUOIA HIGH SIERRA

Backpacking Information: The hike to Pear Lake makes for an ideal (and popular) 2-day trip. Wilderness permits are required and can be obtained from an office next to the visitor center's main entrance, (559) 565-3775. Open June through September daily 7 A.M.–4 P.M. There is a trail quota of 25 people per day but space is usually available. Due to heavy use, no fires are allowed and camping is permitted in designated sites only.

Nearest Campground: Lodgepole Campground, located adjacent to the visitor center (204 sites, $16). Reservations are recommended in summer, and can be made by calling 1-800-365-2267 or going online at *reservations.nps.gov.*

Additional Information: *www.nps.gov/seki*

Hike 99—The Granite Fin

Location	Moro Rock
Agency	Sequoia National Park
Highlights	Surmounting a precipitous granite fin. The Great Western Divide.
Distance	0.6 mile round trip
Total Elevation Gain/Loss	250´/250´
Hiking Time	1 hour
Difficulty	★★
Best Times	June through September
Optional Map	USGS 7.5-min *Giant Forest*

A sharp granite nubbin protruding from the lip of the Giant Forest plateau, Moro Rock protrudes thousands of feet above the Kaweah River gorge. A narrow runway atop its prow offers superlative views of the jagged Great Western Divide.

The Hike climbs to the top of Moro Rock along precipitous ledges and up steps dynamited out of the rock. Among all the trails of Giant Forest with their ubiquitous crowds, this short climb to a unique viewpoint should not be missed. Giant sequoias grow elsewhere in greater seclusion (Hikes 96-97), but there is only one Moro Rock. Crowds are always heavy. Water is available at the trailhead.

To Reach the Trailhead, take Generals Highway to Giant Forest Village and turn east on Crescent Meadow Road—the turnoff is located at the southern end of the complex. In 1.2 miles turn right onto the posted one-way loop for Moro Rock; park in the often crowded parking lot 0.4 mile later. There is a $10 entrance for Sequoia National Park, valid for seven days.

Description: Because Jeffrey pine, incense cedar, white fir, and sugar pine are thick at the outset, bare granite views through the trees provide little hint of

the grandeur that awaits you. At step 21, a sign cries out WARNING—AREA OF EXTREME DANGER! Respect the warning about lightning strikes and postpone your ascent if thunderstorms threaten. Past this sign, the magic begins.

Overhanging sections, narrow cracks, and concrete stairs allow almost everybody—be they sprinters and climbers, walkers and talkers, or huffers and

THE GRANITE FIN

puffers—to surmount the rock. Two of the many informative placards en route identify the peaks of the Great Western Divide (including Sawtooth Peak, Hike 101) and detail the history of Generals Highway, seen twisting tortuously below where it climbs 4,000 feet in 19 miles. The pink flowers of mountain pride penstemon can be spotted in season sprouting from cracks in the rock.

Climbers might also be seen clambering up the rock's steeper faces. At the summit, a 4-foot-wide level walkway with the trail's only bench distinguish the edge of this precipitous granite blade.

Nearest Visitor Center and Campground: please see Hike 98.

Additional Information:
www.nps.gov/seki

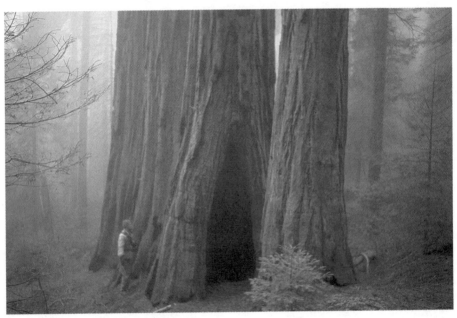

Giant sequoia, tiny man

Hike 100—Crystal Clear

Location	Crystal Lake
Agency	Sequoia National Park
Highlights	Intense verticality above Mineral King. A rugged less-traveled lake basin.
Distance	8.8 miles round trip
Total Elevation Gain/Loss	3100´/3100´
Hiking Time	8–12 hours
Difficulty	★★★★
Best Times	July through September
Optional Map	USGS 7.5-min *Mineral King*

The Great Western Divide towers more than 4,000 feet above the small hamlet of Mineral King in southern Sequoia National Park. The trail climbs up, straight up the Divide's flanks, providing sweeping views of the soaring mountains and precipitous valleys. Beautiful Crystal Lake awaits at your trail's end.

The Hike is extremely strenuous and gains an average of 800 feet per mile. Typically snow-free in mid-June, this route receives heaviest visitation in July and August and becomes optimal after Labor Day. Crystal Lake boils with brook trout but they seldom exceed 8" in length. While no water is available at the trailhead, there is a faucet in front of the ranger station (see below). The first convenient trailside source is 1.3 miles distant and nearly a 1,000 feet up.

To Reach the Trailhead from Hwy. 198 at Hammond, take the road to Mineral King—the turnoff is 4 miles northeast of the town of Three Rivers and 2 miles southwest of the Ash Mountain Entrance Station to Sequoia National Park. While only 23 miles long, the narrow, winding Mineral King Road can take upwards of 90 minutes to drive. You reach the park entrance station 11.2 miles past the turnoff, where a $10

entrance fee is collected. After another 5.6 miles, the road's surface alternates between dirt and pavement. The road soon passes through the tiny settlement of Silver City. A small general store here provides last-minute gas and groceries. You pass Mineral King Ranger Station, where two large parking lots, an outhouse, and a pay phone are located, a short 0.8 mile before the desired trailhead.

WARNING: Beware of lactating marmots! Throughout June and most of July, these critters develop a peculiar craving for antifreeze and brake fluid. Marmots will chew through coolant hoses, brake lines, and even spark plug wires seeking salts from this odd cocktail. Some people fence off the underside of their vehicles with chicken wire to avoid disaster. Some park in a less-risky lot, while others just risk it. A safe parking alternative is the Tar Gap lot located 0.1 mile east of the ranger station, but it means a 0.7-mile road walk to the trailhead. Most active in June, marmots become more lethargic as July progresses. Ask at the ranger station for the most current marmot report.

Description: The trail begins at the end of the north parking lot (0.0/7820), where current trail conditions are posted. The East Fork Kaweah River turns sharply west here, and views south toward its headwaters are highlighted by the striking parabola made by Farewell Gap (10586), bordered west by the red metamorphic pyramid of Vandever Mtn. (11947).

Immediately climbing, the trail's first mile is the steepest, passing through open sage grassland with a few Sierra juniper. The distant pinnacle of Sawtooth Peak (the challenging objective of Hike 101) dominates the skyline east above Monarch Creek. Bouldery staircases help you ascend to a waterfall overlook. Now the trail first traverses west and then—at the junction for Empire Mine Trail (0.6/8320)—east back toward the creek. Ponderosa pine appear here and corn lily, yarrow, Indian paintbrush, and lupine can be spotted underfoot. Climbing along the stream again, you pass a

mossy spring gushing from the opposite hillside before the trail reaches creek level (1.3/8760). Imposing cliffs north, which tower 1,500 feet, actually represent only the lower southwest face of Empire Mountain, whose hidden slopes rise another 1,300 feet to the summit. Refill your water bottles here as this is your last opportunity before Crystal Lake.

Cross the stream and commence switchbacking up the slopes. At the 4th switchback Western white pine appear, and by the 13th you've already ascended 700 feet above the creek. Traversing south, you cross over a small ridgetop and then climb east below the ridgeline to reach the posted junction for Crystal Lake (2.6/9860). (Those out to challenge Sawtooth Peak continue straight on the main trail and see Hike 101.)

Striking southeast over rocky and slightly overgrown terrain, the trail to

CRYSTAL CLEAR & SAWTOOTH

Crystal Lake is obviously less traveled. Foxtail pines dot the open slopes above Chihuahua Mine, whose collapsed tunnel can be located by the small pile of tailings west of the trail. At the blufftop, the trail drops 100 feet to a junction for Cobalt Lakes (3.5/10350), visible below on the hanging lip of the valley. Bearing left at the junction, you make a gradual descending traverse toward cascading Crystal Creek. By a scree slope, the trail abruptly begins its final 400-foot climb to the lake. Occasionally difficult to discern among the boulders, the trail passes two choice campsites just before Crystal Lake (4.4/10780).

Crystal Lake straddles a geologic divide. A granite cliff plunges 800 feet into the lake's south end, while the metavolcanic molar of Mineral Peak (11615) juts out of the northern ridge. With level spots all but non-existent at the lake, even simple navigation around its shores is challenging. In the northern half of this glacial cirque is a small unnamed tarn, most easily accessed by scrambling over the small hill just north of the dam and the trail's end. Look for

granite boulders above this metavolcanic rise. They are glacial erratics, transported and dropped here by the glacier that once carved this high alpine valley. After a serene afternoon here in this crystal-clear basin, descend to Mineral King.

Nearest Visitor Center: Mineral King Ranger Station, (559) 565-3768. Open daily from Memorial Day until the first big snowfall (usually in October) 7 A.M.– 3:30 P.M.

Backpacking Information: Wilderness permits are required and may be obtained only from the ranger station during open hours. A quota of 20 persons per day is enforced for this trailhead, although capacity is typically only exceeded in late August and on the busiest summer holidays.

Nearest Campground: Cold Springs Campground, 0.1 mile west of the ranger station (40 sites, $8). If it's full, try Atwell Mills Campground 4.1 miles farther west (21 sites, $8). Neither is open before Memorial Day.

Additional Information:
www.nps.gov/seki

Hike 101—Sawtooth

Location	Sawtooth Peak
Agency	Sequoia National Park
Highlights	A towering summit of the Great Western Divide.
Distance	11.0 miles round trip
Total Elevation Gain/Loss	4500´/4500´
Hiking Time	12–16 hours
Difficulty	★★★★★
Best Times	July through September
Optional Map	USGS 7.5-min *Mineral King*

Sawtooth Peak dominates, offering expansive views of the southern Sierra from its lofty height. It will challenge but don't let it deter you.

The Hike, an extended variation of Hike 100, ascends Sawtooth Peak (12343) from Mineral King. Epic but brutal, it gains 4,500 feet in less than 7 miles. While the elevation gain is comparable to the popular ascent of Half Dome from Yosemite Valley (Hike 84), the altitude of Sawtooth Peak is considerably higher and the elevation gain more rapid. Exceptional fitness and an early start are required for a one-day ascent. Some degree of acclimatization is important for the rarefied air above 10,000 feet; gaiters are useful for keeping grit out of your boots on Sawtooth's loose slopes. The last 1,500 feet of elevation gain is off-trail and involves considerable boulder-hopping and scrambling. Magnificent and far-reaching views of the Sierra Divide, the Kern River Canyon, and the Great Western Divide reward the hardy adventurer.

To Reach the Trailhead, and for more information on Mineral King, see Hike 100.

Description: The trailhead and first 2.6 miles of the hike are identical to that of Hike 100; refer to its trail description until the Crystal Lake junction

(2.6/9860). From the junction, continue straight on the main trail to recross the small ridge that defines the Monarch Creek watershed. You now begin a dramatic traverse beneath the lower flanks of Mineral Peak. Lower Monarch Lake remains hidden until you're almost upon it, when the red jutting molar of Mineral Peak (11615) also becomes visible for the first time south of the lake.

Lower Monarch Lake (4.4/10380) has several good campsites scattered around the western shore. Food storage lockers are provided for bear and marmot protection. Nearby, flimsy waist-high walls surround the throne of a rustic outhouse. The lake, which can be circumnavigated with some scrambling, boils with small brook trout. Upper Monarch Lake is easily accessed by a use trail at the lake's far shore, north of the small inlet creek. For those wishing to make Sawtooth Peak a two-day trip, this makes an ideal overnight stop. The distinctive rock interface across the lake marks where overlying volcanic rocks have been intruded by Sierra Nevada granite. Rarely is this geologic divide so pronounced. North, the granite mass of Sawtooth Peak rises dramatically above the lake, its summit just visible as the highest point on the ridge more than 2,000 feet above you.

Briefly winding northwest away from the lake at the base of Sawtooth's slope, the posted trail to Sawtooth Pass begins climbing in an obvious spot. It completes five switchbacks before reaching a long swath of grit and dust extending upslope. The trail ascends this via numerous steep switchbacks, gaining 500 feet above the lake before—near the top of the loose sandy slope—spinning off various paths. While the actual trail over Sawtooth Pass heads upward and to the left from here, you should begin slowly bearing right as you ascend to obtain the summit. The last stand of foxtail pine, above you to the right, provides a good landmark for climbing and for the return descent. Continue upward until you are nearly level with these trees, and then climb above and slightly to the right of them until you reach the ridge—a gain of around 1,000 feet from the top of the sandy slope. Incredible views east open up here, but they're better from the top. The peak is now clearly visible southeast, jutting from the ridge. To climb it, traverse below and then approach it from the south; the final scramble to the top is considerably easier from this direction. The last 100 feet require the most scrambling.

The view is epic. East lies the Kern River Canyon and its serrated eastern rampart, the Sierra Divide. Mt. Whitney (14494) can be spotted east-northeast. Looking north, barren and oft-frozen Columbine Lake (10970) lies below you. The Great Western Divide strikes northeast beyond. On the Divide's western slopes, Black Rock Pass Trail zigzags insanely up to its namesake. The large plateau that is home to Sequoia's Giant Forest is visible farther north-northwest, with the seemingly small knob of Moro Rock (Hike 99) on its western edge. On a good day the Minarets and Ritter Range are visible on the northern horizon, a distance of more than 75 miles.

You should find the summit register in an ammo can among the giant slabs of granite. On your return, don't be tempted by sandy routes that drop directly down Sawtooth toward Upper Monarch Lake, because the unseen slope steepens precipitously below. Look for that foxtail pine stand to guide your descent.

Nearest Visitor Center, Campground, and Backpacking Information: Please see Hike 100.

Appendix 1—Hikes by Theme

BACKPACKABLE

SWEEPING 360° VISTAS

LAKES

Appendix 2—Selected Sources & Recommended Reading

Atlases

Benchmark California Road &Recreation Atlas. 2nd ed. Benchmark Maps, 2000.

Northern California Atlas & Gazetteer. 4th ed. Yarmouth, ME: DeLorme, 1998.

Southern California Atlas & Gazetteer. 4th ed. Yarmouth, ME: DeLorme, 1998.

Plant and Animal Identification

Johnson, Sharon G., Pamela C. Muick, Bruce M. Pavlik, and Marjorie Popper. *Oaks of California.* Los Olivos, CA: Cachuma Press, 1991.

Johnston, Verna R. *California Forests and Woodlands.* Berkeley, CA: University of California Press, 1994.

Keator, Glenn, Ruth M. Heady, and Valerie R. Winemiller. *Pacific Coast Fern Finder.* Rochester, NY: Nature Study Guild, 1981.

Lanner, Ronald M. *Conifers of California.* Los Olivos, CA: Cachuma Press, 1999.

Little, Elbert L. *National Audubon Society Field Guide to North American Trees, Western Region.* New York, NY: Alfred A. Knopf, 1998.

Lyons, Kathleen, and Mary Beth Cooney-Lazaneo. *Plants of the Coast Redwood Region.* Boulder Creek, CA: Looking Press, 1988.

Peterson, Roger Tory. *Western Birds.* New York, NY: Houghton Mifflin, 1990.

Spellenberg, Richard. *National Audubon Society Field Guide to North American Wildflowers, Western Region.* New York, NY: Alfred A. Knopf, 1998.

Watts, Tom, *Pacific Coast Tree Finder.* Rochester, NY: Nature Study Guild, 1973.

Geology

General California Geology

Alt, David D., and Donald W. Hyndman. *Roadside Geology of Northern California.* 2nd ed. Missoula, MT: Mountain Press Publishing Company, 2000.

Harden, Deborah R. *California Geology.* Upper Saddle River, NJ: Prentice-Hall, 1998.

McPhee, John. *Assembling California.* New York, NY: Farrar, Straus and Giroux, 1993.

USGS, *Geologic Map of California.* 1:750,000. 1977.

Regional Geology

Durrell, Cordell. *Geologic History of the Feather River Country, California.* Berkeley, CA: University of California Press, 1987.

Galloway, Alan J. *Geology of the Point Reyes Peninsula.* Bulletin 202, California Division of Mines and Geology, 1977.

Konigsmark, Ted. *Geologic Trips: San Francisco and the Bay Area.* GeoPress, 1998.

Moore, James G., Warren J. Nokleburg, and Thomas W. Sisson. *Geologic Road Guide to Kings Canyon and Sequoia National Parks, 1994.*

Wahrhaftig, Clyde. *A Streetcar to Subduction and Other Plate Tectonic Trips by Public Transport in San Francisco.* Revised Edition. Washington, DC: American Geophysical Union, 1984.

Regional Information

The Central Coast, Bay Area, and Coast Ranges

California Coastal Resource Guide. California Coastal Commission. Berkeley, CA: University of California Press, 1987.

Golden Gate National Recreation Area Guide to the Parks. San Francisco, CA: Golden Gate National Parks Association, 1995.

Cassady, Stephen. Spanning the Gate. Santa Rosa, CA: Squarebooks, 1986.

Paddison, Joshua. A World Transformed—Firsthand Accounts of California Before the Gold Rush. Berkeley, CA: Heyday Books, 1999.

Schaffer, Jeffrey P. Hiking the Big Sur Country: The Ventana Wilderness. Berkeley, CA: Wilderness Press, 1988.

Vanderwerf, Barbara. The Coastside Trail Guidebook. El Granada, CA: Gum Tree Lane Books, 1995.

Weintraub, David. East Bay Trails: Outdoor Adventures in Alameda and Contra Costa County. Berkeley, CA: Wilderness Press, 1998.

White, Peter. The Farallon Islands, Sentinels of the Golden Gate. San Francisco, CA: Scottwall Associates, 1995.

Whitnah, Dorothy L. Point Reyes. 3rd ed. Berkeley, CA: Wilderness Press, 1997.

The North Coast and Klamath Mountains

Linkhart, Luther, and Michael White. The Trinity Alps, A Hiking and Backpacking Guide. 3rd ed. Berkeley, CA: Wilderness Press, 1994.

Green, David, and Greg Ingold. Marble Mountain Wilderness. 2nd ed. Berkeley, CA: Wilderness Press, 1996.

Shasta and the Modoc Plateau

Selters, Andy, and Michael Zanger. The Mt. Shasta Book. Berkeley, CA: Wilderness Press, 1997.

Schaffer, Jeffrey P. Lassen Volcanic National Park and Vicinity. 2nd ed. Berkeley, CA: Wilderness Press, 1996.

Boze, M. Jeanne. The Nature of Bidwell Park. 2nd ed. B.C. Publications, 1998.

The Sierra Nevada

Dinkey Creek: A Bridge from Past to Present. [pamphlet] Kings River Ranger District, 1997.

Browning, Peter. Place Names of the Sierra Nevada. 2nd ed. Berkeley, CA: Wilderness Press, 1991.

Jenkins, J.C., and Ruby Johnson Jenkins. Exploring the Southern Sierra: West Side. 3rd ed. Berkeley, CA: Wilderness Press, 1995.

Lamela, Susan and Hank Meals. Yuba Trails. 1993.

Lekisch, Barbara. Tahoe Place Names. Lafayette, CA: Great West Books, 1988.

Moore, James G., Warren J. Nokleburg, and Thomas W. Sisson. Geologic Road Guide to Kings Canyon and Sequoia National Parks, 1994.

Morey, Kathy. Hot Showers, Soft Beds, and Dayhikes in the Sierra. Berkeley, CA: Wilderness Press, 1996.

Schaffer, Jeffrey P. Desolation Wilderness and the South Lake Tahoe Basin. Berkeley, CA: Wilderness Press, 1996.

Schaffer, Jeffrey P. The Tahoe Sierra, A Natural History Guide to 112 Hikes in the Northern Sierra. 4th ed. Berkeley, CA: Wilderness Press, 1998.

Schaffer, Jeffrey P. Yosemite National Park, A Natural-History Guide to Yosemite and Its Trails. 4th ed. Berkeley, CA: Wilderness Press, 1999.

Schifrin, Ben. Emigrant Wilderness. Berkeley, CA: Wilderness Press, 1996.

Secor, R.J. The High Sierra, Peaks, Passes, and Trails. 2nd ed. Seattle, WA: The Mountaineers, 1999.

Whitney, Stephen. The Sierra Nevada. San Francisco, CA: Sierra Club Books, 1979.

Winnett, Thomas, Jason Winnett, Kathy Morey, and Lyn Haber. Sierra South, 100 Back-country Trips in California's Sierra. 6th ed. Berkeley, CA: Wilderness Press, 1993.

Index

PARKS AND WILDERNESS AREAS